T0159249

Recipes from
A MEXICAN
GRANDMOTHER'S
KITCHEN

Recipes from

A MEXICAN GRANDMOTHER'S KITCHEN

More than 150 authentic and
delicious dishes, shown in over
750 photographs

JANE MILTON

LORENZ BOOKS

This edition is published by Lorenz Books
an imprint of Anness Publishing Ltd
info@anness.com
www.lorenzbooks.com
www.annesspublishing.com

If you like the images in this book and would like to investigate using them for
publishing, promotions or advertising, please visit our website
www.practicalpictures.com for more information.

A CIP catalogue record for this book is available from the British Library.

Publisher: Joanna Lorenz
Executive Editor: Joanne Rippin
Designer: Nigel Partridge, *Jacket design:* Adelle Mahoney
Photography: Simon Smith (recipes) and Janine Hosegood (reference)
Food for Photography: Caroline Barty (recipes) and Annabel Ford (reference)

ACKNOWLEDGEMENTS
Thanks to my Mum for typing my recipes and to Dad for proof-reading everything.
I would never have made my deadlines without your help.
Thanks too to Tom Estes of Cafe Pacifico, for sharing his knowledge of tequila
and much more, and for his enthusiasm for this project.
The publishers would like to thank South American Pictures for the use of their
photographs in the book: 1m; 8bl, tr; 9tl, br; 10t; 11tl, br; 12tl, tr, bl; 13tl, m, br; 14tr,
ml, bl; 15tl, br; 16tr, bl; 17tl, br; 18tr, mr, bl; 19tr, ml, bl.

PUBLISHER'S NOTE
Although the advice and information in this book are believed to be accurate and true
at the time of going to press, neither the authors nor the publisher can accept any legal
responsibility or liability for any errors or omissions that may have been made nor for
any inaccuracies nor for any loss, harm or injury that comes about from following
instructions or advice in this book.

COOK'S NOTES
Bracketed terms are intended for American readers.
For all recipes, quantities are given in both metric and imperial measures and, where
appropriate, in standard cups and spoons. Follow one set of measures, but not a
mixture, because they are not interchangeable.
Standard spoon and cup measures are level. 1 tsp = 5ml,
1 tbsp = 15ml, 1 cup = 250ml/8fl oz.
Australian standard tablespoons are 20ml. Australian readers should use 3 tsp
in place of 1 tbsp for measuring small quantities.
American pints are 16fl oz/2 cups. American readers should use
20fl oz/2.5 cups in place of 1 pint when measuring liquids.
Electric oven temperatures in this book are for conventional ovens. When using a fan
oven, the temperature will probably need to be reduced by about 10–20°C/20–40°F.
Ovens vary, so check with your manufacturer's instruction book for guidance.
The nutritional analysis given for each recipe is calculated per portion (i.e. serving or
item), unless otherwise stated. If the recipe gives a range, such as Serves 4–6, then
the nutritional analysis will be for the smaller portion size, i.e. 6 servings. The analysis
does not include optional ingredients, such as salt added to taste.
Medium (US large) eggs are used unless otherwise stated.

CONTENTS

INTRODUCTION   6

INGREDIENTS   22

THE RECIPES   **64**

SALSAS   66

SOUPS AND SNACKS   92

MEAT DISHES   122

FISH AND SEAFOOD   150

VEGETABLES   176

DESSERTS AND SWEETMEATS   204

DRINKS   230

INDEX   254

INTRODUCTION

Mexican food mirrors the culture of the country – it is colourful, rich, stimulating and festive. From the wild and barren north to the sultry heat of the south, this vast country offers the food lover a feast of flavours. The waters of the Gulf of Mexico and the Pacific Ocean teem with fish, while the sub-tropical regions that adjoin them yield abundant fruit, including pineapples and papayas. From the gardens of the high plateau come wonderful vegetables, while the north is cattle country. Chillies of every shape, colour and size are everywhere, their flavours ranging from subtle to strident, providing the signature to one of the world's most exciting cuisines.

HISTORY OF COOKING IN MEXICO

Food is a very important aspect of the Mexican way of life. Producing and purchasing the raw materials, preparing food and eating it account for a large part of each day, and wonderful dishes are created to mark special occasions and celebrations.

Some Historical Influences on the Mexican Diet

In pre-Columbian Mexico there was already an established pattern of agriculture. Foods such as corn (maize), beans, chillies and (bell) peppers were widely cultivated, along with avocados, tomatoes, sweet potatoes, guavas and pineapples. Vegetables such as *jicama*, *chayote* and *sapote* were also grown.

During the Mayan era, the priests, who were the ruling class, allocated land for the growing of crops. They also arranged for the storage of seed and the distribution of surplus food. The warlike Aztecs, who came to power in the 15th century, were less inclined to share. Their rulers appropriated food for themselves, including chocolate, which was made into a frothy drink, believed to be an aphrodisiac.

The Aztecs inherited a rich culinary tradition. The central market in Tenochtitlan was famous for its fabulous array of foods and it is reported that

Montezuma often required of his servants that they prepare more than two dozen dishes daily for his delectation. The emperor would then stroll among the groaning tables, discussing the ingredients with his chefs, before making his selection. During the subsequent meal, young women, chosen for their beauty, would bring him hot tortillas and gold cups filled with frothy chocolate.

Columbus Comes to Mexico

When the Spaniards first arrived in Mexico in 1492, they had few cooks with them, and so local people were hired to prepare food. Dishes made with corn, chillies, beans, tomatoes and chocolate were prepared and the Spaniards became particularly fond of chillies, chocolate and vanilla. With the Spanish came livestock, which was warmly welcomed. Until this time, the native turkeys and the occasional wild boar were the only source of meat.

The introduction of the domestic pig was significant not merely for its meat, but also for the lard, which was used for frying and became a staple ingredient in Mexican kitchens. Frying had not been possible before, due to the absence of

Below: A modern mural by Diego Rivera showing pre-Columbian corn sellers.

Above: Corn cultivation in Mexico's pre-Columbian era. Mural by Diego Rivera.

animal fats and oils. The Spaniards began to adapt their own recipes to the local ingredients, and the local people in turn adapted their cooking to include meat, which had been such a rarity in the past. The fusion began.

In 1519 the Spanish adventurer Hernando Cortés landed near the site of present day Veracruz. Within three years he had conquered Mexico, and the country was ruled as a viceroyalty of Spain for the next three hundred years. Cortés portrayed himself as the liberator of the tribes oppressed by the Aztecs and used his fanatical missionary zeal to justify his own exploitation of the Mexicans. Monks and nuns were sent from Spain to convert the pagan Mexicans to Catholicism. When they reached the New World, these religious missionaries had more than missals in their luggage; they also brought seeds, and soon citrus fruit, wheat, rice and onions augmented the supplies that served the Mexican kitchen.

Texas is Lost to the USA

Mexican independence from Spain was finally gained in 1821, after a lengthy war. Three years later, on the death of General Iturbide, a new republic was established. At that time Mexico possessed large tracts of land in what is

Above: Hernando Cortés, the Spanish conqueror of Mexico.

now the United States, including Texas. In 1836 Texas formed an independent republic, joining the USA some nine years later. This triggered the Mexican Civil War, as a result of which Mexico ceded to the United States all territories north of the Rio Grande. From a culinary perspective, this is significant, as it helps to explain the historic links between Mexico and the "Lone Star" State, and the origin of the Tex-Mex style of cooking. It also accounts for the popularity of the Mexican style of cooking in California and New Mexico.

French Occupation of Mexico

The Civil War proved costly in financial terms, and put the country greatly in debt to France, England and Spain. When they could no longer repay the debt to France, that country seized the opportunity to take control of Mexico. Austrian-born Maximilian Hapsburg, a relative of Napoleon, was put in charge of the French occupation. The French met with considerable resistance and the *Cinco de Mayo* (5th May) holiday commemorates a famous Mexican victory over their forces. However, this success was short-lived, and France installed Maximilian as Emperor of Mexico in 1864. The French occupation lasted only three years, but left a lasting

legacy in the beautiful breads and pastries for which Mexican cooking is now renowned. Following Maximilian's execution in 1867, Mexico experienced another period of unrest, but since 1920 has been more stable.

Other Influences

The Mexican culture is often described as "*mestizo*". The word means "a mixture" and was originally applied only to the offspring of ethnic peoples and Spanish invaders. Today it reflects many culinary influences from beyond its borders, such as the introduction of brewing by German settlers. The Germans also introduced a cheese, now called *queso de Chihuahua* after the town in northern Mexico where the settlers lived. The presence of many sweet-and-sour

Below: Maya Indians in traditional dress perform the dance of the Mestizos.

dishes in the Mexican cuisine reflects an Oriental influence, as does the Mexican classification of foods as "hot" or "cold". This has nothing to do with the temperature at which these foods are served, but relates instead to the effect they have on the body. "Hot" foods are considered to be easily digested and warming, whereas foods designated as "cold" are held to be difficult to digest and likely to lower body heat. Examples of hot foods are coffee, honey and rice, while fish, limes and boiled eggs would all be regarded as cold. A proper balance between hot and cold foods is believed to be vital for good health.

Mexican cuisine is sure to continue to evolve, adapt and embrace foreign influences. It is also likely to become more homogenous as regional recipes are absorbed in the national repertoire. Like its language, the food and eating habits of a country are never static.

REGIONAL COOKING IN MEXICO

Mexico has not one single cuisine, but many. It is a vast country, the third largest in Latin America, with a wide diversity of landscapes, from snow-capped mountains to citrus groves, and a distinct range of climatic zones. These geographical factors have helped to shape a variety of different styles of cooking within the same country. The extremely mountainous nature of the landscape led in the days before the Spanish Conquest to the development of a large number of isolated and completely distinct Indian communities, each with its own style of cooking. When the Spanish invaded, they certainly had a considerable impact on the cuisine in the areas where they were most active, but parts of the country remained impervious to their influence, and the people there continued to cook in much the same

Above: Bananas and mangoes on sale in a street market in Chihuahua.

way as their parents and grandparents had done before them.

Even today, when tourism has introduced new ingredients and ideas, there remain pockets of Mexico where contact with the outside world is limited, and where old dishes, some of which hark back to Aztec times, are preserved.

The altitude, rather than the latitude, determines the climate in Mexico. The coastal region below 914m/3000ft is *tierra caliente* – the hot zone. Here the climate is sub-tropical, and mangoes, pineapples and avocados flourish. Next comes *tierra templada*, the temperate zone, which rises to 1800m/6000ft.

Culinary Regions

Even in present-day Mexico, regional foods are still very apparent. This is due in some measure to the different climates, which mean certain things cannot grow in every area, or to favourable geographic locations: in Vera Cruz, a coastal area, fish dishes are prevalent. In the coming years this is likely to be eroded more as improved transportation allows products from the different regions to be transported more easily and quickly between areas.

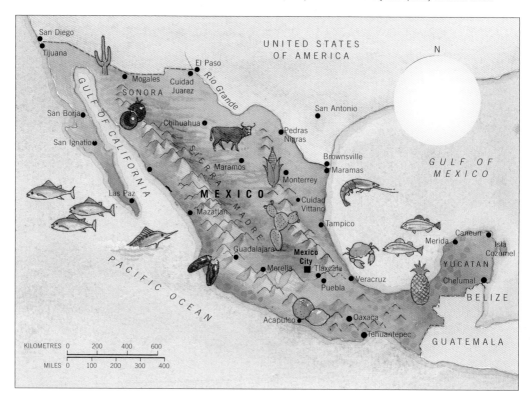

Above: Cooking tortillas in a Mexican street-cafe.

Many familiar vegetables and fruits are grown in Mexico, including green beans, (bell) peppers, tomatoes, cabbages, cauliflowers, onions, and courgettes (zucchini). At the greatest altitude lies the cold zone (*tierra fria*).

These areas of Mexico are all very different from each other, and when it is considered that the rainfall varies from as little as 5cm/2in a year in the north-west to over 300cm/120in in parts of the south-west, it is easy to comprehend how so many diverse styles of cooking came to evolve. Better infrastructure may mean that the regionality of the cuisine will be eroded in time, but at the moment each region has a strong individual identity.

The North

The northern area of Mexico, stretching from Sonora, near the Gulf of California, to Monterrey in Nuevo León, has some striking contrasts. The mountain areas are sparsely populated and life here is very tough. Sonora and Chihuahua are the cattle rearing parts of Mexico. Good grazing encouraged the Spanish to establish herds of their hardy longhorns here, and specialities of the region

include a beef stew called *Caldiddo* and the famous dried beef or *carne seca*. This is produced by first salting the beef, then drying it and finally treating it with lemon juice and pepper.

The ubiquitous beans are as popular in the north as they are elsewhere. A favourite dish of the local *charros* or cowboys is *frijoles* (beans), cooked with scraps of meat, chillies, herbs and spices over an open fire. So well loved is the dish that it is often served in homes and restaurants.

Monterrey is the industrial heart of the region. Brewing employs a large percentage of the population, and this is the home of *frijoles borrachos*, a dish that consists of beans cooked in beer with onion, spices and garlic. The flavour of the beer permeates the beans, earning them their name, which translates as "drunken beans".

The north of Mexico is also the main cheese-producing region. Cheese was introduced by monks who travelled with the Spanish conquerors. Chihuahua is known for *chiles con queso* – melted cheese with chilli strips.The greatest treasure of the north is the soft flour tortilla, produced here because this is the only part of Mexico where wheat is grown. Burritos, portable parcels of meat, beans and rice wrapped in wheat flour tortillas, are typical of this region.

Baja California is a peninsula in the north-western corner of the country, bordering the Pacific and the Gulf of California. It is the oldest continuously producing wine-making region of Mexico. In recent years the region's wines, particularly the whites, have won international acclaim.

The Coastal Regions

The northern Pacific coast has some magnificent beaches. The sea is well stocked with fish, especially bass, tuna and swordfish. *Ceviche*, that delicious dish made of raw fish "cooked" by the action of lime juice, is very popular in the region. It is often made from prawns (shrimp) or other local shellfish.

This area generally has good soil, and grains of various types are widely cultivated, as well as chillies and other vegetables. So famous are the tomatoes produced in this region that the state basketball team is called *Tomateros* (the tomato growers). There are a number of coconut plantations along the coast, and dishes such as coconut soup are popular. Further south is the state of Jalisco, the home of tequila. Red snapper are caught on this part of the coast and cooked over open fires.

Below: Maguey, growing here in the Oaxaca valley, is used in tequila.

Above: Strings of chillies drying in the sun on the Pacific coast of Mexico.

Inland is the colonial town of Guadalajara, famous for *pozole*, a pork stew thickened with hominy – yellow or white corn which has been dried and has had the husk and germ removed, and which has been eaten by the Indians in Mexico for centuries. Another speciality is *birria*, a stew made from lamb or kid.

Down the coast is Acapulco, a very cosmopolitan city with Latin, Oriental and indigenous Indian influences. The cuisine of this area – Oaxaca – has strong Spanish influences, but is also home to some of the most traditional Mexican dishes, such as the *moles* – gloriously rich meat stews which incorporate nuts and chocolate. This is orange country, too, and citrus fruit features strongly in the recipes of the region. *Asadero*, a supple curd cheese similar to the Italian cheese, *Provolone*, originated in Oaxaca.

Chiapas, the southernmost state bordering Guatemala, exhibits some influences from that country. Chillies are commonly served alongside dishes, as accompaniments, rather than as integral ingredients.

The eastern seaboard, lapped by the Caribbean Sea, is known as the Gulf Coast. The climate here is tropical, and this is reflected in the food. Bananas, vanilla, avocados, coffee and coconuts grow on the coast, mangoes and pineapples in the south, and to the north are orchards of apples and pears.

The Gulf Coast has abundant fish stocks. The southern state of Tabasco, on the isthmus of Tehuantepec, is

Below: A palm tree in Chetumal with coconuts ready for harvesting.

Above: Prickly pear cactus growing at Santa Bulalia.

particularly famous for its fish. The catch includes sea bass, striped bass, crabs, lobsters and prawns (shrimp). The port of Veracruz has a famous fish market, with red snapper the local speciality. The cuisine in this area is rich, and many of the towns have lent their names to dishes or ingredients.

In this part of Mexico, *tamales* (little filled parcels) are rolled in banana leaves, rather than the corn husks which are used elsewhere. Another local speciality is *jicama*, a crisp vegetable, which is served raw with a sprinkling of lime juice and ground chillies.

The Bajio, Central Mexico and Mexico City

To the north of Mexico City is the Bajio, a fertile area bordered by mountains. This is sometimes referred to as Colonial Mexico, and many of the local specialities are distinctly Spanish in origin, such as stuffed tongues and rich beef stews. Traditional Mexican foods are to be found here too, especially *nopales* (cactus paddles) and prickly pears (cactus fruit). *Pulque* – the drink made from the juice of the agave (or century) plant – is popular in this area. Pork is the favourite meat, often served as *Carnitas*. These are pieces of pork which are cooked in lard flavoured with orange, until the outside of each piece is crisp, while the inside is beautifully tender and succulent.

Central Mexico, a land-locked area, lies to the south of Mexico City, and includes the towns of Puebla and Tlaxcala. Puebla is the home of the classic dish, *Chiles en Nogada*, which

consists of stuffed chillies dipped in batter, then fried and served with a walnut sauce. Puebla is also associated with the famous *Mole Poblano*, which was said to have been invented by nuns in a local convent. *Mole Poblano* is a wonderfully complex dish in which turkey or chicken is cooked in a paste made by mixing crushed dried chillies, cinnamon and cloves, with sesame seeds and ground nuts, as well as onion, garlic and sometimes tomatillos.

Tlaxcala, which means "the place of many tortillas" is a town renowned for its food. Chicken stuffed with fruit and nuts is one popular dish, while another consists of lamb cooked in agave leaves. Both are usually washed down with the local *pulque*.

Vast, sprawling and vibrant, Mexico City is one of the most cosmopolitan places on earth, a fact that is reflected in its food. It is often said that Mexicans love to eat and would eat all day if they could, and in Mexico City there is nothing to stop them. The streets are filled with vendors selling all sorts of snacks. Some offer tortas and tortillas filled with various meats (including the chorizo for which nearby Toluca is famous), cheeses, beans and chillies. Others sell *tamales*, *sopes* and tacos to the commuters who rush past on their way to work. Another item available on

Above: Dried chillies and other fruit for sale on the streets of Mexico City.

Below: Thick tortillas are served here with cooked meats, chillies and beans.

market stalls is *cuitlacoche*, a corn fungus which tastes like a flavoursome mushroom. This has been regarded as a delicacy since pre-Columban times. *Cuitlacoche* is cooked and used to fill *crepas* (crepes), which the Mexicans adopted into their cuisine after the French occupation in the 19th century.

The South

Although there are differences between all the regions of Mexico, it is in the Yucatán that these are most marked. This is partly due to the isolation of the area, which was for centuries cut off from the rest of the country by dense

jungle and swampland. The Maya lived here before the conquistadors came to Mexico, and their influence on the cooking can still be seen, particularly in *pibil*-style dishes, which got their name from the *pib* or pit in which they were steamed in Mayan times.

Although the poor soil does not readily support agriculture, corn is grown in areas where the vegetation has been cut and burned, and is ground to make meal, *masa harina*, which is used for corn tortillas and a host of other Mexican dishes. The pungent herb *epazote* is used in the cooking of this region, imparting a distinctive flavour.

Good fish, squid and shellfish, including the large prawns (jumbo shrimp) for which the area is famous, are available along the coast. *Ceviche* is a popular dish, made from several different types of fish and shellfish, either singly or in combination.

Huevos Motuleños, a dish of eggs with refried beans and tomato sauce, is a well known Yucatec dish. Also typical of the area are dry spice pastes, called *recados*. These are mixtures of dried spices and vinegar or citrus juice, which are rubbed on to meat before it is cooked. *Recados* are made throughout the country, but they are particularly popular in the Yucatán. Some include ground achiote seed (annatto powder), which is valued for the earthy flavour and bright yellow colour it imparts. Another hallmark of Yucatec cooking is the habañero, a fiery chilli which is grown exclusively in the region.

Below: A field of corn on the cob drying on the plants.

MEXICAN MEAL PATTERNS

Many of the traditional Mexican dishes are very labour-intensive, reflecting the old society where the women worked all day long collecting the food required and then preparing it. Today, despite industrialization, the traditional meal patterns are still observed, especially in rural areas. Most Mexicans still eat their main meal in the middle of the day, and follow it by a siesta. Even in the cities, where meals are beginning to conform to the international pattern of breakfast, lunch and dinner, the biggest meal of the day is still eaten at lunchtime.

Desayuno

This is a light meal eaten first thing in the morning, soon after waking. It usually consists of a cup of coffee and a bread or pastry – perhaps *churros* or *pan dulce* (sweetened bread).

Almuerzo

Having started work very early in the morning, most Mexicans are ready for something fairly substantial by about 11am. Almuerzo is more brunch than

Above: Prickly chayote, *used in Mexican salads and vegetable dishes.*

Below: Green chillies for sale in a Mexican market.

breakfast, and usually includes an egg dish such as *Huevos Rancheros* or scrambled eggs with salsa and cheese. Tortillas are served, and coffee, milk or fruit juice washes everything down.

Comida

This is the main meal of the day, generally eaten at a leisurely pace from about 3pm. The meal is made up of several courses. Soup is almost always served, and this is followed by a rice or pasta dish. The aptly named *platillo fuerte* – the phrase means "heavy dish" – is the main attraction. This dish is accompanied by tortillas, salad and pot beans or Refried Beans. The clay pot used to cook the pot beans – *Frijoles de Olla* – adds flavour to them. Garlic, coriander (cilantro), onion and stock with chillies are additional ingredients, and cream or cheese is stirred in before serving. The meal closes with *postre* (dessert) and an after-dinner coffee.

Merienda

A light supper, this is often made up from the leftovers of the lunchtime *comida* dishes, which are wrapped in a tortilla to make a burrito. If a more substantial meal is required, a stew or *mole* might be served, with *Cafe con Leche* or hot chocolate to follow the food. *Merienda* is usually eaten between 8 and 9pm.

Above: Women prepare the main family meal in a rural Mexican kitchen.

Cena

This more elaborate meal – dinner – is served when entertaining guests in the evening or on special occasions. It replaces the *merienda* and is made up of two or three courses served any time between 8pm and midnight.

The Main Event

Comida – the main meal of the day – provides the perfect opportunity for relaxing with family or friends. Here are some suggestions of suitable dishes to serve at this time:

Sopa

A hearty soup would not be appropriate, as this is the prelude to a large meal. *Thalpeno*, a thin soup with chicken and avocado, would be ideal, as would a cold coconut soup.

Sopa Seca

Translating as "dry soup" this is actually a rice or pasta dish, served after the conventional soup and before the main course. Rice or vermicelli is cooked in a little oil and then simmered in a broth with onions, garlic, tomatoes and other vegetables. Most of the liquid used is absorbed by the rice or pasta, hence

(the unrefined dark brown cane sugar typical of Mexico) and stirred with a cinnamon stick. A delicious alternative, which packs rather more punch, is coffee with a shot of Kahlúa or tequila.

Snack Foods

Mexicans love to snack. Street food is very popular throughout the country. In towns, stalls equipped with steamers sell *tamales* – little corn husk parcels filled with spiced meat or cheese – from first thing in the morning, so that shift workers can still have their *almuerzo* even if they cannot get home. Later in the day, the stalls sell corn soup or *menudo*, a soup made with tripe. Still more stalls are set up at lunchtime by women who serve home-made food to the workforce. The food is very similar to what would be eaten at home: soup, rice or pasta dishes, stews with tortillas or bread, and desserts. In the evening, the stalls sell *quesadillas*, enchiladas and *antojitos* (little whims or nibbles). On the coast, traders sell prawns (shrimp) on skewers, *Ceviche* (marinated raw fish) threaded on sticks or *elotes* – tender cobs of cooked corn dipped in cream and sprinkled with well-flavoured crumbly cheese.

the name. The rice dishes vary – peas are sometimes added to the basic recipe, and coriander (cilantro), and chillies are used to make the popular "Green Rice". In another variation, yellow rice is flavoured with achiote (annatto), a golden colouring made from the ground seeds of a flowering tree.

Pescado y Legumbres

Sometimes a fish course is served before the main dish. Typically this would be *Ceviche* – raw fish "cooked" by the action of lime juice. Alternatively, a vegetable dish might be offered; perhaps a native vegetable such as *jicama*, served as a salad with a chilli and lime dressing. Plantains are also popular, and either these or courgettes (zucchini) might be fried along with cheese and green chillies.

Platillo Fuerto

The "heavy dish" is typically a stew, served with corn tortillas and a salad. Meatballs in a tomato and chilli sauce is one option; pork with green cactus sauce another. A fisherman's stew of mussels, scallops, prawns (shrimp) and cod would also be suitable. For the accompaniment, a cactus or *chayote* salad would be ideal, or a fresh-tasting salsa of *rajas con limon* – strips of chilli and lime.

Above: A family eating their main meal in an open-air restaurant in Mexico City.

Frijoles

Cooked dried beans are an inevitable – and important – part of the main meal. Traditionally, they formed a very big part of the staple diet of the indigenous people, so the number and variety of bean dishes is exhaustive. Most people, if asked to name a Mexican bean dish, suggest Refried Beans, which is all too often a flavourless mush of badly seasoned pinto beans. The home-cooked equivalent couldn't be more different: tender beans deliciously flavoured with bay leaves, garlic and chillies. Equally delicious are pot beans, *Frijoles de Olla* – dry pinto beans put into a pot and cooked very slowly with water and a little lard until they melt in the mouth. These are traditionally served with Guacamole, salsa, soured cream and crumbled fresh cheese.

Postre y Cafe

After such a heavy meal, the dessert often consists of a fruit platter or a simple, refreshing *Flan* – similar to a crème caramel. A cake made from ground pecan nuts and honey is another favourite. *Comida* traditionally concludes with a drink of coarsely ground coffee sweetened with *piloncillo*

Below: Corn on the cob is cooked and sold as a snack in street stalls.

FEASTS AND FESTIVALS

Long before Christianity came to Mexico, the Indians worshipped gods whom they believed provided their food. The Aztecs were convinced that the world would come to an end unless the gods were constantly propitiated with prayers, sacrifices and rituals. Corn (maize) was regarded as a divine gift – a miraculous staple food which grew in all climates and soils.

Feast days, when people cooked particular dishes or brought specific foods as offerings to the gods, were frequent events. When Christianity spread through Mexico many of these days were appropriated by the Church and either assigned as saints' days or linked to celebrations marking important days in the religious calendar.

January 6th – *Día de los Santos Reyes*

As the culmination of two weeks of Christmas festivities, January 6th marks the meeting between the Magi – the Three Kings – and the infant Jesus. Mexicans commemorate that exchange of gifts with ceremonies of their own, and this is the day on which Christmas presents are given and received. Central to the celebration is King's Day Bread, a yeasted sweet bread ring filled with crystallized fruit, covered with icing and decorated with candied fruit jewels.

Right: Maya Indians in traditional dress perform a bottle dance.

Below: A Mexican dancer wearing a Spanish-influenced traditional dress.

February – Carnival

The weekend before the beginning of Lent sees the beginning of a five-day carnival, a final fling before the period of self-denial. Processions of brightly coloured floats, dancing in the street and feasting are all characteristic of this celebration.

April – *Semana Santa*

Holy week – the period leading up to Easter Day – is an important time in the Mexican calendar, particularly for the many Catholics in the country. One custom peculiar to Mexico is the breaking of confetti-filled eggs over the heads of friends and family.

May 5th – *Cinco de Mayo*

This day commemorates the defeat of the French army at the Battle of Puebla in 1862. After the defeat Napoleon sent 30,000 soldiers into the country, and after a year the French had taken power. *Cinco de Mayo* is of particular importance in the state of Puebla, but is celebrated in other parts of the country and in some American states with large Mexican populations such as southern central California and Texas. Nowadays the holiday is a celebration of Mexican culture, drink and music.

Above: Sugar skulls on sale for the celebration of one of Mexico's most important festivals, The Day of the Dead.

September 16th – Mexican Independence Day

A holiday to mark the day in 1810 when the revolt against Spanish rule began. Outside Mexico, the festival is often promoted by commercial outlets, such as Mexican restaurants and bars.

November 1 & 2 – *Los Días de los Muertes*

Commonly called The Day of the Dead, this is in fact a two-day festival, that combines in one both the ancient Aztec tradition of worship of the dead and the Christian festival of All Saints' Day.

The festival originally came about because of a widely held belief that the souls of the dead are permitted to spend a brief period on earth every year – like a holiday – to give their families a chance to spend time with them. Family members gather at the graveside, bringing the favourite foods of the deceased person, as well as other symbolic dishes that are traditionally eaten on this day. The foods include a sweet pumpkin dessert and *tamales*. At the grave candles are lit, incense is burned, special prayers are said and the food and drink are eaten in a party atmosphere. Although the festival commemorates the dead, it is seen by everyone as a joyous occasion. The Mexican attitude is that life is to be lived to the full, and death is simply a part of the cycle.

December 25th – *Navidad*/Christmas Day

For 12 days before Christmas Day, the festival is heralded by processions – called "*posadas*" – depicting Joseph, with Mary on the donkey, searching for a room at the inn. Christmas Day sees

Below: A shop window advertises "bread of the dead" for the festival.

the start of a two-week family holiday for most Mexicans. On the afternoon of the day itself families share a special meal. This traditionally starts with the sharing of the *rosca* – a sweet ring-shaped loaf with a small ceramic doll representing the infant Jesus baked inside it. Whoever finds the doll in their slice of cake must host a party on February 2nd, *Día de Candelaria* (Candlemas). The high point of the Christmas feast is the main course, when *Mole Poblano*, a rich turkey dish made with chillies, nuts, tomatoes, garlic, cinnamon and chocolate is served. It is accompanied by *tamales blancos* – corn husk parcels filled with a flavoured mixture that is based on white cornmeal.

Mexican Weddings

These almost always take place in church. It is traditional for the bride and groom to be united during the ceremony with a *lazo* – a large rosary which is wrapped around them both. Gold or silver coins, a Bible and a rosary are given to the couple during the service by the "*padrinos*", a man and woman especially chosen by the bride and groom for this task. The coins symbolize prosperity. Mexican wedding cookies are served at the subsequent feast. Made from almonds and butter, baked and then sprinkled with sugar, these have a shortbread-like texture.

MEXICAN COOKING OUTSIDE MEXICO

Over the past decade in the UK and for a longer period in the USA there has been a tremendous growth in the number of Mexican restaurants and establishments serving what has come to be known as Tex-Mex food – Mexican food with a Texan influence. Sadly, these restaurants are not always very representative of the wonderful and varied cuisine Mexico has to offer, but what they have done is to stimulate interest in Mexican food and therefore a demand for more authentic Mexican ingredients and equipment. The growing popularity of Mexico amongst tourists has created even more of an interest in the country's varied cuisine.

USA

Mexicans who have emigrated to the United States for political, economic or personal reasons have created their own communities within that country. Parts of the United States such as southern California and Texas, which have strong historical links to Mexico as well as sharing a common border, have large communities of Mexicans and offer some of the best Mexican food. The Mexican cuisine in these areas has

Below: Mexican chillies, when dried, are exported all over the world.

Above and below: Fast-food stalls serving Mexican or Tex-Mex food are a common sight all over America, especially in the South. These two stalls are in New Mexico.

evolved over time to please the palates of local residents. Authentic Mexican ingredients are used, but American products are as well. This style of cooking is often referred to as "fusion", the mixing together of ingredients and flavours from several cultures in one dish, a practice that carries with it the real danger of diluting each country's contribution and distorting the diners' perceptions of each cuisine. In southern California and Texas, however, authentic Mexican ingredients tend to be readily available, thanks to demand and to the proximity to the border, and improved transportation links across Mexico and into the United States ensure that products arrive fresh and undamaged.

The same cannot be said for the rest of the United States. Availability of authentic Mexican ingredients varies from state to state, and some fruits and types of chilli are difficult, if not quite impossible, to obtain.

Other items, such as pinto beans, squash, avocados and chocolate, have become such an integral part of the American diet that few people would consider them to be Mexican foods.

Europe

With the growing number of European people taking holidays in Mexico, the trend for new culinary flavours or

experiences and the increasing market for travel features on television and in magazines, interest in Mexican cuisine has escalated. Nowhere is this more apparent than in Scandinavia, where Mexican food is enormously popular.

Increased demand has led to more varieties of fresh and dried chillies becoming available in both major supermarkets and specialist stores, and this in turn has persuaded more people to experiment with cooking Mexican food at home. The most significant advance in recent years has been the introduction of ready-made corn and flour tortillas in supermarkets and in heat-sealed packs which can be kept in the store cupboard until needed, when they are heated very briefly in the microwave. These have made many dishes much more accessible to the average home cook. People for whom Mexican food meant serving chilli in a taco shell – and who were put off by the sheer messiness of this awkward dish –

Above: Tequila husks. Tequila has grown in popularity around the world.

Below: An American fast-food stall selling Mexican-inspired roasted corn.

discovered ready-made tortillas and were soon experimenting with making fajitas and enchiladas, at first using prepared sauces and ready meals, but then becoming more adventurous. Supermarkets sell ready-made Guacamole, but in order to give this the required shelf life, add extra ingredients such as mayonnaise which dull the fresh, clean taste of the original dish. More discerning cooks prefer still to make their own.

Burritos, nachos and chimichangas are becoming well known, with cooks beginning now to differentiate between Mexico's regional cuisines. Just as the more regional Indian restaurants have persuaded the public that the whole of India cannot be represented by "chicken curry", so people are becoming familiar with the variety and depth of Mexican cuisine and are beginning to seek out more authentic Mexican dishes.

Good quality, reasonably priced Mexican ingredients are available by mail order from a number of specialist suppliers, and this has made it much easier for the enthusiast to recreate genuine dishes at home. Traditional Mexican cooking equipment such as *metates* (used for grinding *masa harina*) and the *molcajete* and *tejolote* (the

Above: Chocolate is now so widespread that people don't necessarily link it with its country of origin, Mexico.

Mexican pestle and mortar) are also available through mail order, but many of the functions for which these utensils are intended are either not necessary or can be carried out just as quickly and efficiently in a food processor.

Restaurants

In America and to a lesser extent in Europe, a number of restaurant chains specializing in Mexican and Tex-Mex food have been established. Tex-Mex restaurants tend to offer burgers and steaks alongside predominantly tortilla-based dishes, so it is not surprising that many people perceive these as being all that Mexico has to offer. Even some restaurants purporting to serve authentic Mexican food perpetuate the myth that Mexicans eat plates piled high with indistinguishable mounds of food, all fairly bland, covered with melted cheese, dollops of soured cream, Guacamole and salsa. In the United States there is an increasing number of small restaurants serving authentic dishes from all over Mexico. A welcome trend indeed.

EQUIPMENT

You need very little by way of specialist equipment in order to cook Mexican food. Most modern Mexican kitchens today have a food processor to do much of the chopping and grinding. However, the items listed below will make many of the tasks easier and are worth investing in if you make a lot of Mexican food.

Tortilla Press

Traditionally, tortillas were always shaped by hand. Skilled women were able to make an astonishing number of perfectly shaped tortillas in a very short time, but this is something of a dying art today. Most people now use metal tortilla presses. Cast iron presses are the most effective, but they must be seasoned (oiled) before use and carefully cared for, so many people today prefer steel presses. These come in various sizes and are heavy, in order to limit the leverage required to work them. Cover the plates with plastic bags or waxed paper and it will be easier to lift the tortillas once they are pressed. Tortilla presses are available in good specialist kitchenware shops and by mail order.

Comal

This is a thin, circular griddle, traditionally used over an open fire to cook tortillas. A cast iron griddle or large frying pan will do this job equally well.

Right: Tortilla press

Above: Metate

Below: Comal

Metate

A *metate* is a grinding stone used to grind corn to make *masa*. It is also used to grind cocoa and *piloncillo* (unrefined cane sugar). The design has not changed for centuries. Made from a sloping piece of volcanic rock, it has three short legs. Before a new *metate* can be used, it must be tempered. A mixture of dry rice and salt is placed on the grinding surface and the *muller* – the implement that does the actual grinding – is used to press the mixture into the surface and remove any loose pieces of sand or grit. The *muller* is made of the same stone as the *metate* and is called a *mano* or *metlapil*. These are quite difficult to locate outside Mexico, but are available by mail order.

Molcajete and *Tejolote*

The mortar and pestle of Mexico, the *molcajete* and *tejolote* are made from porous volcanic rock and must be tempered in the same way as the *metate* before being used. They are ideal for grinding spices such as achiote (annatto) or for grinding nuts and seeds when making *Mole Poblano*.

Tortilla Warmer

Ideal for keeping tortillas warm at the table, this is a small round basket or clay dish with a lid. The size most readily available outside Mexico is suitable for 15cm/6in tortillas. Look for them in specialist kitchenware shops.

Below: Molinollo and wire whisk

Right: Molcajete and Tejolote

Left: Dishes

Ollas

These are the clay pots traditionally used for cooking stews and sauces. They give food a unique flavour, but are seldom to be found outside Mexico, as they are quite fragile. Sadly, they are becoming relatively rare in Mexico too. Flat earthenware dishes decorated around the edge are used for serving and are more easily found than *ollas*.

Molinollo

A carved wooden implement used for whisking drinking chocolate. Some of these are beautiful and are popular with tourists. A wire whisk can also be used.

Above: Ollas

INGREDIENTS

Across the length and breadth of Mexico, the very different types of terrain and variations in climate provide a remarkable range of ingredients. Mexicans are very resourceful, and have made good use of their native foods, as well as adapting many of the ingredients and recipes brought by successive settlers. Some of their favourite foodstuffs will be familiar; others will be unusual; still more may seldom be seen outside their country of origin, but as the popularity of Mexican food continues to soar, demand increases and ingredients that were once rare become commonplace. This chapter is a guide to key ingredients, and offers advice on purchasing, preparing and storing, as well as cooking tips.

CORN (MAIZE AND FLOUR)

The native Indians of Mexico regarded corn as a gift from the gods. How else would they have come by such a versatile food, so hardy and adaptable and able to flourish in all the different climates and soils of their country? They offered up gifts to the god of corn, celebrated him on feast days and even added tiny grains of corn pollen to their traditional sand paintings to give the artworks healing powers. A popular myth held that corn was in fact the very stuff from which the gods created people. Even now, corn accounts for almost 20 per cent of the world's calories taken from food.

In the traditional Navajo Indian wedding ceremony, the bride's

Above: White corn

grandmother presents the couple with a basket of cornmeal and the couple exchange a small handful with each other – such is the significance of corn in their culture.

Every part of the corn cob is used in Mexican culture: the husks for wrapping *tamales*, the silk in medicines, the kernels for food and the stalks for animal feed.The husks from corn cobs are most commonly used for *tamales*, but are also used for wrapping some other foods before cooking. When they are ready, the husks will peel away from the filling. The husks are not eaten, but are discarded once the *tamales* are cooked. In Oaxaca *tamales* are wrapped in banana leaves, which impart a distinctively different flavour.

Varieties and Uses

Corn is the common name for a cereal grass. With wheat and rice, it is one of the world's key grain crops. A native of the Americas, it was introduced into Europe by Columbus, who brought it to Spain. A wide variety of products are produced from corn, including corn syrup, bourbon and starch.

Hybrid varieties of corn can be produced very easily as corn mutates

and adapts to different surroundings readily. There are a few main types of corn used for food, each with several different varieties.

Flint corn This is also known as Indian corn and is described as "flint" because of the hard texture of the kernel. This can be red, blue, brown or purple, which has made this type of corn a popular choice for some of the more novel foods such as blue or red corn tortilla chips. Popcorn is made from a type of flint corn. Predominantly, however, flint corn is used for industrial purposes and animal feed.

Yellow corn A type of "dent" corn, so called because the sides of the kernel are composed of a hard starch and the crown of a softer starch which shrinks to form the characteristic depression or dent. Yellow corn has large, full-flavoured kernels and is used for making many processed foods. It is also the basic ingredient used in corn syrup, cornstarch and corn oil.

White corn is used to make *masa*, a type of dough that is widely used in Mexican cooking. It may seem odd to call it white corn, when the resulting *masa* is actually quite yellow, but the kernels are noticeably whiter than those of yellow corn varieties.

Flour corn is composed largely of soft starch and can readily be ground to make flour for use in baked products.

Below: Red corn

Above: Blue corn

Below: Corn husks; fresh and dried

Preparing Dried Corn Husks

If you are able to buy dried corn husks you will need to make them soft and pliable before using.

Soak the corn husks in a bowl of cold water for several hours. When they are soft, remove them from the bowl and pat dry.

Place the husks flat on a dry surface. Pile on the filling, then tie in neat parcels before steaming.

Grinding produces the very white cornflour (cornstarch) with which we are familiar, and which is the main constituent of custard powder.

Sweetcorn contains more natural sugar than other types of corn. The kernels can be eaten straight from the cooked cob and in Mexico a favourite snack is *elotes con crema*, where the corn cobs are dipped in cream and sprinkled with fresh cheese before being served. The kernels can also be stripped from the cobs and used in soups and vegetable dishes. As soon as the cob is picked, the sugar in the kernels starts to convert to starch. This reduces the natural sweetness, so it is important that the corn is eaten as soon as possible after being picked. Strip off the husks and remove the silks (the thread-like stigmas that catch the pollen) before boiling or steaming the cobs, or baking them in the oven. Sweetcorn can also be cooked on a grill (broiler) or barbecue, which gives the crisp kernels a delicious smoky taste. This is how the Mexicans cook corn on the street as a fast food snack.

Masa/Masa Harina

Masa is the Mexican word for dough, and specifically refers to the fresh corn dough used to make corn tortillas and other corn dishes. The flour – or *masa harina* is traditionally made with sun-dried or fire-dried white corn kernels which have been cooked in water mixed with lime (calcium oxide, not the fruit). They are then soaked in the lime water overnight. The lime helps to swell the kernels and brings about a chemical change which greatly improves the flavour of the *masa*. The wet corn is subsequently ground, using a *metate* – a traditional grinding stone which no self-respecting Mexican kitchen would be without. The resulting *masa* can be used for making corn tortillas – for *tamales*, other ingredients, such as chicken stock and lard need to be added.

In America it is possible to buy fresh *masa* from the factories producing tortillas, but it is not available elsewhere. You can make your own *masa*, but it is a lengthy process and the essential lime is not easy to come by. If you do decide to have a go, it is well worth making a large batch of it and freezing the surplus. *Masa* freezes well, although it will only keep in the refrigerator for a few days.

Right: Two types of Masa harina

Above: Wet corn being ground on the traditional metate.

In some parts of Mexico they serve blue corn *masa* dishes, using the same dough-making process, but a less common corn type.

Corn Tortillas

Have ready a tortilla press and two clean plastic bags, slit if necessary so that they will lie flat. Tortillas are more traditionally cooked on a special griddle called a *comal*, but a cast-iron griddle or large heavy-based frying pan will work just as well.

MAKES 12 × 15CM/6IN TORTILLAS

INGREDIENTS
    275g/10oz/2 cups *masa harina*
    pinch of salt
    250ml/8fl oz/1 cup warm water

1 Place the *masa harina*, salt and water in a large bowl and mix together using a wooden spoon until it forms a dough.

2 Turn out the dough on to a lightly floured surface and knead well for 3–4 minutes until firm, smooth and no longer sticky. Cover the bowl with clear film (plastic wrap) and leave the dough to stand at room temperature for 1 hour.

3 Pinch off 12 pieces of dough of equal size and roll each piece into a ball. Work with one piece of dough at a time, keeping the rest of the pieces of dough covered with clear film (plastic wrap) so that they do not dry out.

4 Open the tortilla press and place a plastic bag on the base. Put a dough ball on top and press with the palm of your hand to flatten slightly.

5 Lay a second plastic bag on top of the round of dough and close the press. Press down firmly several times to flatten the dough into a thin round.

6 Place a large frying pan or griddle over a moderate heat. Open the press and lift out the tortilla, keeping it sandwiched between the plastic bags. Carefully peel off the first bag, then gently turn the tortilla over on to the palm of your hand. Carefully peel off the second plastic bag.

7 Flip the tortilla on to the hot frying pan or griddle and cook for about 1 minute or until the lower surface is blistered and is just beginning to turn golden brown. Turn over using a palette knife and keep warm until ready to serve.

8 Place a clean dish towel in a large ovenproof dish. Transfer the cooked tortilla to the dish, wrap the dish towel over the top and cover with a lid. Keep warm while you cook the remaining tortillas in the same way.

COOK'S TIP
If you do not have a tortilla press, you can improvise by placing the dough between two clean plastic bags and rolling it out with a rolling pin.

Basic *Masa*

Traditionally, tortillas are made with *masa*. *Masa* is made by mixing dried white corn with food grade calcium oxide, although this is difficult to locate in small quantities. For making tortillas, most cooks, even in Mexico, find it easier to use *masa harina*, which is the flour made when *masa* is dried and ground. *Masa harina* should not be confused with cornmeal, polenta or maize meal, all of which are made from corn, but without being soaked or cooked with lime. The taste of tortillas made with *masa harina* is slightly different from that of tortillas made from fresh *masa*, but the flour is much easier to cook with and does away with the need for a *metate*.

Flour Tortillas

Wheat flour tortillas are more common than corn tortillas in the north of Mexico, especially in the areas around Sonora and Chihuahua, where wheat is grown. Flour tortillas differ from corn tortillas in that they include lard, which gives them more pliability and elasticity. For best results, make sure you use a good quality plain (all-purpose) flour.

MAKES ABOUT 12 × 25CM/10IN TORTILLAS

INGREDIENTS
  500g/1¼ lb/5 cups plain flour, sifted
  2.5ml/½ tsp baking powder
  pinch of salt
  100g/3¾ oz/scant ½ cup lard
  about 120ml/4fl oz/½ cup
    warm water

1 Mix the flour, baking powder and salt in a large bowl. Rub in the lard, then gradually add enough water to draw the flour together into a stiff dough.

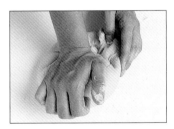

2 Turn out the dough on to a lightly floured work surface and knead it for 10–15 minutes until it is elastic.

3 Divide the dough into 12 even-size pieces and roll into balls using the palms of your hand. Cover the pieces with clear film (plastic wrap) while you are working to stop them drying out.

4 Roll out each ball on a lightly floured surface. Give the dough a quarter turn after each roll to keep the round even. Keep rolling until the round is about 30cm/12in.

5 Warm a large heavy-based frying pan or griddle over a medium heat. Cook one tortilla at a time, placing each one in the ungreased pan or on the griddle and cooking it for 45 seconds–1 minute or until the lower surface begins to blister and brown. Turn over and cook the other side for about 1 minute.

6 Wrap the cooked tortillas in a clean, dry dish towel to keep them soft and warm while you make the rest.

COOK'S TIPS
• If the corn tortillas crack when they are pressed, remove the dough from the press, return it to the bowl and add a little extra water.
• To reheat cold tortillas, sprinkle them with a few drops of water, wrap them in foil and place in an oven preheated to 140°C/275°F/Gas 1 for 10 minutes. Alternatively, wrap them in clear film (plastic wrap) and microwave on maximum power for about 20 seconds.

Quick and Easy Tortilla Fillings
• Cut a skinned chicken breast into thin slices and stir fry with slices of red and yellow (bell) pepper. When the chicken is cooked add the juice of a lime and some fresh oregano, add salt and pepper to taste then use the mixture to fill freshly warmed tortillas. Add some grated cheese if you wish and a spoonful of sour cream.
• If you have some rice and refried beans left from the previous day, mix them together and reheat in a frying pan with a little oil. When the mixture is thoroughly heated spoon into tortillas with grated cheese, slices of tomato and chopped spring onions (scallions).
• Stir fry some mushrooms with plenty of black pepper. Add a dash of soy sauce and a little double (heavy) cream, season to taste then spoon into the tortillas.

FOLDING AND COOKING TORTILLAS

Many Mexican dishes are made with tortillas. The difference lies in the filling, folding and cooking.

Burritos

These are flour tortilla envelopes enclosing various fillings and then folded into the classic shape and the edges sealed with flour and water.

Chimichangas

A chimichanga is a burrito that has been folded, chilled to allow the edges to seal and then deep fried in hot oil until crisp and golden.

Chalupas

Chalupas are pieces of *masa* shaped to resemble canoes or boats and fried until opaque and golden. They are topped with beans, salsa and cheese.

Enchiladas

These can be made from either corn or wheat tortillas. A little filling is laid down the centre of a tortilla, which is then rolled to make a tube, rather like cannelloni. Filled tortillas are laid side by side in a baking dish before being topped with a sauce and baked in the oven or finished under the grill.

Fajitas

These are ideal for informal dinner parties, as various fillings are placed on the table with the hot tortillas, and guests fill and roll their own. The tortilla is then folded to form a pocket around the filling.

Flautas

Corn tortillas are filled with a pork or chicken mixture, rolled tightly into flute shapes, then fried until crisp.

Quesadillas

These tasty treats are made by placing a corn or flour tortilla in a warm frying pan and spreading one half lightly with salsa. A little chicken or a few prawns (shrimp) can be added, and fresh cheese is sprinkled on top. The other half of the tortilla is then folded over, and the quesadilla is cooked for 1–2 minutes, on both sides.

Tacos

The crisp tortilla shells which are often sold in supermarkets as tacos are in fact a Tex-Mex invention. True Mexican tacos are corn tortillas that have been filled and folded in half; they still remain soft. *Taquitos* are miniature tacos – ideal for picnics or parties.

Tostadas

These are individual corn tortillas fried until crisp and then topped with shredded meat, Refried Beans, salsa, Guacamole, sour cream and a little fresh cheese. The finger-food versions are called *tostaditas*.

Totopos

Triangles of corn tortilla, fried until crisp, are called *totopos*. Serve them with a salsa – they are delicious served while still warm.

READY-MADE TORTILLAS

Making Mexican meals is much easier than it once was, thanks to the availability of ready-made tortillas and tortilla chips.

Corn Tortillas

Many supermarkets stock 15cm/6in fresh corn tortillas. Look for them in the bread section. They are ideal for making tacos, tostadas, *totopos* and enchiladas. They do not have a very long shelf life but they do freeze well. Follow the manufacturer's instructions for warming them as methods vary.

Flour Tortillas

These are available in 15cm/6in, 20cm/8in and 25cm/10in sizes, and the packaging is usually marked in inches rather than centimetres. The smallest ones are perfect for fajitas or flour tortilla quesadillas, while the 20cm/8in tortillas are a good size for large quesadillas (to share). Use the largest tortillas for burritos and chimichangas as they allow more room for the filling. Like corn tortillas, fresh flour tortillas are sold in the bread section of supermarkets or in vacuum packs beside the ethnic food ingredients.

The longer-life products tend to be a bit drier and less pliable than the fresh variety, which can be frozen. Flour tortillas sold in shops often contain lard, which makes them softer than the ones that use vegetable oil or fat.

Taco Shells

A Tex-Mex invention, these are so awkward to eat that they are responsible for putting many people off eating Mexican food. They are, however, an excellent substitute for *chalupas*, if making your own seems too much like hard work. Fill them with salsa, beans and fresh, crumbly cheese.

Tortilla Chips

The quality and authenticity of these vary greatly. The best are often to be found in the ethnic food sections of supermarkets rather than with the crisps and snacks. Many of the ones sold in the snack food section have added flavourings, some of which are not remotely Mexican. Plain, lightly salted chips are best for dipping with salsa. Many specialist food stores and health food stores sell organic corn chips and naturally coloured red and blue corn chips (made from coloured corn kernels). These look especially good mixed with yellow corn chips in a dish. Warm them in a low oven or microwave before serving.

Above: Blue and yellow tortilla chips. Plain, lightly salted chips are best for dipping with salsa.

Below: Taco shells are difficult to eat but do have their uses.

Above: Corn tortillas

Below: Wheat flour tortillas

BEANS AND RICE

The importance of beans in the Mexican diet cannot really be overestimated. Indigenous to the country, they were cultivated by the Indians along with corn, and the two staple crops coexisted in a remarkable fashion. Successive plantings of corn soon deplete the soil; beans enrich it by introducing nitrogen. The early inhabitants of Mexico sensed this, and planted both together. They ate them together too, and benefited from the fact that beans supplied nutrients corn lacked, and, unlike corn, were also an excellent source of protein. Rice was first introduced to Mexico by the Spanish and is also an important staple ingredient.

BEANS

Beans continue to be a staple food in Mexico, and there will be a pot of dried beans simmering daily on the cooker top in every home. Fresh beans are eaten, too, of course, but it is the dried beans, with their better keeping properties, that are most widely used. They make a colourful display on market stalls, and there are many different varieties to choose from.

Popular Varieties

Pinto beans and black beans are the most commonly used dried beans in Mexico, although lima beans, which are sold both fresh and dried, are used in a number of dishes and side dishes.

Chick-peas, which in Mexico are called garbanzos, are not native to the country, but were brought in from the Middle East. They have become popular, however, and feature in several dishes.

Pinto beans Pinto is Spanish for "painted" and refers to the speckles of red-brown on the pale pink skins. These beans are native to Latin America and are now widely used in most Spanish-speaking countries. A rich source of protein and iron, they are only available dried. Mexicans use them for all sorts of dishes, but it is as *Frijoles de Olla*, the simple bean dish that is eaten daily in most homes, that they are most familiar. The cooked beans are also the basis of *Refritos* (Refried Beans), and are used in salsas.

Black beans Small, with black skins and cream-coloured flesh, these beans have a wonderfully sweet flavour. Do not confuse them with black-eyed beans, which are white, with a small black eye. The glossy skins look particularly attractive after cooking. They are used in soups and salsas, and are often substituted for pinto beans in *Frijoles de Olla*. Despite their small size, black beans can take quite a long time to

Above: Pinto beans

soften when cooked, so always test before draining, to ensure that they are perfectly tender.

Buying and Storing

Dried beans keep very well, but not indefinitely, so it is best to buy them in relatively small quantities, from a shop with a rapid turnover. That way, they are likely to be tender and full of flavour when soaked and cooked, unlike beans that have been kept for too long, which become dry and so hard that they are only fit for use as weights in pastry cases. Store beans in tightly closed containers in a cool, dry place.

Preparation

Before you use dried beans, put them in a colander or sieve (strainer) and pick them over, removing any foreign bodies, then rinse them thoroughly under cold running water. Drain, tip into a large bowl and pour over plenty of cold water.

Above: Black beans

Leave to soak for several hours, and preferably overnight. Alternatively, you can boil the beans in plenty of water for 3–4 minutes, then cover the pan and set it aside for an hour before cooking. This is very useful when you have forgotten to soak beans for a particular dish, although the long cold soak is preferable.

Main Uses and Cooking Tips

In Mexico, beans are widely used in soups, as fillings for tortillas, in many meat dishes and on their own, either freshly cooked or refried.

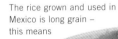

To cook pre-soaked dried beans, simply drain them thoroughly, then put them in a clean pan with plenty of water. Do not add salt, as this would cause the skins on the beans to toughen. Bring the water to the boil and then cook for the time recommended in the individual recipes, usually 1–1¼ hours.

Right: Long grain (top) and ground rice

Cooking times can vary considerably, so always taste for tenderness before finally draining and serving the beans.

RICE

Mexicans have been using rice since it was introduced to the country by the Spanish in the 16th century. It was originally brought to Mexico from the Philippines and was also shipped on to Spain itself.

Description and Varieties

The rice grown and used in Mexico is long grain – this means that each grain is four times longer than its width. White long grain rice that has had the husk removed is most common, although it is often not as refined as the white rice most widely sold in the West.

Buying and Storing

Most rice for sale in the West comes in packets. It keeps extremely well in a cool, dry place, but once packets are opened, any unused rice should be transferred to an airtight container and used as soon as possible. For Mexican food, it is important to use a rice that absorbs the flavours of other ingredients well. It is usual to use ordinary long grain rice, but you may like to experiment with other types.

Main Uses and Cooking Tips

Rice is used in a variety of Mexican dishes, from *sopa seca* (dry soup), which is served as a separate course in the *comida* or main meal, to rice pudding. When served as an accompaniment, rice is usually mixed with other ingredients, as in the popular Green Rice, which includes chillies, and Yellow Rice, which owes its colour to achiote (annatto). Ground rice is used as a flour (*harina de arroz*) in cakes or biscuits. *Horchata* is a drink made with rice that has been soaked and then finely ground. Most Mexicans tend to soak their rice in boiled water for a minimum of 10 minutes before they cook it. This reduces the cooking time and also encourages the rice to absorb other flavours. After soaking, it should be drained thoroughly before being cooked.

CHOCOLATE, NUTS AND SEEDS

Sweets, puddings, cakes and pastries are much loved by the Mexicans, but the sweet ingredients that go into these are also used in savoury dishes, and chocolate, along with various types of nuts and seeds are very important elements of Mexican cooking.

CHOCOLATE

When the Spanish reached Mexico, they discovered a wealth of unfamiliar ingredients, including potatoes, vanilla, avocados and squash. One of their greatest finds, however, was chocolate. The Aztecs were very partial to a drink made from the beans of the cacao tree, which they flavoured in many different ways, and the Spanish, like the rest of the world after them, embraced this wonderful new taste with enthusiasm,

developing a fondness for a variation that included corn, honey and spices.

The conquistadors took chocolate back to Spain, and it was not long before all the most fashionable resorts and cities in Europe boasted cocoa houses. Initially it was served as a drink, but Spanish women also prepared it as a sweetmeat, mixing it with sugar, cinnamon, eggs and almonds. Europeans started producing chocolate in slabs some two hundred years later, but women in Guatemala began pressing chocolate powder into bars for storage some time before this. When slabs of chocolate were finally produced in Mexico, the chocolate was sweetened and spiced in Spanish style.

Mexican Chocolate

This is made using dark and bitter chocolate mixed with sugar, ground nuts and cinnamon, and pressed into discs. The chocolate has a grainy quality, thanks to the sugar and almonds, and is crumbly when broken. One of the most popular brands is *Ibarra*, which comes in a distinctive yellow hexagonal box. Some specialist suppliers outside Mexico stock this product.

Buying and Storing

Mexican chocolate comes in packs, each containing five or six discs that are wrapped individually in waxed paper. Check the packet for a use-by date. Store in a cool, dry place.

Left: Ibarra chocolate

Making Mexican Chocolate

If you cannot buy Mexican chocolate, you can still make an acceptable substitute, using dark bitter chocolate with a minimum of 70 per cent cocoa solids.

Break 115g/4oz dark chocolate into pieces and put it in a food processor. Add 25g/1oz/¼ cup ground almonds, 50g/2oz/¼ cup caster (superfine) sugar and 10ml/2 tsp cinnamon. Process to a fine powder, then tip into an airtight container, close the lid tightly and store in the refrigerator for up to 2 weeks, using as required.

Main Uses and Cooking Tips

The main use for chocolate in Mexico is still as a beverage. Mexicans are very partial to *Champurrada*, a chocolate corn drink, and the classic Mexican Hot Chocolate, which is whisked to a froth with a special whisk called a *molinollo*. Mexican Hot Chocolate is served with *Churros*, long fritters which are dunked in the drink, or *Pan Dulce*, the sweet bread that Mexicans eat for breakfast or as a snack late in the day. The extra ingredients make Mexican chocolate unsuitable for *moles*, the rich stews to which chocolate is traditionally added, so bitter chocolate or cocoa is used.

NUTS AND SEEDS

The three types of nut that are most widely used in Mexican cooking are the pecan, walnut and almond. Pine nuts are used in some desserts and pastries, and coconuts are valued both for their flesh and the cooling liquid they contain. Pecans grow in Northern Mexico. Walnuts, which were introduced from Europe, are cultivated in the colder, central highlands. The Spanish introduced almonds into Mexican cooking during the colonial era, but ensured that the trade with Spain was not disrupted by making it illegal for Mexicans themselves to cultivate them on a large scale.

Seeds from various types of pumpkin and squash have been important ingredients in Mexican cooking for centuries. At one time, pumpkins were grown mainly for their seeds; the flesh was discarded. Sesame seeds are also used, both in pastes and as a garnish on dishes such as *Mole Poblano*.

Buying and Storing

All types of nuts have a limited shelf life once they have been shelled. The oil in them quickly turns rancid, so they should only be bought as required, and stored in a cool, dry place for as short a time as possible. Nuts can, however, be frozen.

Main Uses and Cooking Tips

Salted or coated with sugar, pecans are eaten as a snack food, but their primary use is in desserts such as Pecan Cake. Almonds are used extensively, either whole, chopped or ground, in sweet and savoury dishes, including soups. Mexicans use ground almonds to thicken sauces, and substitute ground almonds for flour in some cakes and biscuits. Walnuts are also used in biscuits, including *Polvorones de Nuez*, which are traditionally eaten at Christmas time (Christmas Cookies with Walnuts). They also feature in savoury dishes such as Stuffed Chillies in a Walnut Sauce (*Chiles en Nogada*). Roasted salted pumpkin seeds are often served as snacks, while ground pumpkin seeds are used in sauces such as *Pepián* (Pumpkin Seed Sauce). Pine nuts, known as *piñon* seeds in Mexico, are added to dishes like *Picadillo* and are also ground for use in desserts and cakes.

Above: Pecans, almonds and walnuts

PILONCILLO – MEXICAN SUGAR

Mexico produces an unrefined brown cane sugar called *piloncillo*. It comes as small cones and adds a distinctive flavour and colour to any dish to which it is added. Unfortunately, *piloncillo* is still not readily available outside Mexico, but soft brown sugar can be used in recipes as a substitute.

Roasting Seeds

When dry roasting or toasting pumpkin or sesame seeds, watch them carefully so that they do not burn. Use a heavy-based pan placed over a low heat, and stir or shake the pan frequently to keep the seeds on the move at all times. If they are allowed to burn, they will taste bitter and will spoil the flavour of any dish to which they are added.

Left: clockwise from top left: pumpkin seeds, sesame seeds and pine nuts

FRUITS

Visit any Mexican market and what will strike you first are the colourful displays of fruit of every size, shape and colour. Some, such as mangoes, papayas and limes, will be familiar, but others may not look or taste like anything you have ever seen before. Fruit is an important part of the Mexican diet, providing the vitamins to balance the corn and beans that are the staple foods. Most of the fruit consumed in Mexico is grown in the country, and some of the surplus is exported to Europe.

CITRUS FRUIT

All types of citrus grow well in Mexico, and because the fruit is allowed to ripen naturally on the trees, it tends to have a very good flavour.

Description and Varieties

Limes have very thin skins which would eventually turn yellow if they were left on the tree long enough. The pulp is green and juicy. Mexican limes – limones – are smaller than other varieties. Almost round in shape, they taste very

Below: Lemons and limes

aromatic. **Lemons** are more oval, and have thicker skins with a dense layer of white pith just below the surface. Their pulp is yellow and acidic, but tastes markedly different to that of lime. **Oranges** grow well in Mexico and freshly squeezed orange juice is widely available, especially in the south. The fruits tend to look much paler than their brightly coloured counterparts in American markets, but are very sweet and juicy.

Buying and Storing

Mexican limes are seldom available outside the country, but any other type of lime can be substituted in recipes. Select limes with smooth, dark green skins, and avoid any that look wizened. The fruit should be heavy for its size. Small brown patches on the skin are harmless and will not affect the flavour or the juiciness of the fruit. Store uncut limes in a plastic bag in the refrigerator or a cool room. They will keep for up to 10 days in their peak condition. Lemons should be plump, with unblemished bright yellow skins. Avoid any whose skins are tinged with green, as this would indicate that the fruit is under-ripe. Oranges should feel heavy for their size. Avoid any that are damaged, shrivelled or have mouldy skins. Oranges keep well at room temperature.

Above: Oranges

Preparation

The rind on citrus fruit is often thinly pared or grated and used for decoration or flavouring. When paring the rind, take care to remove only the coloured outer layer, leaving the bitter white pith behind. The pith must be removed before the fruit is sliced or segmented.

Main Uses and Cooking Tips

Limes, lemons and oranges are used extensively in cooking. Both lime and lemon juice are used to preserve vegetables, as in Onion Relish (*Cebollas en Escabeche*) and are added to casseroles, fruit platters and fresh vegetable dishes to heighten the natural flavours. The most famous use of limes – other than with tequila – is in *Ceviche*. Raw fish or shellfish is marinated in the juice until the texture of the flesh changes, becoming as firm and white as if it had been cooked. Citrus juices are also used to prevent vegetables or fruits, such as avocados, from discolouring on contact with the air. The skins of oranges, lemons or limes are often ground, and the oil is used as a flavouring.

GRANADILLAS

These fruits are the largest members of the passion fruit family. Native to South America, they are round, with a small stalk attached at one end, so that they resemble Christmas tree baubles. The tough, shell-like outer skin is bright orange, while the pulp inside is green and very seedy. It smells and tastes like citrus fruit and is not as fragrant as the pulp of the smaller, purplish-black passion fruit.

Buying and Storing

Unlike passion fruit, which are wrinkled and dimpled when ripe, granadillas should be smooth, with no marks. They can be stored at room temperature for up to 1 week. When ripe, the pulp is moist and juicy, but it dries out if they are stored for too long.

Preparation

Cut the fruit in half and scoop out the pulp with a teaspoon. The seeds are edible, but strain the pulp if you prefer.

Main Uses and Cooking Tips

Granadilla pulp can be used in desserts, either with the seeds, or strained. It is often poured over ice cream or fruit salad, either on its own or in a dessert sauce. It also makes a superb fruit drink and the strained pulp is often mixed with fresh orange juice.

Right: Granadillas

GUAVAS

These fruits – known as *guayabas* in Mexico – are native to the tropical areas of South America and grow in the warmer parts of Mexico. The guava tree grows to a height of about 10m/30ft and has smooth bark and fragrant white flowers. Guavas are an extremely good source of vitamin C. Purées or pastes made from the fruit have been popular in Mexico for centuries, and are still eaten today. They are either served alone or as accompaniments to fresh, soft cheeses.

Description

Guavas vary considerably in colour, shape and size. The variety most popular in Mexico is the yellow guava. When it is ripe the yellow guava has a slightly musky, not particularly pleasant smell. The skin is quite thick, and is referred to as the shell. Inside is a creamy pulp, which is full of edible seeds. The flesh has a clean, sweet, slightly acidic flavour.

Buying and Storing

Guavas should be bought when they are still firm and unblemished. You will find that under-ripe fruit will ripen quite quickly at room temperature. Ripe fruit, however, should be kept in a cool, dark place – or in the refrigerator – as guavas readily ferment and will soon become inedible.

Left: Guavas

Preparation

Cut the fruit in half and scrape out the flesh with a spoon. The seeds can be eaten, or the pulp can be pressed through a sieve (strainer) if preferred.

Main Uses and Cooking Tips

Guavas are usually used in desserts, but their flavour is such that they are equally good in savoury dishes. Sweet guava sauces are served with cakes; savoury ones are excellent with fish.

In Mexico, guava flesh is often boiled with sugar, lemon juice, cinnamon and other spices to make a thick fruit purée. The purée is then poured into a shallow dish and left to cool, then cut into pieces to eat either on its own or with cheese. The fruit is also made into a preserve or relish.

Preparing a Mango

1 Place the mango narrow side down on a chopping board. Cut off a thick lengthways slice, keeping the knife as close to the stone as possible. Turn the mango round and repeat on the other side. Cut off the flesh adhering to the stone.

2 Score the flesh on each thick slice with criss-cross lines at 1cm/½in intervals, taking care not to cut through the skin.

3 Fold the mango halves inside out. The flesh will stand proud, in neat dice. Slice these off, or, for a "hedgehog", leave attached and serve.

MANGOES

Perhaps the most popular of all tropical fruits, mangoes have a wonderful perfume when ripe. The buttery flesh can be absolutely delicious, although some Mexican mangoes have a slightly resinous flavour.

Description and Varieties

There are thousands of varieties of mango. All start off green, but most will change to yellow, golden or red when they are ripe.

Buying and Storing

The best way of telling whether a mango is ripe is to sniff it. It should have a highly perfumed aroma. Next, press it lightly. If it is ripe, the fruit will just yield under your fingertips. Mangoes will ripen at home if placed in a paper bag with a banana. Eat them as soon as they are ripe.

Preparation

It has been said that the best way to eat mango is in the bath. Failing that, use a sharp knife to take a lengthways slice off either side of the fruit, as close to the stone as possible. Scoop out the flesh from each slice, then cut the rest of the flesh off the stone so that none is wasted.

Main Uses and Cooking Tips

Mexicans eat mangoes just as they are, but also use them in a range of desserts and drinks, with or without alcohol. A wonderful way to enjoy mango is in a Mango and Peach Margarita.

PINEAPPLES

Pineapples originated in South America and were introduced to other tropical areas by the Spanish and Portuguese. Historians have found records that prove that pineapples were cultivated by the indigenous peoples of Mexico long before the Spanish conquest.

Description and Varieties

Pineapples have hard, scaly skin and a crown of green leaves on top. The colour of the skin varies. Although most ripe pineapples are yellow or orange, some, such as the Sugar Loaf that grows in Mexico, are green when fully ripe. The flesh is yellow and very juicy, with a sweet flavour that can be tangy or even slightly tart.

Above: Mangoes

Main Uses and Cooking Tips

Mexican pineapples are deliciously sweet, and are usually served quite simply, as dessert. Pineapple is often combined with rice, in savoury dishes as well as sweet, and is used in puddings and sweetmeats. Pineapple juice is very popular, and is widely used in *agua frescas*, the fresh fruit drinks made at home and sold by street vendors.

Buying and Storing

Choose a pineapple that is slightly soft to touch, with a strong colour and crisp, green leaves.
Pineapples must be picked ripe as the starch doesn't convert to sugar after it has been picked. Store in a refrigerator for up to 3 days.

Preparing a Pineapple

1 Use a sharp knife to cut away the green leaves that form the crown and discard it.

2 With a sharp knife, remove the skin from the pineapple cutting deeply enough to remove most of the "eyes".

3 Use a small knife to take out carefully any "eyes" that remain in the pineapple flesh.

4 Cut the pineapple lengthways into quarters and remove the core section from the centre of each piece. Chop the pineapple flesh or cut it into slices and use as required.

Above: Pineapple

PRICKLY PEARS

Prickly pears are the fruits of several different types of cactus. Popular all over South America, they grow wild and are also cultivated, and serve as a staple food in some of the poorer rural areas of Mexico. The fleshy leaves of prickly pears – *nopales* – are treated as a vegetable, and you will find more information about them under the heading of Fruit Vegetables in the latter part of this introduction.

Description

Prickly pears are shaped like grenades and range in colour from deep red to greenish orange. Their name is well earned, for the tough outer skin has tiny tufts of hairs or prickles, which can be very sharp. The fruit is valued for its pulp, which has a sweet aromatic flavour, rather like that of melons, but even more subtle. The pulp contains small brown seeds, which are edible raw, but which become hard when cooked.

Right: Prickly pears

Buying and Storing

To tell whether a prickly pear is ripe, squeeze it carefully (avoiding the prickles!). Do not buy soft fruit or under-ripe fruit which is dark green in colour and very hard. Fruit that is slightly firm will ripen if left at room temperature for a few days.

Preparation

The prickles on these fruit are usually removed before they are sold, but if not, they can be scrubbed off with a stiff brush before the fruit is peeled. It is essential to wear kitchen gloves while carrying out this operation.

Main Uses and Cooking Tips

The peeled fruit should be halved and the flesh scooped out with a teaspoon. It can be strained and used as a sauce, or the fruit can be served as part of a fruit platter. Lime juice and chilli powder are sometimes added to enliven the flavour. Prickly pears can also be made into jelly or jam.

Peeling Prickly Pears

1 Having scrubbed off the prickles, put on a pair of kitchen gloves and hold the fruit down with one hand while you cut off the skin.

2 Alternatively, hold down the prickly pear with a fork and cut a thin slice from the top and bottom of the fruit, then slit the fruit from top to bottom on either side. Peel away the skin, then cut the flesh and arrange on a plate, or simply eat the pear whole.

3 If you prefer, cut the pear in half without removing the skin and scoop out the flesh with a teaspoon. You can eat the flesh in this way as you scoop, or transfer the pulp to a bowl and serve with lime juice.

Above: Coconut

1 Cut off a thin slice from one end.

2 Stand the fruit upright. Cut downwards through the skin at intervals, using a small sharp knife.

3 Bend back the segments and use your fingers to push the seeds into a bowl.

4 Remove all the bitter pith and membrane and use as required.

Other Tropical Fruit Treats

Other fruits popular in Mexico include **papayas**, which are valued for the tenderizing qualities of their skins as well as delicious flesh. These pear-shaped fruits, with vivid yellow skins, are also used in drinks sold by street vendors to quench commuters' thirsts on hot afternoons. Mexicans eat fruit with ground chillies and lime juice as a snack, or part of a meal and slices of papaya are often included. The peppery, round black seeds are edible but are seldom used in dishes. **Pomegranates**, which are used in sauces including the famous dish of Stuffed Chillies in a Walnut Sauce called *Chiles en Nagada*, which is often prepared for special occasions. Pomegranates are also used in refreshing drinks called *Agua Frescas* sold by street vendors. Be careful only to use the seeds and not the bitter-tasting white pith. **Sapodillas** have luscious honey-coloured flesh and taste like vanilla-flavoured banana custard. **Coconuts** are grown in parts of Mexico and pieces are often sold from bowls, cooled with iced water on street corners in busy towns. A chilled coconut soup is often made in the northern Pacific areas. One of the most popular fruits in Mexico is the **sapote**, which has dark salmon-pink flesh. It is very sweet and rather cloying, but makes excellent marmalade, which accounts for its alternative name of marmalade plum.

Above: Papayas

FRUIT VEGETABLES

There are some fruits which are used so often in savoury dishes that we tend to think of them as vegetables. Tomatoes are the obvious example, but avocados, (bell) peppers and chillies also come into this category. Mexico seems to have more than its fair share of these fruit vegetables, including the tomatillo, which is often called the Mexican green tomato, although it is actually related to the physalis.

AVOCADOS

It is believed that the Aztecs introduced avocado seedlings to Mexico during the 13th and 14th centuries, calling them *ahuacatl*, a name whose Spanish version was first corrupted to alligator pear and then to the name by which the fruit vegetable is known today.

Description and Varieties

There are several varieties of avocado. Most are pear-shaped and contain a central stone. The flesh ranges in colour from creamy yellow to bright green and has a buttery texture and mild but distinctive flavour.

The indigenous Mexican avocado has fragrant green flesh around a large stone. The thin skin can be eaten, which is unusual, since most avocados have skins that are tough and inedible, and some, like the Hass variety, have

Left: Avocado

knobbly black skins that are almost shell-like. Hass avocados have creamy flesh and a very good flavour. Another variety is the fuerte avocado, which has glossy green skin and yellow-green flesh.

Buying and Storing

To confirm that an avocado is ripe, press the top end of the fruit gently. It should just yield. If it is soft, the fruit is over-ripe, will prove messy to peel and will have flesh that is soft and mushy. Avocados that are bruised will have blackened flesh.

Finding the perfect avocado is partly a matter of luck, however. Even if you have chosen carefully and have taken great care not to let the fruit get bruised on the journey from the shop to your home, the flesh may still be flecked with brownish spots when you finally cut it open.

Store ripe avocados in the refrigerator; under-ripe fruit will ripen if left for a few days in a warm room. Cut avocados discolour quickly. Although this process can be delayed slightly, it is much more advisable not to prepare the fruit until you are ready to serve it.

Main Uses and Cooking Tips

Avocados are used extensively in Mexican cookery, most famously in Guacamole, the mashed avocado dip. They are also used in soups – both hot and cold – or to make a hot sauce for meat. Fresh avocado tastes wonderful in salads and with seafood. It is often used in tortilla dishes and is also a favourite ingredient in a range of *tortas* – Mexican sandwiches.

As soon as an avocado is cut, the flesh begins to blacken. Sprinkling the slices or chunks with lemon or lime juice delays the process somewhat, and Mexicans swear that burying the avocado stone in the mashed avocado flesh has the same effect.

Avocado Leaves

In Mexico and other countries where the fruit flourishes, fresh or dried avocado leaves are used for their flavouring properties, much as bay leaves are used elsewhere. They can either be crushed and added to dishes or put in whole and then removed just before the dish is served. Dried avocado leaves are usually toasted before being added to dishes such as Refried Beans, stews and marinades, or used for meat that is going to be grilled or barbecued.

Guacamole

Guacamole originated in Mexico, but has become one of the world's most popular dishes. Mashed avocado is the main ingredient, but other items, such as onion, garlic, diced tomato, chopped chillies, lime or lemon juice as well as seasonings are added. The smooth, buttery taste of the avocado gives this dip a creamy texture, yet it contains no saturated fat. Guacamole is often served with tortilla chips as a simple dip. It is an essential accompaniment to fajitas, is used in *tortas*, and is served alongside meat and fish dishes.

Simple Guacamole

1 Cut two avocados in half. Remove the stones and scoop the flesh out of the shells. Place it in a blender and process until almost smooth. Transfer into a bowl and add the juice of half a lime.

2 Add one-quarter of a small onion, chopped finely, a crushed garlic clove and a handful of fresh coriander (cilantro), also chopped finely.

3 Add salt and other seasoning to taste and serve immediately, with tortilla chips for dipping. The Guacamole will keep in the refrigerator for 2–3 days if it is kept in an airtight container.

VARIATION

Try adding chopped fresh tomatoes and fresh chilli to give your Guacamole added flavour, texture and fire.

Preparing Avocado

1 If a recipe calls for avocado halves or mashed avocado, run a small, sharp knife all the way around the fruit, starting at the top and cutting right in until the knife touches the stone.

2 Gently prise the two halves apart with the knife.

3 Push the knife blade into the stone, then lift it away. If any of the brown skin from the stone remains on the avocado flesh, remove it. The avocado halves can be served with vinaigrette, filled with prawns (shrimp) or topped with thin slices of ham. Alternatively, the flesh can be scooped into a bowl and mashed.

1 For avocado slices, cut the fruit in half, remove the stone, then nick the skin at the top of each half and ease it away until you can peel away the skin completely; if the avocado is ripe, it will come away cleanly and easily.

2 Cut the peeled avocado halves into slices, leaving them attached at one end if you want to fan them on the plate. Sprinkle them with lemon or lime juice to stop them from discolouring too quickly.

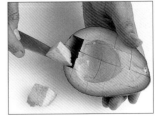

1 For cubes of avocado, score the half of avocado and then with the tip of the knife gently lift each cube out one by one.

Left: Tomatoes

TOMATOES

Tomatoes are native to western South America and were cultivated by the Aztecs long before the Spanish invasion. Hernando Cortés is credited with introducing the first tomatoes – yellow ones – to Europe. They were initially treated with suspicion, but after a pair of Jesuit priests introduced red tomatoes to Italy in the 18th century, they steadily become more and more popular.

Description and Varieties

There are numerous varieties of tomato, ranging from tiny cherry tomatoes to ridged beefsteak tomatoes that measure as much as 10cm/4in across. Great piles of plum tomatoes are a common sight in Mexican markets. Richly flavoured, with fewer seeds than most other varieties, they are a popular choice for salads and salsas.

Buying and Storing

Tomatoes sold in Mexican markets will have ripened naturally, and will be full of flavour, so use ripe home-grown tomatoes or vine tomatoes when cooking Mexican dishes. Over-ripe tomatoes can be used for soups or purées, but avoid any tomatoes which show signs of mould. Avoid buying tomatoes that are still green, but pale ones that have begun to redden can be ripened in a brown paper bag, especially if you add a slice of apple. Try to either store fresh tomatoes at room temperature, or bring them to room temperature before use, as chilling dulls the flavour.

Preparation

If a recipe requires that a tomato be seeded, just cut it in half and squeeze gently, or scoop out the seeds with a teaspoon. To peel, cut a cross in the base of the tomato, immerse it in boiling water for 3 minutes, then plunge into cold water. Drain well. The skins will have begun to peel back from the crosses and will be easy to remove. Chop or slice the tomatoes, as required in individual recipes. If sliced tomatoes are called for, it is better to slice them across, rather than downwards.

Main Uses and Cooking Tips

Mexicans use tomatoes in so many of their recipes that it would be impossible to list them all. They feature in both hot and cold soups, salsas, salads and meat and fish dishes. Chopped tomatoes are added to beans to make *frijoles*, are mixed with avocados in Guacamole, and are used in Sangrita, a popular drink that is sipped alternately with tequila.

TOMATILLOS/TOMATE VERDE

Despite the name by which we know them – and the fact that they are sometimes referred to as Mexican green tomatoes – tomatillos are not members of the tomato family. Instead, they are related to physalis (cape gooseberry), the little orange fruit surrounded by papery lanterns, which are so popular for garnishing. They have been grown in Mexico since Aztec times, when they were known as *miltomatl*. Mexicans seldom use the term "tomatillo", preferring to call these fruit by one of their many local names, which include *fresadilla* and *tomate milpero*.

Description

Ranging in colour from yellowish green to lime, tomatillos are firm, round fruit, about the size of a small tomato, but lighter in weight, as they are not juicy. Fresh ones usually have the brown

*Left: Tomatillos
with husks*

papery husk attached to them at the stem end. The flavour resembles that of tart apples with a hint of lemon, and is enhanced by cooking, although a *salsa cruda* of raw tomatillos has a very pleasant, clean taste.

Buying and Storing

Fresh tomatillos are difficult to come by outside Mexico, but some specialist stores sell them, and they are also available by mail order in season. They can also be grown from seed, a most worthwhile enterprise for anyone who loves their clean, slightly acidic flavour. If you do locate a supply of fresh tomatillos, look for firm fruit with tight-fitting husks, and store them in the refrigerator for up to 1 week.

In the same way that canned carrots bear little resemblance to fresh ones, canned tomatillos are softer and not as tasty as fresh, but they are more readily available and preferable to missing out on this great flavour completely. When buying canned tomatillos, be sure to take account of the loss of weight when the liquid is drained off – it can be as much as a third of the total.

Main Uses and Cooking Tips

Tomatillos are used in table salsas and in the sauce (*tomate verde salsa*) which is poured over enchiladas before they are cooked. They can also be used instead of tomatoes in Guacamole, giving a piquant flavour to the sauce. To cook fresh tomatillos, remove the husks and dry fry them in a heavy-based frying pan until the skins have begun to char and the flesh has softened. Alternatively, put them in a pan with water to cover, bring to the boil, then simmer them until they soften and begin to break down. If the dish in which they are used requires stock, use the cooking liquid.

1 To make a rough textured salsa with tomatillos, process 450g/1lb raw tomatillos in a food processor or chop them finely, then mix with one chopped small onion and one crushed garlic clove. Add two seeded and chopped jalapeño chillies and salt to taste.

2 Finely chop a small bunch of fresh coriander (cilantro) and add it to the tomatillo mixture.

3 Stir well, spoon into a clean bowl and serve at once with freshly made corn tortilla chips.

*Above:
Canned tomatillos*

Right: Plantains

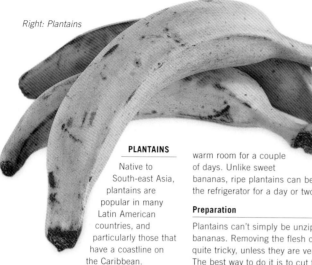

PLANTAINS

Native to South-east Asia, plantains are popular in many Latin American countries, and particularly those that have a coastline on the Caribbean.

Description and Varieties

Plantains are a type of banana, larger than the sweet bananas and with a harder skin. There are several varieties, all initially green, but some ripening to yellow, then black, while others become dark pink or red when ripe. The flesh is fibrous and starchy and must be cooked before being eaten. The flavour can be quite mild, resembling that of a squash, but when plantains are fried, the flesh tastes sweeter and has a more obvious banana flavour.

Buying and Storing

Both green and ripe plantains are used in cooking. Look for them in markets specializing in West Indian or African foods. Ripe plantains are slightly soft to the touch. If a recipe calls for ripe plantains, and you can only get green or yellow ones, they will ripen if left in a

warm room for a couple of days. Unlike sweet bananas, ripe plantains can be stored in the refrigerator for a day or two.

Preparation

Plantains can't simply be unzipped, like bananas. Removing the flesh can be quite tricky, unless they are very ripe. The best way to do it is to cut the plantains into short lengths, then slit the skin along one of the natural ridges so that it can be eased apart and removed. Unless you are going to use the peeled plantains immediately, put them in a bowl of acidulated water (water to which lime juice has been added) to prevent them from discolouring. When slicing plantains for chips, don't remove the skins first. Put the slices into a bowl of salted water for about half an hour, then drain them. It will be quite easy to press the slices of plantain out of their skins.

Main Uses and Cooking Tips

Plantains are used in both sweet and savoury dishes. Fried plantain slices are delicious with a chilli dip or simply a squeeze of lime and a sprinkling of chilli powder. Slices can be cooked in butter and served as a vegetable, the sweet creaminess making them a good partner for a hot, spicy dish. They are good in meat dishes, but make a delectable dessert. Just cook them in butter and cinnamon, with a little sugar and a good measure of rum.

Right: Sweet (bell) peppers

Banana Leaves

In parts of Mexico, banana leaves are used instead of corn husks for wrapping food before cooking. Before use, the leaves should be soaked in water until soft, then dried on kitchen paper. They will impart a unique, slightly lemony flavour to food cooked in them.

SWEET PEPPERS

Sometimes known as bell peppers or capsicums, these are native to Mexico and Central America, and were also a staple food for the Incas in Peru.

Description

Sweet peppers range in colour from green through yellow and orange to deep red, depending on ripeness, and there is even a purplish-black variety. They have a mild, sweet flavour and crisp, juicy flesh. Peppers can be eaten raw or cooked.

Buying and Storing

When buying peppers, try to look for specimens with bright, glossy skins. Avoid any that are limp or wrinkled, or that have "blistered" areas on the skin. Store them in a cool place or in the refrigerator for up to 1 week.

Preparation

Inside each pepper is a core that is surrounded by seeds, which must be removed. If the peppers are to be used whole, this can be lifted out if a neat slice is taken off the top, around the stem. If the peppers are halved or quartered, removing the core and seeds is even easier. Many Mexican recipes call for peppers to be roasted over a gas

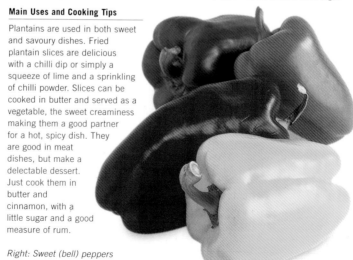

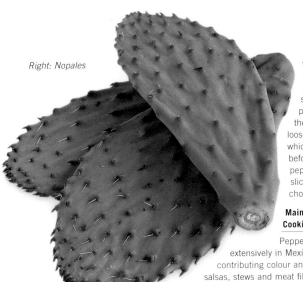

Right: Nopales

flame or in a dry frying pan, then sealed in a plastic bag until the steam loosens the skin, which is removed before the peppers are sliced or chopped.

Main Uses and Cooking Tips

Peppers are used extensively in Mexican cuisine, contributing colour and flavour to salsas, stews and meat fillings, as well as fish dishes, vegetable medleys and salads. For salads, they are usually just cored, seeded and chopped, but for cooked dishes, it is more usual for them to be roasted and skinned first.

NOPALES

Nopales are the edible leaves of several varieties of prickly pear cactus. Fat and fleshy, they are often called cactus paddles. Mexicans have been cooking and eating them for thousands of years.

Description

The leaves – or paddles – are oval in shape, with sharp spines. They range in colour from pale to dark green, depending on variety and age. The flavour is similar to that of a green bean, but with a slightly acidic tang.

Buying and Storing

Fresh *nopales* are quite difficult to locate outside Mexico and the adjoining American states. If you do find them, choose the thinnest, smallest leaves with the palest colour, as older leaves can be very woody, even when cooked. Store fresh *nopales* in the refrigerator for up to 1 week. Bottled *nopales* – called *nopalitos* – have had the spines removed and are sliced before being preserved in brine or vinegar. They are available from specialist food shops.

Preparing Peppers

1 To serve (bell) peppers whole, use a sharp knife to cut a ring around the stem at the top of each pepper. Lift out the core and surrounding seeds. If the peppers can be cut into halves or quarters, do this taking care not to cut into the core, then cut around it and remove.

2 For roasted peppers, roast over a gas glame or in a dry frying pan or griddle.

3 Place them in a strong plastic bag and seal the bag. Leave until the steam loosens the skin. Remove the skin and slice or chop the peppers.

Preparing *Nopales*

1 Wearing gloves or holding each paddle in turn with kitchen tongs, cut off the bumps that contain the thorns with a sharp knife. Try not to remove the whole of the green outer surface; just the parts containing spines.

2 Cut off and discard the thick base from each paddle. Rinse the paddles well and either chop them or cut them into strips.

Main Uses

Nopales are used in stews and soups, particularly in the Tlaxcala area of Mexico, and are pickled for use in salsas and salad dishes. They are even added to scrambled eggs.

Cooking Nopales

Cactus can be slimy when cooked. Mexican cooks often add onion and garlic at the start of cooking, removing them after the sliminess has gone. You can also boil *nopales* in water, drain them, then rinse under cold water. Cover with a damp dish towel and leave for 30 minutes, by which time the gumminess will have disappeared.

CHILLIES

Chillies have been grown in South America for thousands of years. Over 150 indigenous varieties are found in Mexico alone. In 1492 Columbus brought chillies to Europe, and from there they spread around the world.

Mexican food is often perceived as being very hot, and some of the dishes certainly live up to their reputation, but it is possible to find many dishes that are only mildly flavoured with chillies. The heat level of a chilli is determined by the amount of capsaicin it contains. This compound is concentrated mainly in the ribs and seeds, so you can reduce the fieriness considerably by removing these parts. Chillies that have been pickled, or that are used raw, tend to have more heat than cooked chillies.

Below: Jalapeño and serrano chillies

Left: Poblana chillies

The heat level of a chilli is measured in Scoville units, on a scale where 0 is the heat level of a sweet pepper and 300,000 is the hottest chilli, the habañero. In many instances, the ratings have been simplified to a scale of 1–10, to make them easier to remember.

The heat level of a particular chilli will vary according to where it was grown, when it was picked, the irrigation, the weather during the growing season and a host of other factors, so Scoville units can only be a guide. Each crop from the same plant will be different.

Fresh Chillies

The following are the most commonly used fresh chillies:

Serrano Heat level 8. This is a small chilli, about 4–5cm/1½–2in long and 1cm/½in wide, with a pointed tip. Serrano chillies change from green to red when ripe, and are sold at both stages of their development. The flavour is clean and biting. Serranos are used in cooked dishes, Guacamole and salsas.

Jalapeño Heat level 6. One of the most common – and most popular – types of chilli, this is about the same length as a serrano, but plumper. Jalapeños are sold at all stages of ripeness, so you are as likely to find red as green. Green jalapeños are often pickled. One method of preparing jalapeños is to stuff with fresh cheese, coat in a light batter and deep fry.

Poblano Heat level 3. Like many chillies, poblanos are initially green, and ripen to a dark red. They are large chillies, being roughly 8cm/3½in long

Roasting and Peeling Chillies

1 Dry fry the chillies in a frying pan or griddle until the skins are scorched. Alternatively, spear them on a long-handled metal skewer and roast them over the flame of a gas burner until the skins blister and darken. Do not let the flesh burn.

2 Place the roasted chillies in a strong plastic bag and tie the top to keep the steam in. Set aside for 20 minutes.

3 Remove the chillies from the bag and peel off the skins. Cut off the stalks, then slit the chillies and scrape out the seeds.

Above: Fresno chillies

and 5.5cm/2¼in wide, and are sometimes said to be heart-shaped. Although not very hot, poblanos have a rich, earthy flavour which is intensified when the chillies are roasted and peeled. They are widely used in Mexican cooking, notably in Stuffed Chillies (*Chiles Rellenos*). Anaheim chillies, which are widely available in the United States and sometimes in the UK, can be substituted for poblanos.

Fresno Heat level 8. Looking rather like elongated sweet peppers, fresnos are about 6cm/2½in long and 2cm/¾in wide. They have a hot, sweet flavour and are used in salsas, as well as in meat, fish and vegetable dishes. They are particularly good in Black Bean Salsa and Guacamole.

Buying and Storing Fresh Chillies

Look for firm fresh chillies, with shiny skins. Try to avoid any specimens that are dull or limp, as they will be past their best. Fresh chillies can be successfully stored in a plastic bag in the refrigerator for up to 3 weeks. If they are to be chopped and added to cooked dishes, they can be seeded, chopped and then frozen, ready for use until required.

COOK'S TIP

If you bite into a chilli that is uncomfortably hot, swallow a spoonful of sugar. Don't be tempted to gulp down a glass of water or beer; this will only spread the heat further.

Preparing Fresh Chillies

Be very careful when handling fresh chillies as the capsaicin that they contain can cause severe irritation to sensitive skin, especially on the face. Either wear gloves when working with them, or wash your hands thoroughly with soap after handling them. If you touch your skin by mistake, wash your hands quickly and then splash the affected area with plenty of fresh cold water. Avoid scratching or rubbing enflamed skin, as this could aggravate the problem.

1 Holding the chilli firmly at the stalk end, cut it in half lengthwise with a sharp knife.

2 Cut off the stalk from both halves of the chilli, removing a thin slice of the top of the chilli as you do so. This will help to free the white membrane and make it easier to scrape out.

3 Carefully scrape out all of the seeds and remove the core with a small sharp knife.

4 Cut out any white membrane from the inside of the chillies. Keep the knife close to the flesh so that all the membrane is removed.

5 At this point make sure you carefully discard all of the seeds and membrane that are now lying on the board. Then take each half chilli and cut as required. To chop finely first cut the chilli half into thin strips. Then bunch the strips together and cut across them to produce tiny pieces. If the chilli is being added to a dish that will be cooked for some time you can chop it less finely.

DRIED CHILLIES

Dried chillies are nothing new. The convenience of a product that could be stored and rehydrated when needed was realised centuries ago. Chillies were originally sun-dried, but today are more likely to be dried in an oven. Either way, they are a valuable ingredient, and are extensively used in this book because they are so much easier to obtain than fresh chillies are.

In many cases, drying intensifies the flavour of chillies. Depending on the process used, drying can also impart extra flavour, as when jalapeños are dried and smoked. Not only does the flavour deepen to a rich smokiness, but the name of the chilli changes, and it becomes a chipotle. The fact that the same chilli can have two names,

Below: Cascabel chillies

depending on whether it is fresh or dried, can be confusing, and it may be simpler to think of dried chillies as separate varieties. The heat rating given for the dried chillies in the list that follows is based on the same scale as that used for the fresh chillies on the previous pages.

Drying seems to spread the capsaicin through the chillies, so removing the seeds and membrane will do little to alter their heat. The seeds of a dried chilli add very little to the flavour, however, so if they are loose, discard them. Dried chillies can be ground to a powder or cut into strips before being used. Unless the chillies are to be added to a dish with a high proportion of liquid, they are usually soaked in water before use.

Buying and Storing Dried Chillies

Good quality dried chillies should be flexible, not brittle. Store them in an airtight jar in a cool, dry place. For short term storage, the refrigerator is ideal, although they can also be frozen. Do not keep dried chillies for more than a year or the flavour may depreciate.

The following is a list of some of the more common dried chillies, all of which feature in this book.

Ancho Heat scale 3. The most common dried chilli in Mexico, the ancho is a dried red poblano chilli, and has a fruity, slightly sharp flavour. When rehydrated, anchos can be used to make Stuffed Chillies (*Chiles Rellenos*), but should not be peeled first.

Cascabel Heat scale 4. The name means "little rattle" and refers to the noise that the seeds make inside the chilli. This chilli has a chocolate brown skin, and

Above: Chilli powder

Above: Ancho chillies

Right: Chipotle chillies

Grinding Chillies

This method gives a distinctive and smoky taste to the resulting chilli powder.

1 Soak the chillies, pat dry and then dry fry in a heavy-based pan until crisp.

2 Transfer to a mortar and grind to a fine powder with a pestle. Store in an airtight container.

remains dark, even after soaking. Cascabels have a slightly nutty flavour and are often added to salsas such as *tomate verde*.

Chipotle Heat scale 6. These are smoked jalapeños. They add a

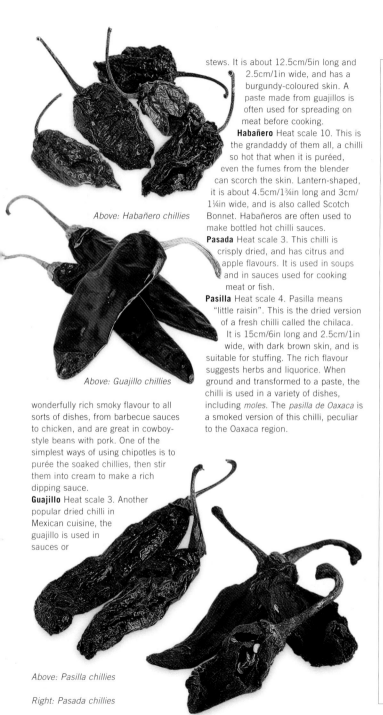

Above: Habañero chillies

Above: Guajillo chillies

wonderfully rich smoky flavour to all sorts of dishes, from barbecue sauces to chicken, and are great in cowboy-style beans with pork. One of the simplest ways of using chipotles is to purée the soaked chillies, then stir them into cream to make a rich dipping sauce.

Guajillo Heat scale 3. Another popular dried chilli in Mexican cuisine, the guajillo is used in sauces or

Above: Pasilla chillies

Right: Pasada chillies

stews. It is about 12.5cm/5in long and 2.5cm/1in wide, and has a burgundy-coloured skin. A paste made from guajillos is often used for spreading on meat before cooking.

Habañero Heat scale 10. This is the grandaddy of them all, a chilli so hot that when it is puréed, even the fumes from the blender can scorch the skin. Lantern-shaped, it is about 4.5cm/1¾in long and 3cm/1¼in wide, and is also called Scotch Bonnet. Habañeros are often used to make bottled hot chilli sauces.

Pasada Heat scale 3. This chilli is crisply dried, and has citrus and apple flavours. It is used in soups and in sauces used for cooking meat or fish.

Pasilla Heat scale 4. Pasilla means "little raisin". This is the dried version of a fresh chilli called the chilaca. It is 15cm/6in long and 2.5cm/1in wide, with dark brown skin, and is suitable for stuffing. The rich flavour suggests herbs and liquorice. When ground and transformed to a paste, the chilli is used in a variety of dishes, including *moles*. The *pasilla de Oaxaca* is a smoked version of this chilli, peculiar to the Oaxaca region.

Soaking Dried Chillies

In order to appreciate their full flavour, it is recommended that dried chillies which are not being ground should be soaked before being used. The amount of time chillies need to rehydrate depends on the type, the thickness of the skin and how dry they are. The longer they soak the better, so if there is time, leave them in the water for 1 hour before cooking.

1 Wipe them to remove any dirt, and brush away any seeds that are accessible.

2 Soak the dried chillies in a bowl of hot water for about 10 minutes (longer if possible) until the colour is restored and the chilli has swelled and softened.

3 Drain, cut off the stalks, then slit the chillies and scrape out the seeds with a small sharp knife. Slice or chop the flesh. If the chillies are to be puréed, put them in a blender or food processor with a little of the soaking water and process them until smooth.

VEGETABLES

Mexico's indigenous peoples were very good agriculturists, and when the Spanish invaded they found a country blessed with abundant vegetables, including corn (maize), sweet potatoes, *jicama*, pumpkins and courgettes (zucchini). The Spanish introduced onions, garlic, green beans, cabbage and cauliflower, all of which were integrated into the Mexican cuisine.

CORN (MAIZE)

The vegetable we know as sweetcorn has been grown in the Americas for over five thousand years. It was brought to Europe by the Spanish in the late 15th century, but long before that it was a staple food of the indigenous peoples of Mexico, who used every part of the corn, including the husks and silks.

Description

An ear of corn consists of yellow, plump kernels on a firm cob, sheathed in long green leaves or husks. Between the leaves and the kernels are long thin threads called silks. Mexicans traditionally use these for tying *tamales*, but elsewhere they are usually discarded.

Buying and Storing

Look for ears whose outer leaves are a fresh, tender green. They should not be limp or faded. One way of testing whether the corn is fresh is to squeeze one of the kernels gently. A milky liquid should ooze out. Corn should be cooked within 24 hours of being purchased, because the sugar starts turning to starch the moment it is cut. The older the corn, the less sweet it will be.

Preparation

Peel off the husks, then pull off the silks. (If necessary, scrub the cobs with a vegetable brush to remove any remaining silks.) If the corn is to be cooked on the barbecue, the husks can be pulled back, then replaced after removing the silks.

Main Uses and Cooking Tips

Corn cobs can be cooked in boiling water, but do not add salt or the kernels will toughen. They can also be cooked in the oven or on the barbecue. In Mexico, corn is a popular street food. The cooked cobs are dipped in cream, then sprinkled with cheese. A similar dish involves removing the kernels from the cobs and cooking them in cream with pickled jalapeños and cheese.

GREEN BEANS

Green beans have been growing in the Americas for hundreds of years. In Mexico lima beans, sometimes called fava beans, are widely used, as are French or string beans.

Buying and Storing

Beans pods should be bright and crisp. Use on the day bought if possible.

Preparation

Top and tail the beans (cut off both ends) and remove any strings on the sides of the pods. Lima beans and broad beans must be removed from their soft, fleshy pods before use, and are sometimes blanched.

Main Uses and Cooking Tips

Mexicans use beans in salads and vegetable dishes. A favourite dish is lima beans with a tomato sauce. Beans are best cooked briefly in boiling water, or steamed until they are tender. Both these methods ensure the beans retain maximum colour, texture and flavour.

Above: Beans

Above: Corn

Right: Sweet potatoes

skins, or, if you prefer, peel them just before boiling and mashing them.

Main Uses and Cooking Tips

Sweet potatoes are used in both sweet and savoury dishes, either cooked slowly in their skins or peeled and boiled. Try them boiled and mashed with a little butter and cream, and some nutmeg, salt and black pepper. A sweet potato mash, with tomatoes and chillies, is a wonderful accompaniment to barbecued food. Roast sweet potatoes are excellent with roast pork. They are also used in stews and casseroles.

SWEET POTATOES

One of the staple foods of the indigenous peoples of Mexico in pre-Columbian times, sweet potatoes are still a very important food.

Description and Varieties

Sweet potatoes are starchy tubers, and need to be cooked before being eaten. There are many different varieties, ranging from pale-skinned sweet potatoes with pale crumbly flesh to darker tubers with thick skins and moist flesh. The skin colour can be anything from pink to deep purple, and the flesh can range from creamy white to the more familiar vivid orange. As their name suggests, they have a sweet flavour, but with a hint of spice.

Buying and Storing

Sweet potatoes have smooth skins and should not be damaged or soft. Smaller specimens often have finer flavour than large ones. They can be stored in a cool, dark place for up to 1 week.

Preparation

Cook sweet potatoes in their

JICAMAS

The *jicama* – or yam bean – is a native of Central America. It was introduced to the Philippines by the Spanish, and from there it spread to China, where it is still popular today. In fact, Chinese supermarkets are a good source of *jicama*. The Chinese name for it is *saa got,* but you may also find it labelled Chinese turnip.

Description

Jicama is the root of a climbing bean plant. The young beans are edible, but older ones are poisonous. It looks like a turnip or beetroot (beets), but has a conical base. The skin is light brown and quite thin. The moist, creamy-coloured flesh tastes slightly fruity, and the texture resembles that of a crisp green apple or a water chestnut. *Jicama* can be eaten raw or cooked.

Buying and Storing

Look for firm *jicamas* that are about the size of a large turnip; larger ones may be a bit woody. To keep the crisp texture, store them in the refrigerator for up to 1 week.

Preparation

Peel away the thin, papery skin by hand or with a sharp knife, then slice the *jicama* thinly.

Below: Jicamas

Main Uses and Cooking Tips

Raw *jicama* makes a refreshing snack when it is sprinkled with freshly squeezed orange juice and served with chilli powder and salt. It is also delicious added to salads and used in salsas. *Jicama* retains its pleasingly crisp texture when boiled, as long as it is not overcooked. Mexicans sometimes like to use grated *jicama* in desserts.

SQUASH

Pumpkins and other types of squash, cucumbers and *chayotes* all belong to the same family, and have been cultivated since ancient times. Pumpkin seeds dating back as far as 7000BC have been found in Mexico. The word "squash" comes from an Indian word, "askutasquash" meaning raw or uncooked, which may seem odd to those of us accustomed to eating squash cooked. However, there are numerous types of squash, and some are indeed delicious eaten raw.

Description

There are two main classifications of squash – summer and winter. Many of the summer squash are now available all the year round, but it can still be useful to differentiate between the two distinct groups.

Summer squash grow on bushes and have thin, edible skins and soft seeds. Examples include courgettes (zucchini), patty pans and marrows. The flesh

Above: Summer squash

is soft, generally pale in colour and has a high water content. It only needs a little cooking, and has a mild flavour. The seeds are dispersed through the flesh, and are usually eaten with it. Courgettes can be eaten raw, in salads. Winter squash have harder, thicker skins and tough seeds. They may grow on bushes, but are often the fruit of vine plants. The skin is usually cut off and discarded, although if the squash is roasted, its skin may be soft enough to eat. Acorn, butternut, spaghetti, onion squash and pumpkin are some of the better known varieties. The flesh is often yellow or deep orange, is firmer and requires longer cooking than that of summer squash. The seeds are generally removed and discarded before cooking, although some,

Above: Pumpkin

such as pumpkin seeds, are a valuable food in their own right.

The blossoms or flowers from both winter and summer squash are edible, and there are a number of Mexican recipes for cooking squash blossoms. In Mexico you can buy the blossoms separately, and they are sold in some speciality food shops elsewhere, but most cooks who want to try them will have to harvest them from home-grown vegetables. They are delicious coated in light batter and fried.

Buying and Storing

Summer squash, and courgettes in particular, are best when they are small, slim and still tender. They should have bright, smooth, unblemished skins with no bruising. They should be stored in the refrigerator, and will only keep for 3–4 days. The thicker skins of winter squash make them much better keepers. They can be stored in a cool room for up to 1 month, depending on how mature they were when picked and on how old they were when sold. When buying winter squash, choose specimens that are heavy for their size and that have unmarked skins.

Main Uses and Cooking Tips

Summer squash can be steamed, stir-fried, boiled, baked or even coated in batter and deep fried. As the flesh is soft, it will only need to be cooked for a few minutes and should still retain some bite. Popular Mexican recipes include Courgette Torte and Courgettes with Cheese and Green Chillies.

Winter squash are often cut into pieces, seeded and baked, steamed or boiled. They need to be cooked for longer than summer squash because the flesh is firmer. The skin is usually discarded, and this can be done either before cooking or after.

Mexicans often roast pumpkins in large chunks. They also cook pumpkin in water and sugar, as a dessert, or bake it with sugar and spices in the oven. Other types of squash are used in similar ways, and cooked squash often features as a filling in both sweet and savoury *empanadas*.

Left: Chayote

CHAYOTES

The *chayote* is native to Mexico. A member of the squash family, it grows on a vine, and goes under several names, including vegetable pear, *chocho* or *chow-chow*, *mirliton* and *choko*. In France it is called a *christophene*.

Chayotes are pale green and pear-shaped, with smooth and leathery skins, which are often furrowed and may be covered with short spines. Inside is a large, flat seed, similar in appearance to that found in a mango. *Chayote* seeds are, however, edible. The flesh is pale and crisp, like that of a tart green apple or a water chestnut.

Buying and Storing

Choose a firm *chayote* with a smooth, unwrinkled skin that is free from blemishes or bruising. Smaller chayotes will be more flavourful than large ones. They keep well in the refrigerator and can be stored for up to 1 month.

Main Uses and Cooking Tips

Chayotes have a fairly mild flavour and are best peeled and served simply in salads or salsas, with a squeeze of lime or orange juice and some chillies. If they are cooked, they should be seasoned well. The mild flavour makes them ideal for combining with other, more strongly flavoured ingredients. To cook *chayotes*, either peel and cook them in the same way as summer squash, or bake them.

Above: Winter squash

Baked Chayote

Cut them in half, brush the cut sides with oil, then either fill them with a vegetable stuffing or simply sprinkle them with salt, pepper and a little spice, if liked. Bake in a pre-heated oven at 190°C/375°F/ Gas 5 for 25 minutes, or until tender all the way through when pierced with a skewer.

CHORIZO, DRIED MEAT AND SALT FISH

In hot countries dried and preserved foods are an important part of the diet. Mexico's traditional dried ingredients are very popular and are used to flavour many dishes.

CHORIZO

Chorizo is a highly seasoned pork sausage made from coarsely ground pork, garlic and spices. It is widely used in Mexican cooking in dishes as varied as Eggs with Chorizo (*Huevos con Chorizo*), soups, stews and casseroles. Mexican chorizo is made from fresh pork, unlike the Spanish chorizo, which is based upon smoked pork. The sausage mixture can be made up as needed and cooked immediately, just as it is, or packed into sausage skins. It can then be hung in a cool place and kept until required.

DRIED MEATS

Machaca is meat, usually beef, that has been salted and sun-dried before being shredded. This way of preparing meat is typical of northern Mexico, from Sonora in the west to Monterrey in the east. *Machaca* is often mixed with scrambled eggs, beans and cheese and wrapped in a flour tortilla. *Carne seca* (the term simply translates as "dried meat") is cut into chunks and served as an appetizer with fresh lime juice. It is one of the most popular dishes of the northern part of Mexico.

Below: Chorizo

Making Fresh Chorizo

As is so often the case, bought sausages can be good, but there is little comparison to the homemade product. Chorizo is easy to make, and you can prepare it in bulk, then freeze the surplus. Air-drying is best left to the experts.

MAKES ABOUT 900G/2LB

INGREDIENTS
    900g/2lb minced (ground) pork
    10ml/2 tsp each salt and ground
      black pepper
    2.5ml/½ tsp freshly grated nutmeg
    5ml/1 tsp dried thyme
    2.5ml/½ tsp ground anise
    2.5ml/½ tsp ground bay leaf
    3 garlic cloves, crushed
    120ml/4fl oz/½ cup sherry
      or brandy
    juice of 2 limes

1 Place the meat in a large bowl and mix in all the other ingredients. Cover and chill in the refrigerator for at least 4 hours or overnight, so that all the flavours blend together.

2 Fill sausage skins with the meat mixture to make individual sausages. Use the sausages immediately or freeze until required.

3 Cook by pricking the skins in several places, then immersing the sausages in a pan of boiling water. Continue to boil for 10 minutes or until the meat is thoroughly cooked.

4 If you prefer, you can shape the sausagemeat into small patties and fry these in a little fat, turning them once to ensure even cooking. Serve the sausages hot, with a spicy tomato-based sauce.

SALTED MEAT AND FISH

Salting was a useful way of preserving meat for long periods in the days before people had refrigerators. If a family slaughtered a pig or cow, every piece of the animal was utilized; by drying surplus meat or making it into sausages, it would have been possible to make it last for several months. Fish was salted for much the same reason, but what began as a necessity is now a delicacy as Mexicans became very fond of fish prepared in this manner. Today, when the need for preserving fish is not as pressing, salt fish, particularly cod, is still popular in Mexican, Spanish, Caribbean and even French cooking.

Soaking Salted Fish

To make it edible, salted fish should be soaked for several hours, preferably overnight. The fish will also have picked up grit and dirt, and is hard and stiff, and needs to be cleaned and softened before it is cooked. Place the fish in a large bowl of fresh water. Change the water frequently. After the fish has soaked for some time, test the water to see how salty it is. As it soaks the fish will become soft and pliable.

SALT COD

Buying and Storing

Salt cod is available from ethnic food stores and some supermarkets, and can be kept in a cupboard for several months before use. The pieces on display look incredibly unappetizing and are rock hard. They are also usually unwrapped and might have a slightly grimy appearance. Don't let this put you off, when it has been cleaned and rehydrated salt fish is perfectly safe to cook with and consume.

Main Uses and Cooking Tips

Before cooking, salt cod must be soaked in water for several hours, or overnight if possible. Change the water frequently to get rid of any dirt and to reduce the salt content. *Bacalao a la Vizcaína* is a salt cod stew which originated in Spain, but is now the traditional dish for Christmas Eve dinner in Mexico. Salt cod can also be cooked and served with a chilli sauce or a classic fresh tomato or citrus salsa.

Right: Salt cod

Making *Machaca* at Home

This might seem an unusual technique for preparing beef, but the results make for a totally authentic experience of Mexican food.

INGREDIENTS
 900g/2lb sirloin steak, about
  5mm/¼in thick
 45ml/3 tbsp medium ground
  sea salt

1 Trim away any gristle from the meat and then sprinkle both sides with the sea salt.

2 Make a hole in each piece of meat and thread string through, or hang the meat from a butcher's hook.

3 Hang the meat for about 3 days in a cool dry place so it can dry out. Alternatively, place the meat on a raised grill pan or suspend it from a rotisserie bar, so that the air can circulate around it, and dry it out in an oven heated to the lowest setting.

4 When the meat is completely dry, place it in a bowl and pour over water to cover. Leave it to rehydrate for about 30 minutes.

5 Drain the meat, and shred it with two forks.

6 Spread it out to dry again. When it has dried, store it in a covered box in the refrigerator until required.

CHEESE

Being a complete protein, cheese was an important addition to the Mexican diet. Until its arrival, Mexicans' main sources of protein were beans and corn, both of which are incomplete. Cheese is widely used in Mexican cooking. The type for each dish is carefully chosen, and the properties – crumbling, melting, grating – are as important as the flavour.

In terms of the history of Mexican cuisine, cheese arrived on the scene fairly late. Before the Conquest in 1521, the main source of meat was the pig, and there was therefore no milk. The Spanish invaders established vast estates and introduced dairy cattle to the country. Milk, cream and butter were produced, and the monks who travelled with the conquerors taught the local people how to make cheeses. At first these were based on traditional Spanish cheeses such as Manchego, but the Mexicans soon developed several cheeses of their own. Today, the range includes cheeses made from goat's and ewe's milk, and also includes varieties that were introduced to Mexico by later immigrants.

There are many different cheeses available in Mexico, but there are a few types that deserve special mention. Unfortunately, Mexican cheeses are seldom sold outside

Below: Feta and ricotta can be used as substitutes for Mexican cheeses.

the country, so acceptable substitutes are suggested for cooks who are unable to access the authentic ingredient.

Below: Mozzarella can be used as a substitute for Asadero.

QUESO FRESCO

As the name suggests, *queso fresco* (fresh cheese) is young and unripened. *Queso fresco* is actually the generic name for a number of different cheeses, of all which share some common characteristics, being moist and creamy in colour, with a very mild flavour and a crumbly texture. The cheese is often used for crumbling over dishes such as scrambled eggs, cooked *nopales* (cactus leaves) or other vegetables. It is also used in tacos and other snacks based on tortillas. *Queso fresco* has a clean, sharp taste and is a good melting cheese. If you can't locate it, substitute a good quality ricotta or mozzarella, preferably bought from a specialist Italian food store.

ASADERO

The name means "roasting cheese" and this is a mild curd cheese which is beautifully supple. *Asadero* is best when it is melted, and is ideal for stuffing chillies or other vegetables or meats, as it is unlikely to leak out. The closest equivalent is mozzarella.

Left: Queso Anejo

QUESO ANEJO

Anejo means "aged". This is a very mature, hard, dry cheese. Sharp and salty, it can be grated easily. *Anejo* is often used for sprinkling on the top of enchiladas. Parmesan cheese makes a good substitute.

QUESO CHIHUAHUA

This cheese resembles *anejo*, but is less salty. Substitute medium Cheddar cheese for it in recipes.

QUESO DE OAXACA

This is another stringy cheese that is ideal for cooking as it has good melting properties. It tastes slightly tart. Monterey Jack is recommended as a substitute in recipes.

Monterey Jack

Monterey Jack is a Californian cheese which originated as *queso del pais* ("country cheese"). Spanish missionaries taught the people of California to make it in the early part of the 18th century. The recipe, which is still being used today, was actually refined in Monterey, California, about 200 years ago. The "Jack" part of the name is reputed to owe its origin to David Jacks, who made the cheese in his dairy, the "s" being dropped when it was felt that the name Monterey Jack was more catchy.

The cheese has a mild flavour and creamy texture and is good to eat on its own as well as being a useful cooking cheese. It matures well, developing a sweet, nutty flavour as it ages. Monterey Jack can be substituted in any recipe calling for *Queso de Oaxaca*, *asadero* or *Chihuahua* cheese. Monterey Jack is very popular all over North America, and is now available in other countries too. If you can't locate Monterey Jack, a mild Cheddar cheese can be used.

Minguichi

Chillies and cheese make an excellent partnership, and the pairing is especially celebrated in dishes called *minguichi* in Michoacán and *chiles con queso* (chillies with cheese) in other areas. There are innumerable variations on the basic theme, using whatever ingredients are to hand. Serve *chiles con queso* on its own with corn tortillas or tortilla chips, or stir in some *Frijoles de Olla* to add more body to the dip. This dish is also very good if chipotle chillies (smoked jalapeños) are used instead of anchos.

In Mexico, the dip would be made with *crema*, a thick cream with a slightly acidic flavour. *Crema* is not readily available outside Mexico, so crème fraîche has been used instead.

MAKES ABOUT 750ML/1¼ PINTS/3 CUPS

INGREDIENTS
250ml/8fl oz/1 cup crème fraîche
225g/8oz/2 cups grated medium
  Cheddar cheese
2 ancho chillies, seeded and
  toasted until crisp

1 Spoon the crème fraîche into a heavy-based pan and cook over a low heat until warmed.

2 Add the cheese and stir until it melts. Crumble in the chillies and mix well, then pour into a bowl and serve immediately.

HERBS, SEASONINGS AND SPICES

Mexican cooking makes use of a wide range of flavourings. Chillies are clearly top of the list. There are so many different varieties that fresh and dried chillies, chilli powders and pastes can create a wide range of flavours, from fiery or merely spicy to supremely subtle. Chillies are by no means the only flavourings used in Mexico, however. Spices like cinnamon and allspice are popular and herbs also play an important role. Some, such as *epazote*, are native to the country, while others were first introduced by Spanish and other immigrant groups.

Achiote

This is the hard red-orange seed of the annatto tree, which is native to the warmer parts of South America, including some areas of Mexico. The seed is ground and added to food to give colour and flavour. Good quality, fresh achiote seeds give food a distinctive, earthy flavour.

Achiote is used a lot in the Yucatán, where it is included in pastes that are spread on meats before cooking.

Allspice

This tree is native to Jamaica, although it may also have grown naturally in the coastal area of Mexico around Tabasco. Columbus is reputed to have brought it to Europe from Jamaica, having mistaken the berries for peppercorns – the Spanish call the spice *pimienta*, which means pepper. Allspice berries are picked, dried and ground or used whole. They are used in various types of *Escabeche* to add flavour to vegetables or fish which is being pickled, and are also added to meat dishes. They even feature in desserts and drinks.

Below: Cumin, right, coriander, left and cloves, bottom right.

Above: Allspice, top, cinnamon quills and ground cinnamon, and achiote, bottom.

Cinnamon

Sri Lankan cinnamon is used quite extensively in Mexican cookery in both sweet and savoury dishes. It was introduced during the colonial era, and is a favourite spice in chorizo sausages. It is also used in rice pudding and is added to such drinks as *Rompope*. Mexican chocolate, which is used to make hot drinks, contains cinnamon. Both ground cinnamon and sticks are used in Mexican cooking.

Cloves

Cloves were brought to Mexico from Asia, via Spain. They are used in the complex spice mixes that are so important in making *moles* and *pepiáns* for cooking with meat and poultry.

Coriander

Fresh coriander leaves, cilantro in Mexico and US, are used in a number of savoury dishes and salsas. The herb

Right: Oregano

Cumin Seeds

Cumin seeds are ground with other spices in some savoury dishes, but are neither used alone nor used in large quantities, as their taste would overpower other, more delicate flavours. Native to Egypt, cumin was introduced in Mexican cuisine during colonial times.

Tamarind

The dark brown, bean-shaped pod comes from the tamarind tree, which has grown in India for centuries. The Spanish introduced it to the West Indies in the 17th century, and it has been growing there ever since. Tamarind is usually marketed as a pressed block of pods and pulp – rather like a block of pressed stoned dates – and is often sold in Indian food shops. The taste is a refreshing mixture of sweet and sour.

Vanilla

Records depicting Aztec life reveal that they were familiar with vanilla, and there is also evidence that it was used

is native to Europe, but is grown in South America too. It has a wonderful flavour and aroma. Coriander seeds are also used in some Mexican recipes, but the two should not be confused, nor should one be substituted for the other, as they have very different flavours.

Right: Vanilla

in Mexico in the 16th century as a flavouring for hot chocolate. Vanilla pods (beans) grow on vines, and until the 1800s, the spice was grown exclusively in Mexico. Good quality pods are very dark brown, waxy and malleable. The spice has a rich aroma and a sweet taste. It is perfect for adding to desserts and is also used to flavour drinks.

Epazote

This herb is widely used in Mexican cooking, but is, unfortunately, not available outside Mexico unless you grow it yourself. There is no real substitute for the distinctive, sharply pungent flavour of this fresh herb. *Epazote* is also useful because when it is cooked with beans such as black beans, it can help to relieve flatulence.

Oregano

There are several varieties of oregano grown in Mexico. The most popular type is from the verbena family; its flavour is stronger and more aromatic than that of the European varieties. Sold fresh or dried in markets across Mexico, oregano adds a delightful sweet note to *Escabeche*, stews and meat dishes.

Right: Tamarind

Vanilla Sugar

Place a vanilla pod (bean) in a large jar full of caster (superfine) sugar. It gives the sugar a wonderful flavour, which is great in cakes, puddings and other sweet dishes, and one pod will flavour several jars full of sugar before it is exhausted.

ALCOHOLIC DRINKS

Mexico has a large number of fermented beverages, mainly derived from fruit or a plant called the agave. Many of these are an acquired taste and not particularly popular outside the country.

BEER

Mexicans were introduced to the brewing process by the German settlers who came to their country and many of the brewing companies in existence today have German roots. Mexican beer production centres largely around the north of the country, although there are breweries everywhere. The city of Monterrey in Nuevo León is renowned as the beer capital of Mexico. Many people are employed in brewing and subsidiary industries such as glass making, carton manufacture and label printing,

Above: Beers

and the beer industry is an important part of the economy. Mexican beer brands such as Dos Equis, Sol and Corona are exported, although these are often brewed outside Mexico on licence. Other brands, such as Tecate, which are less readily available, are worth trying.

WINE

Wine production on a large scale was actively discouraged during the years of Spanish rule as the conquerors wanted to promote wines and spirits from Spain. A wine industry finally did grow up, however, in Baja California, and even today, the major vineyards are in the north-west of the country, although there is some wine production further south. New World wines have become an important part of the wine market in recent years and there is increased interest in wines from Mexico, which are very reasonably priced. The popular grapes for the production of white wine are Chardonnay, Sauvignon Blanc,

Left: Red wine

Right: White wine

Riesling and Chenin Blanc, while established red grape varieties include Cabernet Sauvignon, Pinot Noir and Grenache, as well as Merlot.

PULQUE

Records from the time of Cortés make reference to *pulque* being drunk by the Aztecs. It is a beer-like drink made from the sap of the agave plant, which is commonly called *maguey* in Mexico. While chocolate drinks were the preserve of the ruling classes in 16th century Mexico, *pulque* was drunk by the common people. The drink is still popular today, and *pulquerìas*, small bars selling *pulque* are widespread. These bars were once reputed to be wild, dangerous places, and women, children and people in uniform were not allowed to frequent them.

The traditional method for making *pulque* has changed little since the days of the Aztecs. The sap is extracted from the plant, allowed to ferment for a few weeks, then drunk. If left, it would continue to ferment and would quite soon become undrinkable. The short life span of the product means that it is seldom sold outside Mexico.

Pulque, which is between 6 and 8 per cent proof, has a unique, slightly earthy flavour, and is very definitely an acquired taste. In Mexico, efforts to make it more universally acceptable include blending it with a fruit juice such as pineapple and selling it in cans.

Right: Pulque

KAHLÚA

This is a coffee liqueur made in Mexico city and popular throughout the world. It is added to fresh coffee to make after-dinner coffee and often features in cocktails. Kahlúa is delicious when drunk from a straight liqueur glass with a thin layer of cream floated on the top, and is also irresistible when blended with vanilla ice cream.

MESCAL

This is the generic name for agave spirit. Tequila, which will be discussed in more detail later, is just one type of *mescal*. Unfortunately, in western Europe, the name *mescal* is synonymous with one particular brand of the spirit, which has a *maguey* worm in the bottle. This has led to some monumental drinking

sessions as individuals competed to see who would be landed with the worm, and the reputation of *mescal* suffered in the process. For the record, the worm was originally placed in the bottle to demonstrate the alcoholic proof of the *mescal*, the argument being that the preservation of the worm (actually a moth larva) proved the potency of the alcohol. Oaxaca is largely credited by aficionados as being one of the best areas for *mescal* production. The traditional way of producing the spirit involves taking the heart or *piña* from a number of plants and cooking them in a large pit. An average *piña* will weigh about 50kg/110lb. The procedure begins with the digging of the pit. A large fire is built in the bottom and a layer of rocks is piled on top. When the fire has been burning under the rocks for about a day, the *piñas* are added. They are left to cook for 2–3 days. The cooking plays a large part in determining the flavour, aroma and smoothness of the *mescal*,

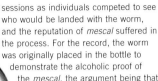

Left: Kahlúa

and is a skilled job. After cooking, the *piñas* are removed from the pit and crushed to release the juice. This, together with the fibrous part of the plant, is mixed with water and left to ferment. More modern methods, involving special ovens, are now used by commercial producers to cook the *piñas* and control the all-important fermentation process.

TEQUILA

Tequila is, without doubt, the Mexican spirit which is best known outside the country. A specific type of *mescal*, it is becoming steadily more popular, especially among younger drinkers.

The Spanish taught Mexicans the art of distilling. *Pulque*, the national drink made from the agave plant, was the perfect subject, and they began by distilling it to make *mescal*. This was then distilled a second time to produce tequila. If *mescal* is brandy, then tequila is Cognac, and is subject to similar

controls to those that are imposed by the French government on their famous spirit. There are also parallels with the production of Champagne, in that tequila production is tightly regulated and may only take place in specially designated areas.

Tequila takes its name from the eponymous town in Jalisco where it was first made. The name means "volcano" in the local Indian dialect. Jalisco is also the home of *mariachi* music, which possibly explains how tequila gained its image as a fun, party drink.

Production

Tequila is made from the sap of the blue agave plant, which is not a cactus, as is commonly believed, but is related to the amaryllis. The leaves of each plant are cut away to leave the *piña*,

which is then steam cooked. The juice is fermented, then distilled twice, the second time in a copper still, after which it is bottled or matured in casks. All aspects of the process are rigidly controlled and documented.

Flavour Variations

There are several different types of tequila, and innumerable brands of all of these. Each brand has a different flavour, determined by the soil and the climate where the agave was grown, the amount of sugar the agave contained and the finer details of the processing, including the cooking of the *piña* and the fermentation of the juice. Some tequilas are matured in casks, and the type of wood used, together with the duration of the ageing process, will also influence the flavour of the finished product.

Not all tequilas are 100 per cent agave spirit; some are blended with cane spirit, but by law tequila must contain at least 51 per cent agave spirit. Blended tequilas are becoming less popular in foreign markets as consumers become more discriminating. At one time

Left: Mescal

Right: Tequila

Left: Tequila blanco

Below: Tequila and lime

Right: A bottle of Tequila anejo

Types of Tequila

Joven or blanco tequila has been bottled immediately after distillation. It is usually clear, but can sometimes be golden in colour. This classification also includes tequilas that have been aged for less than 60 days.

Reposada tequila is golden in colour and has been aged in oak for 2–6 months. It has a more rounded flavour than joven tequila.

Anejo tequila has been aged in oak for a year or more and has a rich golden colour.

Curados is the name given to blanco or joven tequila that has been naturally flavoured. Cinnamon sticks, chillies, almonds and vanilla pods are among the whole flavourings used, but essences and syrups can also be used.

Developing a Taste for Tequila

The best way to become a discriminating tequila drinker is to try as many different brands and types as possible. Compare and contrast them in terms of their appearance, bouquet, viscosity and flavour. Few tequilas taste of only one thing; most are a complex blend of flavours. They may taste sweet, earthy, woody, smooth or even smoky. It is a good idea to taste a new tequila against a familiar brand to give a standard for comparison.

Tequila Drinking

Drinking a shot of tequila in the classic manner, with a lick of salt beforehand and a wedge of lime after, is one of the best ways for Europeans to sample this drink. The method was originally adopted because the spirit was so crude that salt and lime were deemed necessary to make it palatable.

A natural progression from the tequila shot was the margarita. The rim of the glass is dipped in salt, the lime juice and tequila are combined and

triple sec – orange liqueur – is added. A margarita may be served neat, as it comes out of the bottle, or over ice cubes, or "frozen" with crushed ice.

In Mexico, tequila is often sipped alternately with a glass of *sangrita*, a tomato juice flavoured with chillies and other seasonings. When the tequila and tomato juice are combined, the drink becomes a Bloody Maria.

Below: Two types of Curados; bottles of blanco tequila that have had flavouring added. Here a few red chillies have been added to the bottle on the left, and three vanilla pods to the one on the right. The tequila will take on the flavour of the chilli or vanilla in just a few days.

you could walk into a bar in Britain or Europe and find only one type of tequila – and that was primarily used for making margaritas. However, the increasing popularity of Mexican food has led to a gradual rise in the popularity of tequila and a greater appreciation of the various types, and in some places today there are even specialist tequila bars, which stock a vast range of different types and brands of this exciting spirit.

Left: Margarita

THE RECIPES

Mexican cooking is so much more than enchiladas and empanadas, although these are both worthy of mention. Until relatively recently, many Mexican restaurants outside the country tended to serve Tex-Mex food, which owed its origins to Mexico, but had been modified by the country's northern neighbours. Today, discerning diners seek out places that serve true Mexican food – colourful, imaginative and not necessarily fiery – and are keen to recreate their favourite dishes at home.

Supermarkets, gourmet stores and mail-order suppliers have responded to the changing market by stocking specialist ingredients – even such unusual items as tomatillos and the less common varieties of chilli – and this has made it much easier for enthusiastic cooks. The recipes that follow are a cross section of all the different regional dishes available in this exciting country, and illustrate the diversity of flavours, textures and cooking methods that make Mexican cooking so fascinating and delicious.

SALSAS

Salsa simply means sauce, and Mexico is home to some of the finest. Hot and spicy, cool and refreshing, cooked or fresh, all are as versatile as they are varied. Some are poured over food, others are served as relishes. There are a number of classic salsas which are widely used. Chief among the cooked sauces is Pumpkin Seed Sauce, or Pepián, in which the seeds are roasted to give a rich, nutty flavour. Green Tomatillo Sauce, known as Salsa Verde, is very tasty when served over enchiladas or with pork. Of the many uncooked sauces, Classic Tomato Salsa, known as Salsa Ranchera, or Salsa Mexicana, is probably the most popular. This combination of tomatoes, onion, coriander (cilantro) and lime makes a superb accompaniment which appears on almost every table. Unlike commercial sauces, many Mexican salsas contain neither oil nor added sugar, but rely for their flavour on fresh raw fruit and vegetables, making them an excellent choice for the health-conscious. The bright colours, incomparable flavours and adaptability of salsas make them indispensable to any good cook, and their usefulness extends far beyond the boundaries of Mexican cuisine.

Classic Tomato Salsa

This is the traditional tomato-based salsa that most people associate with Mexican food. There are innumerable recipes for it, but the basics of onion, tomato, chilli and coriander are common to every one of them. Serve this salsa as a condiment with a wide variety of dishes.

SERVES SIX AS AN ACCOMPANIMENT

INGREDIENTS
  3–6 fresh serrano chillies
  1 large white onion
  grated rind and juice of 2 limes, plus
    strips of lime rind, to garnish
  8 ripe, firm tomatoes
  large bunch of coriander (cilantro)
  1.5ml/¼ tsp caster (superfine) sugar
  salt

4 Remove the chillies from the bag and peel off the skins. Cut off the stalks, then slit the chillies and scrape out the seeds with a sharp knife. Chop the flesh roughly and set aside.

7 Dice the peeled tomatoes and put them in a bowl. Add the chopped onion which should have softened, together with the lime mixture. Chop the fresh coriander finely.

1 Use three chillies for a salsa of medium heat; up to six if you like it hot. To peel the chillies spear them on a long-handled metal skewer and roast them over the flame of a gas burner until the skins blister and darken. Do not let the flesh burn. Alternatively, dry fry them on a griddle pan until the skins are scorched.

2 Place the roasted chillies in a strong plastic bag and tie the top of the bag to keep the steam in. Set aside for about 20 minutes.

3 Meanwhile, chop the onion finely and put it in a bowl with the lime rind and juice. The lime juice will soften the onion.

5 Cut a small cross in the base of each tomato. Place the tomatoes in a heatproof bowl and pour over boiling water to cover.

8 Add the coriander to the salsa, with the chillies and the sugar. Mix gently until the sugar has dissolved and all the ingredients are coated in lime juice. Cover and chill for 2–3 hours to allow the flavours to blend. The salsa will keep for 3–4 days in the refrigerator. Garnish with the strips of lime rind just before serving.

6 Leave the tomatoes in the water for 3 minutes, then lift them out using a slotted spoon and plunge them into a bowl of cold water. Drain. The skins will have begun to peel back from the crosses. Remove the skins completely.

VARIATIONS
Use spring onions (scallions) or mild red onions instead of white onion. For a smoky flavour, use chipotle chillies instead of fresh serrano chillies.

Energy 122kcal/514kJ; Protein 5.3g; Carbohydrate 21.8g, of which sugars 19.9g; Fat 2.1g, of which saturates 0.4g; Cholesterol 0mg; Calcium 144mg; Fibre 7.9g; Sodium 49mg

GREEN TOMATILLO SAUCE

This sauce, with its distinctive green colour and sharp taste, is a popular choice for pouring over enchiladas. When the cream is added, it is perfect for poached fish or with chicken breasts. Fresh tomatillos are difficult to obtain outside Mexico, but the sauce can be made with canned tomatillos. Instructions for both versions are given here.

SERVES FOUR AS A SAUCE
FOR A MAIN COURSE

INGREDIENTS
300g/11oz fresh tomatillos, plus
    120ml/4fl oz/½ cup stock or water
    or 300g/11oz drained canned
    tomatillos, plus 60ml/4 tbsp/¼ cup
    stock or water
2 fresh serrano chillies
4 garlic cloves, crushed
15ml/1 tbsp vegetable oil
small bunch of coriander (cilantro)
120ml/4fl oz/½ cup double (heavy)
    cream (optional)
salt

1 If using fresh tomatillos, remove the husks and cut the tomatillos into quarters. Place them in a pan and add the stock or water. Cook over a moderate heat for 8–10 minutes until the flesh is soft and transparent.

2 Remove the stalks from the chillies, slit them and scrape out the seeds with a small knife. Chop the flesh roughly and place it in a food processor or blender with the garlic.

3 Add the tomatillos to the processor or blender with their cooking liquid and process for a few minutes until almost smooth. If using drained canned tomatillos, simply quarter and put in the blender or food processor with the smaller amount of stock or water and the chopped chillies and garlic. Process until almost smooth.

4 Heat the oil in a heavy-based frying pan and add the processed tomatillo purée. Reduce the heat and cook gently, stirring, for about 5 minutes until the sauce thickens. Be sure to keep stirring the sauce all the time, since it can easily catch and burn.

5 Chop the coriander and add it to the sauce, with salt to taste. Cook for a few minutes, stirring occasionally.

6 Stir in the cream, if using, and warm the sauce through. Do not let it boil after adding the cream. Serve at once.

Energy 43kcal/179kJ; Protein 1.1g; Carbohydrate 2.9g, of which sugars 2.6g; Fat 3.1g, of which saturates 0.4g; Cholesterol 0mg; Calcium 10mg; Fibre 0.9g; Sodium 8mg

GUACAMOLE

ONE OF THE BEST LOVED MEXICAN SALSAS, THIS BLEND OF CREAMY AVOCADO, TOMATOES, CHILLIES, CORIANDER AND LIME NOW APPEARS ON TABLES THE WORLD OVER. BOUGHT GUACAMOLE USUALLY CONTAINS MAYONNAISE, WHICH HELPS TO PRESERVE THE AVOCADO, BUT THIS IS NOT AN INGREDIENT IN TRADITIONAL RECIPES.

SERVES SIX TO EIGHT

INGREDIENTS
4 medium tomatoes
4 ripe avocados, preferably fuerte
juice of 1 lime
½ small onion
2 garlic cloves
small bunch of coriander (cilantro), chopped
3 fresh red fresno chillies
salt
tortilla chips, to serve

1 Cut a cross in the base of each tomato. Place the tomatoes in a heatproof bowl and pour over boiling water to cover.

2 Leave the tomatoes in the water for 3 minutes, then lift them out using a slotted spoon and plunge them into a bowl of cold water. Drain. The skins will have begun to peel back from the crosses. Remove the skins completely. Cut the tomatoes in half, remove the seeds with a teaspoon, then chop the flesh roughly and set it aside.

COOK'S TIP
Smooth-skinned fuerte avocados are native to Mexico, so would be ideal for this dip. If they are not available, use any avocados, but make sure they are ripe. To test, gently press the top of the avocado; it should give a little.

3 Cut the avocados in half then remove the stones. Scoop the flesh out of the shells and place it in a food processor or blender. Process until almost smooth, then scrape into a bowl and stir in the lime juice.

4 Chop the onion finely, then crush the garlic. Add both to the avocado and mix well. Stir in the coriander.

5 Remove the stalks from the chillies, slit them and scrape out the seeds with a small sharp knife. Chop the chillies finely and add them to the avocado mixture, with the chopped tomatoes. Mix well.

6 Check the seasoning and add salt to taste. Cover closely with clear film (plastic wrap) or a tight-fitting lid and chill for 1 hour before serving as a dip with tortilla chips. If it is well covered, guacamole will keep in the refrigerator for 2–3 days.

Energy 108kcal/445kJ; Protein 1.6g; Carbohydrate 3.1g, of which sugars 2.3g; Fat 9.9g, of which saturates 2.1g; Cholesterol 0mg; Calcium 13mg; Fibre 2.3g; Sodium 8mg

BLACK BEAN SALSA

THIS SALSA HAS A VERY STRIKING APPEARANCE. IT IS RARE TO FIND A BLACK SAUCE AND IT PROVIDES A WONDERFUL CONTRAST TO THE MORE COMMON REDS AND GREENS ON THE PLATE. THE PASADO CHILLIES ADD A SUBTLE CITRUS FLAVOUR. LEAVE THE SALSA FOR A DAY OR TWO AFTER MAKING TO ALLOW THE FLAVOURS TO DEVELOP FULLY.

SERVES FOUR AS AN ACCOMPANIMENT

INGREDIENTS

130g/4½oz/generous ½ cup black
   beans, soaked overnight in water
   to cover
1 pasado chilli
2 fresh red fresno chillies
1 red onion
grated rind and juice of 1 lime
30ml/2 tbsp Mexican beer (optional)
15ml/1 tbsp olive oil
small bunch of coriander (cilantro),
   chopped
salt

1 Drain the beans and put them in a large pan. Pour in water to cover and place the lid on the pan. Bring to the boil, lower the heat slightly and simmer the beans for about 40 minutes or until tender. They should still have a little bite and should not have begun to disintegrate. Drain, rinse under cold water, then drain again and leave the beans until cold.

2 Soak the pasado chilli in hot water for about 10 minutes until softened. Drain, remove the stalk, then slit the chilli and scrape out the seeds with a small sharp knife. Chop the flesh finely.

COOK'S TIP
Mexican beer is a lager-type beer. Few brands are to be found in this country, but the most popular, *Dos Equis* (Double X), is readily available.

3 Spear the fresno chillies on a long-handled metal skewer and roast them over the flame of a gas burner until the skins blister and darken. Do not let the flesh burn. Alternatively, dry fry them in a griddle pan until the skins are scorched. Then place the roasted chillies in a strong plastic bag and tie the top to keep the steam in. Set aside for 20 minutes.

4 Meanwhile, chop the red onion finely. Remove the chillies from the bag and peel off the skins. Slit them, remove the seeds and chop them finely.

5 Tip the beans into a bowl and add the onion and both types of chilli. Stir in the lime rind and juice, beer, oil and coriander. Season with salt and mix well. Chill before serving.

Energy 109kcal/461kJ; Protein 6.6g; Carbohydrate 14g, of which sugars 1.1g; Fat 3.4g, of which saturates 0.5g; Cholesterol 0mg; Calcium 49mg; Fibre 2.7g; Sodium 9mg

PINTO BEAN SALSA

THESE BEANS HAVE A PRETTY, SPECKLED APPEARANCE. THE SMOKY FLAVOUR OF THE CHIPOTLE
CHILLIES AND THE HERBY TASTE OF THE PASILLA CHILLI CONTRAST WELL WITH THE TART TOMATILLOS.
UNUSUALLY, THESE ARE NOT COOKED.

2 Soak the chipotle and pasilla chillies in hot water for about 10 minutes until softened. Drain, reserving the soaking water. Remove the stalks, then slit each chilli and scrape out the seeds with a small sharp knife. Chop the flesh finely and mix it to a smooth paste with a little of the soaking water.

3 Roast the garlic in a dry frying pan over a moderate heat for a few minutes until the cloves start to turn golden. Crush them and add them to the beans.

SERVES FOUR AS AN ACCOMPANIMENT

INGREDIENTS
  130g/4½oz/generous ½ cup pinto
  beans, soaked overnight in water
  to cover
  2 chipotle chillies
  1 pasilla chilli
  2 garlic cloves, peeled
  ½ onion
  200g/7oz fresh tomatillos
  salt

1 Drain the beans and put them in a large pan. Pour in water to cover and place the lid on the pan. Bring to the boil, lower the heat slightly and simmer the beans for 45–50 minutes or until tender. They should still have a little bite and should not have begun to disintegrate. Drain, rinse under cold water, then drain again and tip into a bowl. Leave the beans until cold.

COOK'S TIP
Canned tomatillos can be substituted, but to keep a clean, fresh flavour add a little lime juice.

4 Chop the onion and tomatillos and stir them into the beans. Add the chilli paste and mix well. Add salt to taste, cover and chill before serving.

Energy 97kcal/410kJ; Protein 7g; Carbohydrate 16.8g, of which sugars 3.2g; Fat 0.7g, of which saturates 0.2g; Cholesterol 0mg; Calcium 32mg; Fibre 2.9g; Sodium 10mg

CHIPOTLE SAUCE

THE SMOKY FLAVOUR OF THIS SAUCE MAKES IT IDEAL FOR BARBECUED FOOD, EITHER AS A MARINADE OR AS AN ACCOMPANIMENT. IT IS ALSO WONDERFUL STIRRED INTO CREAM CHEESE AS A SANDWICH FILLING WITH CHICKEN. CHIPOTLE CHILLIES ARE SMOKED DRIED JALAPEÑO CHILLIES.

SERVES SIX AS AN ACCOMPANIMENT

INGREDIENTS
500g/1¼lb tomatoes
5 chipotle chillies
3 garlic cloves, roughly chopped
150ml/¼ pint/⅔ cup red wine
5ml/1 tsp dried oregano
60ml/4 tbsp clear honey
5ml/1 tsp American mustard
2.5ml/½ tsp ground black pepper
salt

1 Preheat the oven to 200°C/400°F/ Gas 6. Cut the tomatoes into quarters and place them in a roasting tin. Roast for 45 minutes–1 hour, until they are charred and softened.

2 Meanwhile, soak the chillies in a bowl of cold water to cover for about 20 minutes or until soft. Remove the stalks, slit the chillies and scrape out the seeds with a small sharp knife. Chop the flesh roughly.

3 Remove the tomatoes from the oven, let them cool slightly, then remove the skins. If you prefer a smooth sauce, remove the seeds. Chop the tomatoes and put them in a blender or food processor. Add the chopped chillies and garlic with the red wine. Process until smooth, then add the oregano, honey, mustard and black pepper. Process briefly to mix, then taste and season with salt.

4 Scrape the mixture into a small pan. Place over a moderate heat and stir until the mixture boils. Lower the heat and simmer the sauce for about 10 minutes, stirring occasionally, until it has reduced and thickened. Spoon into a bowl and serve hot or cold.

GUAJILLO CHILLI SAUCE

THIS SAUCE CAN BE SERVED OVER ENCHILADAS OR STEAMED VEGETABLES. IT IS ALSO GOOD WITH MEATS SUCH AS PORK, AND A LITTLE MAKES A FINE SEASONING FOR SOUPS OR STEWS. MADE FROM DRIED CHILLIES, IT HAS A WELL ROUNDED, FRUITY FLAVOUR AND IS NOT TOO HOT.

SERVES FOUR AS AN ACCOMPANIMENT

INGREDIENTS
2 tomatoes, total weight about 200g/7oz
2 red (bell) peppers, cored, seeded and quartered
3 garlic cloves, in their skins
2 ancho chillies
2 guajillo chillies
30ml/2 tbsp tomato purée (paste)
5ml/1 tsp dried oregano
5ml/1 tsp soft dark brown sugar
300ml/½ pint/1¼ cups chicken stock

1 Preheat the oven to 200°C/400°F/ Gas 6. Cut the tomatoes into quarters and place them in a roasting tin with the peppers and whole garlic cloves. Roast for 45 minutes–1 hour, until the tomatoes and peppers are slightly charred and the garlic has softened.

2 Put the peppers in a strong plastic bag and tie the top to keep the steam in. Set aside for 20 minutes. Remove the skin from the tomatoes. Meanwhile, soak the chillies in boiling water for 15 minutes until soft.

3 Remove the peppers from the bag and rub off the skins. Cut them in half, remove the cores and seeds, then chop the flesh roughly and put it in a food processor or blender. Drain the chillies, remove the stalks, then slit them and scrape out the seeds with a sharp knife. Chop the chillies roughly and add them to the peppers.

4 Add the roasted tomatoes to the food processor or blender. Squeeze the roasted garlic out of the skins and add to the tomato mixture, with the tomato purée, oregano, brown sugar and stock. Process until smooth.

5 Pour the mixture into a pan, place over a moderate heat and bring to the boil. Lower the heat and simmer for 10–15 minutes until the sauce has reduced to about half. Transfer to a bowl and serve immediately or, if serving cold, cover, leave to cool, then chill until required. The sauce will keep in the refrigerator for up to a week.

Energy 76kcal/323kJ; Protein 1.1g; Carbohydrate 11.9g, of which sugars 11.9g; Fat 0.5g, of which saturates 0.1g; Cholesterol 0mg; Calcium 13mg; Fibre 1.3g; Sodium 40mg
Energy 55kcal/230kJ; Protein 2.4g; Carbohydrate 10.4g, of which sugars 9.4g; Fat 0.6g, of which saturates 0.2g; Cholesterol 0mg; Calcium 19mg; Fibre 2.3g; Sodium 27mg

ROASTED TOMATO SALSA

SLOW ROASTING THESE TOMATOES TO A SEMI-DRIED STATE RESULTS IN A VERY RICH, FULL-FLAVOURED SWEET SAUCE. THE COSTENO AMARILLO CHILLI IS MILD AND HAS A FRESH LIGHT FLAVOUR, MAKING IT THE PERFECT PARTNER FOR THE RICH TOMATO TASTE. THIS SALSA IS GREAT WITH TUNA OR SEA BASS AND MAKES A MARVELLOUS SANDWICH FILLING WHEN TEAMED WITH CREAMY CHEESE.

SERVES SIX AS AN ACCOMPANIMENT

INGREDIENTS
  500g/1¼lb tomatoes
  8 small shallots
  5 garlic cloves
  sea salt
  1 fresh rosemary sprig
  2 costeno amarillo chillies
  grated rind and juice of ½ small
    lemon
  30ml/2 tbsp extra virgin olive oil
  1.5ml/¼ tsp soft dark brown sugar

3 Leave the tomatoes to cool, then peel off the skins and chop the flesh finely. Place in a bowl. Remove the outer layer of skin from any shallots that have toughened.

6 Soak the chillies in hot water for about 10 minutes until soft. Drain, remove the stalks, slit them and scrape out the seeds with a sharp knife. Chop the flesh finely and add it to the tomato mixture.

1 Preheat the oven to 160°C/325°F/ Gas 3. Cut the tomatoes into quarters and place them on a baking tray.

4 Using a large, sharp knife, chop the shallots and garlic roughly, place them with the tomatoes in a bowl and mix.

7 Stir in the lemon rind and juice, the olive oil and the sugar. Mix well, taste and add more salt if needed. Cover and chill for at least an hour before serving, sprinkled with the remaining rosemary. It will keep for up to a week in the refrigerator.

2 Peel the shallots and garlic and add them to the roasting tin. Sprinkle with sea salt. Roast in the oven for 1¼ hours or until the tomatoes are beginning to dry. Do not let them burn or blacken or they will have a bitter taste.

5 Strip the rosemary leaves from the woody stem and chop them finely. Add half to the tomato and shallot mixture and mix lightly.

COOK'S TIP
Use plum tomatoes or vine tomatoes, which have more flavour than tomatoes that have been grown for their keeping properties rather than their flavour. Cherry tomatoes make delicious roast tomato salsa and there is no need to peel them after roasting.

Energy 67kcal/278kJ; Protein 1.5g; Carbohydrate 6.6g, of which sugars 5.1g; Fat 4.1g, of which saturates 0.6g; Cholesterol 0mg; Calcium 16mg; Fibre 1.6g; Sodium 10mg

JICAMA SALSA

The jicama is a round, brown root vegetable with a texture somewhere between that of water chestnut and crisp apple. It can be eaten raw or cooked, and is always peeled. Look for jicamas in ethnic food stores.

SERVES FOUR AS AN ACCOMPANIMENT

INGREDIENTS
1 small red onion
juice of 2 limes
3 small oranges
1 *jicama*, about 450g/1lb
½ cucumber
1 fresh red fresno chilli

1 Cut the onion in half, then slice each half finely. Place in a bowl, add the lime juice and leave to soak while you prepare the remaining ingredients.

2 Slice the top and bottom off each orange. Stand an orange on a board, then carefully slice off all the peel and pith. Hold the orange over a bowl and cut carefully between the membranes so that the segments fall into the bowl. Having cut out all the segments, squeeze the pulp over the bowl to extract the remaining juice.

3 Peel the *jicama* and rinse it in cold water. Cut it into quarters, then slice finely. Add to the bowl of orange juice.

COOK'S TIP
The juices of citrus fruits are very useful in preserving colour and freshness, and add more than flavouring to a recipe. For instance, lemon juice added to sliced apples keeps them white. Guacamole retains its colour for two to three days if lime juice is added. In this recipe the lime juice will slightly soften the finely sliced onion.

4 Cut the cucumber in half lengthways, then use a teaspoon to scoop out the seeds. Slice the cucumber and add to the bowl. Remove the stalk from the chilli, slit it and scrape out the seeds with a small sharp knife. Chop the flesh finely and add to the bowl.

5 Add the sliced onion to the bowl, with any remaining lime juice, and mix well. Cover and leave to stand at room temperature for at least 1 hour before serving. If not serving immediately, put the salsa in the refrigerator; it will keep for 2–3 days.

Energy 87kcal/371kJ; Protein 2g; Carbohydrate 20.5g, of which sugars 20.1g; Fat 0.3g, of which saturates 0g; Cholesterol 0mg; Calcium 64mg; Fibre 4g; Sodium 9mg

SWEET POTATO SALSA

VERY COLOURFUL AND DELIGHTFULLY SWEET, THIS SALSA MAKES THE PERFECT ACCOMPANIMENT TO HOT, SPICY MEXICAN DISHES.

SERVES FOUR AS AN ACCOMPANIMENT

INGREDIENTS
675g/1½lb sweet potatoes
juice of 1 small orange
5ml/1 tsp crushed dried
 jalapeño chillies
4 small spring onions (scallions)
juice of 1 small lime (optional)
salt

COOK'S TIP
This fresh and tasty salsa is also very good served with a simple grilled salmon fillet or other fish dishes, and makes a delicious accompaniment to veal escalopes or grilled chicken breasts.

1 Peel the sweet potatoes and dice the flesh finely. Bring a pan of water to the boil. Add the sweet potato and cook for 8–10 minutes, until just soft. Drain off the water, cover the pan and put it back on the hob, having first turned off the heat. Leave the sweet potato for about 5 minutes to dry out, then tip into a bowl and set aside.

2 Mix the orange juice and crushed dried chillies in a bowl. Chop the spring onions finely and add them to the juice and chillies.

3 When the sweet potatoes are cool, add the orange juice mixture and toss carefully until all the pieces are coated. Cover the bowl and chill for at least 1 hour, then taste and season with salt. Stir in the lime juice if you prefer a fresher taste. The salsa will keep for 2–3 days in a covered bowl in the refrigerator.

Energy 155kcal/662kJ; Protein 2.3g; Carbohydrate 37.6g, of which sugars 11.1g; Fat 0.6g, of which saturates 0.2g; Cholesterol 0mg; Calcium 46mg; Fibre 4.3g; Sodium 70mg

NOPALES SALSA

NOPALES ARE THE TENDER, FLESHY LEAVES OR "PADDLES" OF AN EDIBLE CACTUS KNOWN VARIOUSLY AS THE CACTUS PEAR AND THE PRICKLY PEAR CACTUS. THIS GROWS WILD IN MEXICO, BUT IS ALSO CULTIVATED. THE MOST FAMILIAR TYPE SOLD IN MEXICAN MARKETS HAS DARK GREEN OVALS WITH TINY THORNS. FRESH NOPALES ARE DIFFICULT TO TRACK DOWN OUTSIDE MEXICO, BUT IF YOU DO LOCATE A SUPPLY, LOOK FOR PADDLES THAT ARE FIRM AND SMOOTH SKINNED.

SERVES FOUR AS AN ACCOMPANIMENT

INGREDIENTS

2 fresh red fresno chillies
250g/9oz *nopales* (cactus paddles)
3 spring onions (scallions)
3 garlic cloves, peeled
½ red onion
100g/3½oz fresh tomatillos
2.5ml/½ tsp salt
150ml/¼ pint/⅔ cup cider vinegar

1 Spear the chillies on a long-handled metal skewer and roast them over the flame of a gas burner until the skins blister and darken. Do not let the flesh burn. Alternatively, dry fry them in a griddle pan until the skins are scorched. Place the roasted chillies in a strong plastic bag and tie the top to keep the steam in. Set aside for 20 minutes.

2 Remove the chillies from the bag and peel off the skins. Cut off the stalks, then slit the chillies and scrape out the seeds. Chop the chillies roughly and set them aside.

COOK'S TIP
Fresh *nopales* are sometimes available from specialist fruit and vegetable stores. Like okra, they yield a sticky gum, and are best boiled before being used. Fresh cactus will lose about half its weight during cooking. Look out for canned *nopales* (sometimes sold as *nopalitos*) packed in water or vinegar.

3 Carefully remove the thorns from the nopales. Wearing gloves or holding each cactus paddle in turn with kitchen tongs, cut off the bumps that contain the thorns with a sharp knife.

4 Cut off and discard the thick base from each cactus paddle. Rinse the paddles well and cut them into strips then cut the strips into small pieces.

5 Bring a large pan of lightly salted water to the boil. Add the cactus paddle pieces, spring onions and garlic. Boil for 10–15 minutes, until the paddle pieces are just tender.

6 Drain the mixture in a colander, rinse under cold running water to remove any remaining stickiness, then drain again. Discard the spring onions and garlic.

7 Chop the red onion and the tomatillos finely. Place in a bowl and add the cactus and chillies.

8 Spoon the mixture into a large preserving jar, add the salt, pour in the vinegar and seal. Put the jar in the refrigerator for at least 1 day, turning the jar occasionally to ensure that the *nopales* are marinated. The salsa will keep in the refrigerator for up to 10 days.

Energy 18kcal/79kJ; Protein 1.5g; Carbohydrate 2.8g, of which sugars 2.4g; Fat 0.3g, of which saturates 0g; Cholesterol 0mg; Calcium 72mg; Fibre 1.5g; Sodium 6mg

MANGO SALSA

THIS HAS A FRESH, FRUITY TASTE AND IS PERFECT WITH FISH OR AS A CONTRAST TO RICH, CREAMY DISHES. THE BRIGHT COLOURS MAKE IT AN ATTRACTIVE ADDITION TO ANY TABLE.

SERVES FOUR AS AN ACCOMPANIMENT

INGREDIENTS
2 fresh red fresno chillies
2 ripe mangoes
½ white onion
small bunch of coriander (cilantro)
grated rind and juice of 1 lime

1 To peel the chillies spear them on a long-handled metal skewer and roast them over the flame of a gas burner until the skins blister and darken. Do not let the flesh burn. Alternatively, dry fry them in a griddle pan until the skins are scorched.

2 Place the roasted chillies in a strong plastic bag and tie the top to keep the steam in. Set aside for 20 minutes.

COOK'S TIP
Mangoes, in season, are readily available nowadays, but are usually sold unripe. Keep in a warm room for 24 hours or until they are just soft to the touch. Do not allow to ripen beyond this point.

3 Meanwhile, put one of the mangoes on a board and cut off a thick slice close to the flat side of the stone. Turn the mango round and repeat on the other side. Score the flesh on each thick slice with criss-cross lines at 1cm/½in intervals, taking care not to cut through the skin. Repeat with the second mango.

4 Fold the mango halves inside out so that the mango flesh stands proud of the skin, in neat dice. Carefully slice these off the skin and into a bowl. Cut off the flesh adhering to each stone, dice it and add it to the bowl.

5 Remove the roasted chillies from the bag and carefully peel off the skins. Cut off the stalks, then slit the chillies and scrape out the seeds.

6 Chop the white onion and the coriander finely and add them to the diced mango. Chop the chilli flesh finely and add it to the mixture in the bowl, together with the lime rind and juice. Stir well to mix, cover and chill for at least 1 hour before serving. The salsa will keep for 2–3 days in the refrigerator.

ROASTED TOMATO AND CORIANDER SALSA

ROASTING THE TOMATOES GIVES A GREATER DEPTH TO THE FLAVOUR OF THIS SALSA, WHICH ALSO BENEFITS FROM THE WARM, ROUNDED FLAVOUR OF ROASTED CHILLIES.

SERVES SIX AS AN ACCOMPANIMENT

INGREDIENTS
500g/1¼lb tomatoes
2 fresh serrano chillies
1 onion
juice of 1 lime
large bunch of coriander (cilantro)
salt

1 Preheat the oven to 200°C/400°F/ Gas 6. Cut the tomatoes into quarters and place them in a roasting tin. Add the chillies. Roast for 45 minutes–1 hour, until the tomatoes and chillies are charred and softened.

2 Place the roasted chillies in a strong plastic bag. Tie the top to keep the steam in and set aside for 20 minutes. Leave the tomatoes to cool slightly, then remove the skins and dice the flesh.

3 Chop the onion finely, then place in a bowl and add the lime juice and the chopped tomatoes.

4 Remove the chillies from the bag and peel off the skins. Cut off the stalks, then slit the chillies and scrape out the seeds with a sharp knife. Chop the chillies roughly and add them to the onion mixture. Mix well.

5 Chop the coriander and add most to the salsa. Add salt, cover and chill for at least 1 hour before serving, sprinkled with the remaining coriander. This salsa will keep in the refrigerator for 1 week.

Energy 55kcal/234kJ; Protein 1.5g; Carbohydrate 12.2g, of which sugars 11.6g; Fat 0.4g, of which saturates 0.1g; Cholesterol 0mg; Calcium 42mg; Fibre 2.8g; Sodium 7mg
Energy 29kcal/123kJ; Protein 1.3g; Carbohydrate 5g, of which sugars 4.8g; Fat 0.5g, of which saturates 0.1g; Cholesterol 0mg; Calcium 32mg; Fibre 1.9g; Sodium 15mg

CHAYOTE SALSA

CHAYOTE — *OR VEGETABLE PEAR, AS IT IS SOMETIMES CALLED — IS A GOURD-LIKE FRUIT, SHAPED LIKE A LARGE PEAR. SEVERAL VARIETIES GROW IN MEXICO, THE MOST COMMON BEING WHITE-FLESHED AND SMOOTH-SKINNED, WITH A TASTE REMINISCENT OF CUCUMBER.* CHAYOTES *SHOULD BE PEELED BEFORE BEING EATEN RAW OR COOKED. THE SEED, WHICH LOOKS RATHER LIKE A LARGE, FLAT ALMOND, IS EDIBLE. THE CONTRAST BETWEEN THE CRISP* CHAYOTE, *COOL MELON AND HOT HABAÑERO SAUCE MAKES THIS A SPECTACULAR SALSA.*

SERVES SIX AS AN ACCOMPANIMENT

INGREDIENTS
1 *chayote*, about 200g/7oz
½ small Galia melon
10ml/2 tsp habañero sauce or similar hot chilli sauce
juice of 1 lime
2.5ml/½ tsp salt
2.5ml/½ tsp sugar

COOK'S TIP
In some countries, *chayotes* are called *christophenes* or *choko*. They are also used in Chinese cooking, so will be found in Oriental stores.

1 Peel the *chayote*, then cut slices of flesh away from the stone. Cut the slices into thin strips. Cut the melon in half, scoop the seeds out, and cut each half into two pieces. Remove the skin and cut the flesh into small cubes. Place in a bowl with the *chayote* strips.

2 Mix the chilli sauce, lime juice, salt and sugar in a bowl or jug. Stir until all the sugar has dissolved. Pour over the melon and *chayote* mixture and mix thoroughly. Chill for at least 1 hour before serving. The salsa will keep for up to 3 days in the refrigerator.

Energy 16kcal/66kJ; Protein 0.4g; Carbohydrate 3.2g, of which sugars 2.9g; Fat 0.2g, of which saturates 0.1g; Cholesterol 0mg; Calcium 15mg; Fibre 0.5g; Sodium 16mg

PUMPKIN SEED SAUCE

THE ANCESTORS OF MODERN-DAY MEXICANS DIDN'T BELIEVE IN WASTING FOOD, AS THIS TRADITIONAL RECIPE PROVES. IT IS BASED UPON PUMPKIN SEEDS, THE FLESH HAVING BEEN USED FOR ANOTHER DISH, AND HAS A DELICIOUS NUTTY FLAVOUR. IT IS GREAT SERVED OVER STEAMED OR BOILED NOPALES (CACTUS PADDLES) AND IS ALSO DELICIOUS WITH COOKED CHICKEN OR RACK OF LAMB.

SERVES FOUR AS AN ACCOMPANIMENT

INGREDIENTS
130g/4½oz raw pumpkin seeds
500g/1¼lb tomatoes
2 garlic cloves, crushed
300ml/½ pint/1¼ cups chicken
  stock, preferably freshly made
15ml/1 tbsp vegetable oil
45ml/3 tbsp red chilli sauce
salt (optional)

1 Preheat the oven to 200°C/400°F/Gas 6. Heat a heavy-based frying pan until very hot. Add the pumpkin seeds and dry fry them, stirring constantly over the heat. The seeds will start to swell and pop, but they must not be allowed to scorch (see Cook's Tip). When all the seeds have popped remove the pan from the heat.

2 Cut the tomatoes into quarters and place them on a baking tray. Roast in the hot oven for 45 minutes–1 hour, until charred and softened. Allow to cool slightly, then remove the skins using a small sharp knife.

3 Put the pumpkin seeds in a food processor and process until smooth. Add the tomatoes and process for a few minutes, then add the garlic and stock and process for 1 minute more.

COOK'S TIP
When dry frying the pumpkin seeds, don't stop stirring for a moment or they may scorch, which would make the sauce bitter. It is a good idea to stand back a little as some of the hot seeds may fly out of the pan.

4 Heat the oil in a large frying pan. Add the red chilli sauce and cook, stirring constantly, for 2–3 minutes. Add the pumpkin seed mixture and bring to the boil, stirring all the time.

5 Simmer the sauce for 20 minutes, stirring frequently until the sauce has thickened and reduced by about half. Taste and add salt, if needed. Serve over meat or vegetables or cool and chill. The salsa will keep for up to a week in a covered bowl in the refrigerator.

Energy 201kcal/838kJ; Protein 6.1g; Carbohydrate 9.5g, of which sugars 4.8g; Fat 15.6g, of which saturates 1.8g; Cholesterol 1mg; Calcium 39mg; Fibre 2.9g; Sodium 50mg

ONION RELISH

THIS POPULAR RELISH, KNOWN AS CEBOLLAS EN ESCABECHE, *IS TYPICAL OF THE* YUCATAN *REGION AND IS OFTEN SERVED WITH CHICKEN, FISH OR TURKEY DISHES.* TRY *IT WITH BISCUITS AND CHEESE – IT ADDS A SPICY, TANGY TASTE AND WON'T CONTRIBUTE ANY ADDITIONAL FAT OR SUGAR.*

MAKES ONE SMALL JAR

INGREDIENTS

2 fresh red fresno chillies
5ml/1 tsp allspice berries
2.5ml/½ tsp black peppercorns
5ml/1 tsp dried oregano
2 white onions
2 garlic cloves, peeled
100ml/3½fl oz/⅓ cup white wine
  vinegar
200ml/7fl oz/scant cup cider vinegar
salt

1 Spear the fresno chillies on a long-handled metal skewer and roast them over the flame of a gas burner until the skins blister. Do not let the flesh burn. Alternatively, dry fry them in a griddle pan until the skins are scorched. Place the roasted chillies in a strong plastic bag and tie the top to keep the steam in. Set aside for 20 minutes.

2 Meanwhile, place the allspice, black peppercorns and oregano in a mortar or food processor. Grind slowly by hand with a pestle or process until coarsely ground.

3 Cut the onions in half and slice them thinly. Put them in a bowl. Dry roast the garlic in a heavy-based frying pan until golden, then crush and add to the onions in the bowl.

4 Remove the chillies from the bag and peel off the skins. Slit the chillies, scrape out the seeds with a small sharp knife, then chop them.

COOK'S TIP
White onions have a pungent flavour and are good in this salsa, Spanish onions can also be used. Shallots also make an excellent pickle.

5 Add the ground spices to the onion mixture, followed by the chillies. Stir in both vinegars. Add salt to taste and mix thoroughly. Cover the bowl and chill for at least 1 day before use.

Energy 218kcal/902kJ; Protein 8.3g; Carbohydrate 37.1g, of which sugars 24.2g; Fat 1.1g, of which saturates 0g; Cholesterol 0mg; Calcium 118mg; Fibre 6.6g; Sodium 25mg

CHILLI STRIPS WITH LIME

THIS FRESH RELISH IS IDEAL FOR SERVING WITH STEWS, RICE DISHES OR BEAN DISHES. THE OREGANO ADDS A SWEET NOTE AND THE ABSENCE OF SUGAR OR OIL MAKES THIS A VERY HEALTHY CHOICE.

2 Meanwhile, slice the onion very thinly and put it in a large bowl. Squeeze the limes and add the juice to the bowl, with any pulp that gathers in the strainer. The lime juice will soften the onion. Stir in the oregano.

3 Remove the chillies from the bag and peel off the skins. Slit them, scrape out the seeds with a small sharp knife, then cut the chillies into long strips, which are called "rajas".

4 Add the chilli strips to the onion mixture and season with salt. Cover the bowl and chill for at least 1 day before serving, to allow the flavours to blend. The salsa will keep for up to 2 weeks in a covered bowl in the refrigerator.

MAKES ABOUT 60ML/4 TBSP

INGREDIENTS
   10 fresh green chillies
   ½ white onion
   4 limes
   2.5ml/½ tsp dried oregano
   salt

COOK'S TIP
This method of roasting chillies is ideal if you need more than one or two, or if you do not have a gas burner. To roast over a burner, spear the chillies, four or five at a time, on a long-handled metal skewer and hold them over the flame until the skins blister.

1 Roast the chillies in a griddle pan over a moderate heat until the skins are charred and blistered. The flesh should not be allowed to blacken as this might make the salsa bitter. Place the roasted chillies in a strong plastic bag and tie the top to keep the steam in. Set aside for 20 minutes.

Energy 39kcal/165kJ; Protein 3g; Carbohydrate 5.9g, of which sugars 4.5g; Fat 0.6g, of which saturates 0g; Cholesterol 0mg; Calcium 40mg; Fibre 0.9g; Sodium 7mg

HABAÑERO SALSA

THIS IS A VERY FIERY SALSA WITH AN INTENSE HEAT LEVEL. A DAB ON THE PLATE ALONGSIDE A MEAT OR FISH DISH ADDS A FRESH, CLEAN TASTE, BUT THIS IS NOT FOR THE FAINT-HEARTED. HABAÑERO CHILLIES, ALSO CALLED SCOTCH BONNETS, ARE VERY HOT. LANTERN-SHAPED, THEY RANGE IN COLOUR FROM YELLOW TO A DEEP ORANGE RED. COSTENO AMARILLO CHILLIES ARE YELLOW WHEN FRESH AND HAVE A SHARP CITRUS FLAVOUR.

3 Put the chillies in a food processor and add a little of the soaking liquid. Purée to a fine paste. Do not lean over the processor – the fumes may burn your face. Remove the lid and scrape the mixture into a bowl.

4 Put the chopped spring onions in another bowl and add the fruit juice, with the lime rind and juice. Roughly chop the coriander.

SERVE SPARINGLY

INGREDIENTS
5 dried roasted habañero chillies
4 dried costeno amarillo chillies
3 spring onions (scallions), chopped
juice of ½ large grapefruit or
   1 Seville orange
grated rind and juice of 1 lime
small bunch of coriander (cilantro)
salt

1 Soak the habañero and costeno amarillo chillies in hot water for about 10 minutes until softened. Drain, reserving the soaking water.

2 Wear rubber gloves to handle the habañeros. Remove the stalks from all chillies, then slit them and scrape out the seeds with a small sharp knife. Chop the chillies roughly.

5 Add the coriander to the chilli mixture and mix thoroughly. Add salt to taste. Cover and chill for at least 1 day before use. Serve the salsa very sparingly.

Energy 52kcal/218kJ; Protein 5.1g; Carbohydrate 5g, of which sugars 4.8g; Fat 1.4g, of which saturates 0g; Cholesterol 0mg; Calcium 145mg; Fibre 3g; Sodium 27mg

ADOBO SEASONING

ADOBO MEANS VINEGAR SAUCE, AND THIS ADOBO IS A CHILLI VINEGAR PASTE USED FOR MARINATING PORK CHOPS OR STEAKS. ADOBOS ARE WIDELY USED IN THE COOKING OF THE YUCATAN.

MAKES ENOUGH TO MARINATE
SIX CHOPS OR STEAKS

INGREDIENTS
  1 small head of garlic
  5 ancho chillies
  2 pasilla chillies
  15ml/1 tbsp dried oregano
  5ml/1 tsp cumin seeds
  6 cloves
  5ml/1 tsp coriander seeds
  10cm/4in piece of cinnamon stick
  10ml/2 tsp salt
  120ml/4fl oz/½ cup white
    wine vinegar

1 Preheat the oven to 180°C/350°F/ Gas 4. Cut a thin slice off the top of the head of garlic, so that the inside of each clove is exposed. Wrap the head of garlic in foil. Roast for 45–60 minutes or until the garlic is soft.

2 Meanwhile, slit the chillies and scrape out the seeds. Put the chillies in a blender or a mortar. Add the oregano, cumin seeds, cloves, coriander seeds, cinnamon stick and salt. Process or grind with a pestle to a fine powder.

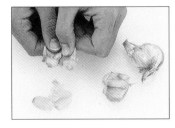

3 Remove the garlic from the oven. When it is cool enough to handle, squeeze the garlic pulp out of each clove and grind into the spice mix.

4 Add the wine vinegar to the spice and garlic mixture and process or grind until a smooth paste forms. Spoon into a bowl and leave to stand for 1 hour, to allow the flavours to blend. Spread over pork chops or steaks as a marinade, before grilling or barbecuing.

Energy 11kcal/45kJ; Protein 1g; Carbohydrate 1.5g, of which sugars 0.2g; Fat 0.1g, of which saturates 0g; Cholesterol 0mg; Calcium 6mg; Fibre 0.3g; Sodium 656mg

RED RUB

This "rub" or dry paste is frequently used in the Yucatan for seasoning meat. The mixture is rubbed on to the surface of the meat, which is then wrapped in banana leaves and cooked slowly in a PIB, a heated stone-lined hole in the ground. Meat cooked this way is referred to as PIBIL-STYLE. Try using the rub on pork chops or chicken pieces before oven baking or barbecuing.

MAKES ENOUGH FOR ONE JOINT OF MEAT
OR FOUR CHICKEN BREASTS

INGREDIENTS
   10ml/2 tsp achiote (annatto) seeds
   5ml/1 tsp black peppercorns
   5ml/1 tsp allspice berries
   5ml/1 tsp dried oregano
   2.5ml/½ tsp ground cumin
   5ml/1 tsp freshly squeezed lime juice
   1 small Seville orange or ½ grapefruit

1 Put the achiote (annatto) seeds in a mortar and grind them with a pestle to a fine powder. Alternatively, use a food processor. Add the peppercorns, grind again, then repeat the process with the allspice berries. Mix in the oregano and ground cumin.

2 Add the lime juice to the spice mixture. Squeeze the orange or grapefruit and add the juice to the spice mixture a teaspoonful at a time until a thick paste is produced. Don't be tempted to substitute a sweet orange if Seville oranges are out of season; the spice mixture must be tart.

3 Allow the paste to stand for at least 30 minutes so the spices absorb the juice. The correct consistency for the paste is slightly dry and crumbly. When ready to use, rub the paste on to the surface of the meat, then leave to marinate for at least 1 hour before cooking, preferably overnight. The rub will keep for up to 1 week in a covered bowl in the refrigerator, after which time some of the flavour will be lost.

COOK'S TIP
Achiote is the rusty red seed of the annatto, a tropical American tree. It is used in Mexico for flavouring and colouring cheeses, butter and smoked fish. It is also used in Indian cooking and can be purchased from ethnic food stores.

RED SALSA

Use this as a condiment with fish or meat dishes, or as a dipping sauce for baked potato wedges. It is often added to rice dishes.

MAKES ABOUT 250ML/8FL OZ/1 CUP

INGREDIENTS
   3 large tomatoes
   15ml/1 tbsp olive oil
   3 ancho chillies
   2 pasilla chillies
   2 garlic cloves, peeled and left whole
   2 spring onions (scallions)
   10ml/2 tsp soft dark brown sugar
   2.5ml/½ tsp paprika
   juice of 1 lime
   2.5ml/½ tsp dried oregano
   salt

1 Preheat the oven to 200°C/400°F/Gas 6. Quarter the tomatoes and place in a roasting tin. Drizzle over the oil. Roast for about 40 minutes until slightly charred, then remove the skin.

2 Soak the chillies in hot water for about 10 minutes. Drain, remove the stalks, slit and then scrape out the seeds. Chop finely. Dry roast the garlic in a heavy-based pan until golden.

3 Finely chop most of the spring onions, retaining the top part of one for garnishing. Place the chopped onion in a bowl with the sugar, paprika, lime juice and oregano. Slice the remaining spring onion diagonally and set aside for the garnish.

4 Put the skinned tomatoes and chopped chillies in a food processor or blender and add the garlic cloves. Process until smooth.

5 Add the sugar, paprika, lime juice, spring onions and oregano to the blender. Process for a few seconds, then taste and add salt as required. spoon into a pan and warm through before serving, or place in a bowl, cover and chill until required. Garnish with the sliced spring onion. The salsa will keep, covered, for up to 1 week in the refrigerator.

Energy 20kcal/82kJ; Protein 0.8g; Carbohydrate 2.5g, of which sugars 0.5g; Fat 0.8g, of which saturates 0g; Cholesterol 0mg; Calcium 49mg; Fibre 1.7g; Sodium 34mg
Energy 158kcal/658kJ; Protein 2.1g; Carbohydrate 12.3g, of which sugars 12.3g; Fat 11.5g, of which saturates 1.6g; Cholesterol 0mg; Calcium 30mg; Fibre 0.6g; Sodium 8mg

SOUPS AND SNACKS

If you found the word "sopas" on a Mexican menu, you might, quite rightly, translate it to mean "soups". However, your order might not be quite what you were expecting. There are two classifications of soup in Mexico: those that conform to the accepted definition, and consist of vegetables, meat or fish cooked in a liquid, and those that come under the heading of sopa seca, or "dry soup". This may sound like a contradiction in terms, but there is actually a perfectly logical explanation. A sopa seca starts out with plenty of liquid, but ingredients such as rice, vermicelli or corn tortilla strips soon absorb the surplus. What remains is a moist, thick, satisfying dish, which serves as a separate course in the comida — the main meal — but may also be served solo.

Bocaditos means "little bites", an apt description for a range of colourful little dishes that Mexicans snack on throughout the day. Several of these may be served together, rather like the Spanish tapas, to make an informal meal, or they may appear as appetizers or starters, or on a brunch or buffet table. Most bocaditos can be prepared quickly and easily, so they make perfect packed lunches or picnic fare.

TLALPEÑO-STYLE SOUP

THIS SIMPLE CHICKEN SOUP ORIGINATES FROM TLALPAN, A SUBURB OF MEXICO CITY. THE SOUP IS MADE MORE SUBSTANTIAL BY THE ADDITION OF CHEESE AND CHICK-PEAS.

SERVES SIX

INGREDIENTS

1.5 litres/2½ pints/6¼ cups
chicken stock
½ chipotle chilli, seeded
2 skinless, boneless chicken breasts
1 medium avocado
4 spring onions (scallions), sliced
400g/14oz can chick-peas, drained
salt and ground black pepper
75g/3oz/¾ cup grated Cheddar
cheese, to serve

1 Pour the stock into a large pan and add the dried chilli. Bring to the boil, add the whole chicken breasts, then lower the heat and simmer for about 10 minutes or until the chicken is cooked. Remove the chicken from the pan and let it cool a little.

2 Using two forks, shred the chicken into small pieces. Set it aside. Pour the stock and chilli into a blender or food processor and process until smooth. Return the stock to the pan.

COOK'S TIP
When buying the avocado for this soup choose one that is slightly under-ripe, which makes it easier to handle when peeling and slicing.

3 Cut the avocado in half, remove the skin and seed, then slice the flesh into 2cm/¾in pieces. Add it to the stock, with the spring onions and chick-peas. Return the shredded chicken to the pan, with salt and pepper to taste, and heat gently.

4 Spoon the soup into heated bowls. Sprinkle grated cheese on top of each portion and serve immediately.

CORN SOUP

QUICK AND EASY TO PREPARE, THIS COLOURFUL SOUP HAS A SWEET AND CREAMY FLAVOUR. CHILDREN LOVE IT.

SERVES SIX

INGREDIENTS

2 red (bell) peppers
30ml/2 tbsp vegetable oil
1 medium onion, finely chopped
500g/1¼lb/3–4 cups corn niblets,
thawed if frozen
750ml/1¼ pints/3 cups chicken stock
150ml/¼ pint/⅔ cup single (light)
cream
salt and ground black pepper

1 Dry fry the peppers in a griddle pan over a moderate heat, turning them frequently until the skins are blistered all over. Place them in a strong plastic bag and tie the top to keep the steam in. Set aside for 20 minutes, then remove the peppers from the bag and peel off the skin.

2 Cut the peppers in half and scoop out the seeds and cores. Set one aside. Cut the other into 1cm/½in dice.

3 Heat the oil in a large pan. Add the onion and fry over a low heat for about 10 minutes, until it is translucent and soft. Stir in the diced pepper and corn and fry for 5 minutes over a moderate heat.

4 Spoon the contents of the pan into a food processor, pour in the chicken stock and process until almost smooth. This processing can be done in batches if necessary.

5 Return the soup to the pan and reheat it. Stir in the cream, with salt and pepper to taste. Core, seed and cut the reserved pepper into thin strips and add half of these to the pan. Serve the soup in heated bowls, garnished with the remaining pepper strips.

COOK'S TIP
Look out for roasted red (bell) peppers in jars. These come ready-skinned and are useful in all sorts of recipes. Used here, they make a quick soup even speedier.

Energy 239kcal/1005kJ; Protein 24.8g; Carbohydrate 11.3g, of which sugars 0.6g; Fat 10.6g, of which saturates 4.2g; Cholesterol 60mg; Calcium 141mg; Fibre 3.4g; Sodium 291mg
Energy 218kcal/914kJ; Protein 4.2g; Carbohydrate 27.4g, of which sugars 12.8g; Fat 11g, of which saturates 4.5g; Cholesterol 17mg; Calcium 39mg; Fibre 2.2g; Sodium 237mg

TORTILLA SOUP

THERE ARE SEVERAL TORTILLA SOUPS. THIS ONE IS AN AGUADA — OR LIQUID — VERSION, AND IS INTENDED FOR SERVING AS AN APPETIZER OR LIGHT MEAL. IT IS VERY EASY AND QUICK TO PREPARE, OR MAKE IT IN ADVANCE AND FRY THE TORTILLA MEZES AS IT REHEATS. THE CRISP TORTILLA PIECES ADD AN UNUSUAL TEXTURE.

SERVES FOUR

INGREDIENTS

    4 corn tortillas, freshly made or a few
      days old
    15ml/1 tbsp vegetable oil, plus extra,
      for frying
    1 small onion, finely chopped
    2 garlic cloves, crushed
    400g/14oz can plum tomatoes, drained
    1 litre/1¾ pints/4 cups chicken stock
    small bunch of coriander (cilantro)
    salt and ground black pepper

1 Using a sharp knife, cut each tortilla into four or five strips, each measuring about 2cm/¾in wide.

2 Pour vegetable oil to a depth of 2cm/¾in into a heavy-based frying pan. Heat until a small piece of tortilla, added to the oil, floats on the top and bubbles at the edges.

3 Add a few tortilla strips to the hot oil and fry for a few minutes until crisp and golden brown all over, turning them occasionally. Remove with a slotted spoon and drain on a double layer of kitchen paper. Cook the remaining tortilla strips in the same way.

4 Heat the 15ml/1 tbsp vegetable oil in a large heavy-based pan. Add the chopped onion and garlic and cook over a moderate heat for 2–3 minutes, stirring constantly with a wooden spatula, until the onion is soft and translucent. Do not let the garlic turn brown or it will give the soup a bitter taste.

5 Chop the tomatoes using a large sharp knife and add them to the onion mixture in the pan. Pour in the chicken stock and stir well. Bring to the boil, then lower the heat and allow to simmer for about 10 minutes, until the liquid has reduced slightly.

6 Chop the coriander. Add to the soup, reserving a little to use as a garnish. Season to taste.

7 Place a few of the crisp tortilla pieces in the bottom of four warmed soup bowls. Ladle the soup on top. Sprinkle each portion with the reserved chopped coriander and serve.

COOK'S TIP
An easy way to chop the coriander is to put the coriander leaves in a mug and snip with a pair of scissors. Hold the scissors vertically in both hands and work the blades back and forth until the coriander is finely chopped.

Energy 142kcal/595kJ; Protein 3.1g; Carbohydrate 19.6g, of which sugars 4.5g; Fat 6.2g, of which saturates 0.8g; Cholesterol 0mg; Calcium 63mg; Fibre 2.4g; Sodium 84mg

CHILLED COCONUT SOUP

REFRESHING, COOLING AND NOT TOO FILLING, THIS SOUP IS THE PERFECT ANTIDOTE TO HOT WEATHER. FOR A FORMAL MEAL, IT WOULD BE AN EXCELLENT CHOICE FOR SERVING AFTER AN APPETIZER, TO REFRESH THE PALATE BEFORE THE MAIN COURSE.

SERVES SIX

INGREDIENTS

1.2 litres/2 pints/5 cups milk
225g/8oz/2⅔ cups unsweetened desiccated (dry, shredded) coconut
400ml/14fl oz/1⅔ cups coconut milk
400ml/14fl oz/1⅔ cups chicken stock
200ml/7fl oz/scant 1 cup double (heavy) cream
2.5ml/½ tsp salt
2.5ml/½ tsp ground white pepper
5ml/1 tsp sugar
small bunch of coriander (cilantro)

COOK'S TIP

Avoid using sweetened desiccated coconut, which would spoil the flavour of this soup.

1 Pour the milk into a large pan. Bring it to the boil, stir in the coconut, lower the heat and allow to simmer for 30 minutes. Spoon the mixture into a food processor and process until smooth. This may take a while – up to 5 minutes – so pause frequently and scrape down the sides of the bowl.

2 Rinse the pan to remove any coconut that remains, pour in the processed mixture and add the coconut milk. Stir in the chicken stock (home-made, if possible, which gives a better flavour than a stock (bouillon) cube), cream, salt, pepper and sugar. Bring the mixture to the boil, stirring occasionally, then lower the heat and cook for 10 minutes.

3 Reserve a few coriander leaves to garnish, then chop the rest finely and stir into the soup. Pour the soup into a large bowl, let it cool, then cover and put into the refrigerator until chilled. Just before serving, taste the soup and adjust the seasoning, as chilling will alter the taste. Serve in chilled bowls, garnished with the coriander leaves.

Energy 597kcal/2474kJ; Protein 10.8g; Carbohydrate 16.9g, of which sugars 16.9g; Fat 54.6g, of which saturates 40.8g; Cholesterol 69mg; Calcium 317mg; Fibre 6.7g; Sodium 188mg

AVOCADO SOUP

THIS DELICIOUS AND VERY PRETTY SOUP IS PERFECT FOR DINNER PARTIES AND HAS A FRESH, DELICATE FLAVOUR. YOU MIGHT WANT TO ADD A DASH MORE LIME JUICE JUST BEFORE SERVING FOR ADDED ZEST.

SERVES FOUR

INGREDIENTS
2 large ripe avocados
300ml/½ pint/1¼ cups crème fraîche
1 litre/1¾ pints/4 cups well-flavoured
   chicken stock
5ml/1 tsp salt
juice of ½ lime
small bunch of coriander (cilantro)
2.5ml/½ tsp freshly ground
   black pepper

COOK'S TIP
Because this soup contains avocados, it may discolour if left to stand, so make it just before serving.

1 Cut the avocados in half, remove the peel and lift out the stones. Chop the flesh coarsely and place it in a food processor with 45–60ml/3–4 tbsp of the crème fraîche. Process until smooth.

2 Heat the chicken stock in a pan. When it is hot, but still below simmering point, stir in the rest of the crème fraîche, with the salt.

3 Add the lime juice to the avocado mixture, process briefly to mix, then gradually stir the mixture into the hot stock. Heat gently but do not let the mixture approach boiling point.

4 Chop the coriander. Pour the soup into individual heated bowls and sprinkle each portion with coriander and black pepper. Serve immediately.

Energy 407kcal/1676kJ; Protein 3.3g; Carbohydrate 3.4g, of which sugars 2.1g; Fat 42.2g, of which saturates 21.7g; Cholesterol 78mg; Calcium 73mg; Fibre 3.2g; Sodium 24mg

CHILLIES RELLENOS

STUFFED CHILLIES ARE POPULAR ALL OVER MEXICO. THE TYPE OF CHILLI USED DIFFERS FROM REGION TO REGION, BUT LARGER CHILLIES ARE OBVIOUSLY EASIER TO STUFF THAN SMALLER ONES. POBLANOS AND ANAHEIMS ARE QUITE MILD, BUT YOU CAN USE HOTTER CHILLIES IF YOU PREFER.

MAKES SIX

INGREDIENTS

6 fresh poblano or Anaheim chillies
2 potatoes, total weight about
   400g/14oz
200g/7oz/scant 1 cup cream cheese
200g/7oz/1¾ cups grated mature
   (sharp) Cheddar cheese
5ml/1 tsp salt
2.5ml/½ tsp ground black pepper
2 eggs, separated
115g/4oz/1 cup plain (all-purpose)
   flour
2.5ml/½ tsp white pepper
oil, for frying
chilli flakes to garnish, optional

1 Make a neat slit down one side of each chilli. Place them in a dry frying pan over a moderate heat, turning them frequently until the skins blister.

2 Place the chillies in a strong plastic bag and tie the top to keep the steam in. Set aside for 20 minutes, then carefully peel off the skins and remove the seeds through the slits, keeping the chillies whole. Dry the chillies with kitchen paper and set them aside.

COOK'S TIP
Take care when making the filling; mix gently, trying not to break up the potato pieces.

VARIATION
Whole ancho (dried poblano) chillies can be used instead of fresh chillies, but will need to be reconstituted in water before they can be seeded and stuffed.

3 Scrub or peel the potatoes and cut them into 1cm/½in dice. Bring a large pan of water to the boil, add the potatoes and let the water return to boiling point. Lower the heat and simmer for 5 minutes or until the potatoes are just tender. Do not overcook. Drain them thoroughly.

4 Put the cream cheese in a bowl and stir in the grated cheese, with 2.5ml/½ tsp of the salt and the black pepper. Add the potato and mix gently.

5 Spoon some of the potato filling into each chilli. Put them on a plate, cover with clear film (plastic wrap) and chill for 1 hour so that the filling becomes firm.

6 Put the egg whites in a clean, grease-free bowl and whisk them to firm peaks. In a separate bowl, beat the yolks until pale, then fold in the whites. Scrape the mixture on to a large, shallow dish. Spread out the flour in another shallow dish and season it with the remaining salt and the white pepper.

7 Heat the oil for deep frying to 190°C/375°F. Coat a few chillies first in flour and then in egg before adding carefully to the hot oil.

8 Fry the chillies in batches until golden and crisp. Drain on kitchen paper and serve hot, garnished with a sprinkle of chilli flakes for extra heat, if desired.

Energy 605kcal/2512kJ; Protein 18.5g; Carbohydrate 30.8g, of which sugars 1.9g; Fat 45.4g, of which saturates 27.7g; Cholesterol 159mg; Calcium 385mg; Fibre 1.5g; Sodium 478mg

TORTAS

THE MULTI-LAYERED FILLING OF TORTAS OFFERS LOTS OF DIFFERENT TASTES AND TEXTURES. TRADITIONALLY THEY ARE MADE USING ROLLS CALLED TELERAS.

SERVES TWO

INGREDIENTS

2 fresh jalapeño chillies
juice of ½ lime
2 French bread rolls or 2 pieces
  of French bread
115g/4oz/⅔ cup Refried Beans
150g/5oz roast pork
2 small tomatoes, sliced
115g/4oz Cheddar cheese, sliced
small bunch of coriander (cilantro)
30ml/2 tbsp crème fraîche

VARIATIONS
The essential ingredients of a *torta* are refried beans and chillies. Everything else is subject to change. Ham, chicken or turkey could all be used instead of pork, and lettuce is often added.

1 Cut the chillies in half, scrape out the seeds, then cut the flesh into thin strips. Put it in a bowl, pour over the lime juice and leave to stand.

2 If using rolls, slice them in half and remove some of the crumb so that they are slightly hollowed. If using French bread, slice each piece in half lengthways. Set the top of each piece of bread or roll aside and spread the bottom halves with the refried beans.

3 Cut the pork into thin shreds and put these on top of the refried beans. Top with the tomato slices. Drain the jalapeño strips and put them on top of the tomato slices. Add the cheese and sprinkle with coriander leaves.

4 Turn the top halves of the bread or rolls over, so that the cut sides are uppermost, and spread these with crème fraîche. Sandwich back together again and serve.

Energy 703kcal/2956kJ; Protein 42.9g; Carbohydrate 72.4g, of which sugars 8.4g; Fat 27.8g, of which saturates 16.4g; Cholesterol 108mg; Calcium 570mg; Fibre 7.8g; Sodium 1329mg

TAQUITOS WITH BEEF

MINIATURE SOFT CORN TORTILLAS MOULDED AROUND A TASTY FILLING AND SERVED WARM. UNLESS YOU HAVE ACCESS TO MINIATURE FRESH CORN TORTILLAS, YOU WILL NEED A TORTILLA PRESS.

2 Mix the *masa harina* and salt in a large bowl. Add the warm water, a little at a time, to make a dough that can be worked into a ball. Knead this on a lightly floured surface for 3–4 minutes until smooth, then wrap the dough in clear film (plastic wrap) and leave to rest for 1 hour.

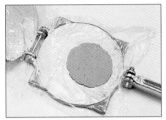

3 Divide the dough into 12 small balls. Open a tortilla press and line both sides with plastic (this can be cut from a new plastic sandwich bag). Put a ball on the press and bring the top down to flatten it into a 5–6cm/2–2½in round. Flatten the remaining dough balls in the same way to make more tortillas.

4 Heat a griddle or frying pan until hot. Cook each tortilla for 15–20 seconds on each side, and then for a further 15 minutes on the first side. Keep the tortillas warm and soft by folding them inside a slightly damp dish towel.

5 Add the oregano, cumin, tomato purée and sugar to the pan containing the reserved beef cubes, with a couple of tablespoons of the reserved beef stock, or just enough to keep the mixture moist. Cook gently for a few minutes to combine the flavour.

6 Place a little of the lettuce on a warm tortilla. Top with a little of the filling and a little onion relish, fold in half and serve while still warm. Fill more tortillas in the same way.

SERVES TWELVE

INGREDIENTS
500g/1¼lb rump steak, diced into
  1cm/½in pieces
2 garlic cloves, peeled and left whole
750ml/1¼ pints/3 cups beef stock
150g/5oz/1 cup *masa harina*
pinch of salt
120ml/4fl oz/½ cup warm water
7.5ml/1½ tsp dried oregano
2.5ml/½ tsp ground cumin
30ml/2 tbsp tomato purée (paste)
2.5ml/½ tsp sugar
salt and ground black pepper
shredded lettuce and Onion Relish,
  to serve

1 Put the beef and whole garlic cloves in a large pan and cover with the beef stock. Bring to the boil, lower the heat and simmer for 10–15 minutes, until the meat is tender. Using a slotted spoon, transfer the meat to a clean pan and set it aside. Reserve the stock.

Energy 109kcal/458kJ; Protein 11.8g; Carbohydrate 10g, of which sugars 0.7g; Fat 2.4g, of which saturates 0.8g; Cholesterol 28mg; Calcium 4mg; Fibre 0.4g; Sodium 36mg

EMPANADAS <u>WITH</u> ROPAS VIEJAS

THE FILLING FOR THESE EMPANADAS IS TRADITIONALLY MADE WITH MEAT THAT IS COOKED UNTIL IT IS SO TENDER THAT IT CAN BE TORN APART WITH FORKS. IT RESEMBLES TATTERED CLOTH, WHICH IS HOW IT CAME TO BE KNOWN AS ROPA VIEJA, WHICH MEANS "OLD CLOTHES".

SERVES SIX (TWELVE EMPANADAS)

INGREDIENTS
150g/5oz/1 cup *masa harina*
30ml/2 tbsp plain (all-purpose) flour
2.5ml/½ tsp salt
120–150ml/4–5fl oz/½–⅔ cup
  warm water
15ml/1 tbsp oil, plus extra, for frying
250g/9oz lean minced (ground) pork
1 garlic clove, crushed
3 tomatoes
2 ancho chillies
½ small onion
2.5ml/½ tsp ground cumin
2.5ml/½ tsp salt

1 Mix the *masa harina*, plain flour and salt in a bowl. Gradually add enough of the warm water to make a smooth, but not sticky, dough. Knead briefly, then shape into a ball, wrap in clear film (plastic wrap) and set aside.

2 Heat 15ml/1 tbsp oil in a pan. Add the minced pork and cook, stirring frequently, until it has browned evenly. Stir in the garlic and cook for 2 minutes more. Remove from the heat and set the pan aside.

3 Cut a cross in the base of each tomato, place them in a bowl and pour over boiling water. After 3 minutes plunge the tomatoes into a bowl of cold water. Drain. The skins will peel back easily from the crosses. Remove the skins completely. Chop the tomato flesh and put in a bowl.

4 Slit the ancho chillies and scrape out the seeds. Chop the chillies finely and add them to the tomatoes. Chop the onion finely and add it to the tomato mixture, with the ground cumin.

5 Stir the tomato mixture into the pan containing the pork and cook over a moderate heat for 10 minutes, stirring occasionally. Season with salt to taste.

6 To make the tortillas, divide the empanada dough into 12 pieces and roll each piece into a ball. Open a tortilla press and line both sides with plastic (this can be cut from a new plastic sandwich bag). Put a ball of dough on the press and bring the top down to flatten it into a 7.5cm/3in round. Use the remaining dough balls to make more tortillas in the same way.

COOK'S TIP
If the empanada dough proves difficult to handle, a little oil or melted lard can be kneaded into the dough to help make it more pliable.

7 Spoon a little of the meat mixture on one half of each tortilla, working quickly to stop the dough from drying out. Dampen the edges of the dough with a little water and fold, turnover-style, to make the empanadas.

8 Seal the edges on the empanadas by pinching them between the index finger and thumb of the left hand and the index finger of the right hand.

9 Heat a little oil in a large frying pan. When it is hot, fry the empanadas in batches until crisp and golden on both sides, turning at least once. Serve hot or cold.

Energy 228kcal/951kJ; Protein 10.4g; Carbohydrate 24.5g, of which sugars 2.2g; Fat 9.7g, of which saturates 1.4g; Cholesterol 21mg; Calcium 16mg; Fibre 1.4g; Sodium 28mg

PANUCHOS

THESE STUFFED TORTILLAS ARE A BIT FIDDLY TO MAKE, BUT WELL WORTH THE EFFORT. THIS DISH IS PARTICULARLY POPULAR IN THE YUCATÁN.

SERVES SIX (TWELVE *PANUCHOS*)

INGREDIENTS

150g/5oz/1 cup *masa harina*
pinch of salt
120ml/4fl oz/½ cup warm water
2 skinless, boneless chicken breasts
5ml/1 tsp dried oregano
150g/5oz/about 1 cup *Frijoles de Olla*, blended to a smooth purée
2 hard-boiled eggs, sliced
oil, for shallow frying
salt and ground black pepper
Onion Relish, to serve

1 Mix the *masa harina* and salt in a large bowl. Add the warm water, a little at a time, to make a dough that can be worked into a ball. Knead this on a lightly floured surface for 3–4 minutes until smooth, then wrap the dough in clear film (plastic wrap) and leave to rest for 1 hour.

2 Put the chicken in a pan, add the dried oregano and pour in water to cover. Bring to the boil, then lower the heat and simmer for 10 minutes or until the chicken is cooked. Remove the chicken from the pan, discard the water and let the chicken cool a little. Using two forks, shred the chicken into small pieces. Set it aside.

3 Divide the dough into 12 small pieces and roll into balls. Open a tortilla press and line both sides with plastic (this can be cut from a new plastic sandwich bag). Put a dough ball on the press and flatten it into a 6cm/2½in round. Use the remaining dough balls to make more tortillas in the same way.

4 Cook each tortilla in a hot frying pan for 15–20 seconds on each side. After a further 15 seconds on one side remove and wrap in a clean dish towel.

5 Cut a slit in each tortilla, about 1cm/½in deep around the rim. Put a spoonful of the bean purée and a slice of hard-boiled egg in each slit.

6 Heat the oil for shallow frying in a large frying pan. Fry the tortilla pockets until they are crisp and golden brown on all sides, turning at least once during cooking. Drain them on kitchen paper and place on six individual serving plates. Top with a little of the shredded chicken and some onion relish. Season to taste and serve immediately.

Energy 258kcal/1080kJ; Protein 19.4g; Carbohydrate 24.9g, of which sugars 0.4g; Fat 9g, of which saturates 1.4g; Cholesterol 98mg; Calcium 20mg; Fibre 1.7g; Sodium 55mg

SOPES <u>WITH</u> PICADILLO

THESE ARE SMALL, THICK TORTILLAS MADE WITH MASA HARINA *WITH CRIMPED EDGES, WHICH ARE FILLED LIKE TARTS. THEY ARE AN ACQUIRED TASTE AS THEY REMAIN "DOUGHY" WHEN COOKED, BUT THEY CAN BECOME QUITE ADDICTIVE. THE FILLING –* PICADILLO *– IS VERY POPULAR IN* MEXICO *AND IS USED IN MANY DIFFERENT RECIPES.*

SERVES SIX

INGREDIENTS
250g/9oz/scant 2 cups *masa harina*
2.5ml/½ tsp salt
50g/2oz/¼ cup chilled lard
300ml/½ pint/1¼ cups warm water
15ml/1 tbsp vegetable oil
250g/9oz lean minced (ground) beef
2 garlic cloves, crushed
1 red pepper (bell), seeded and chopped
60ml/4 tbsp dry sherry
15ml/1 tbsp tomato purée (paste)
2.5ml/½ tsp ground cumin
5ml/1 tsp ground cinnamon
1.5ml/¼ tsp ground cloves
2.5ml/½ tsp ground black pepper
25g/1oz/3 tbsp raisins
25g/1oz/¼ cup slivered almonds
fresh parsley sprigs, to garnish

1 Put the *masa harina* and salt in a large bowl. Grate the chilled lard into the bowl and rub it into the dry ingredients until no visible pieces remain. Add the warm water, a little at a time, to make a dough that can be worked into a ball. Knead the dough on a lightly floured surface for 3–4 minutes until smooth. Set aside.

2 Heat the oil in a large pan. Add the minced beef and cook over a high heat, stirring until it has browned. Stir in the garlic and continue cooking for 2–3 minutes, stirring occasionally.

3 Stir in the red pepper, sherry, tomato purée and spices. Cook for 5 minutes more, then add the raisins and the slivered almonds. Lower the heat and simmer for 10 minutes. The meat should be cooked through and the mixture moist, but not wet. Keep hot.

4 Divide the dough into six balls. Open a tortilla press and line both sides with plastic (this can be cut from a new plastic sandwich bag). Put a ball on the press and bring the top down to flatten it into a 10cm/4in round, thicker than the conventional tortilla. Use the remaining dough balls to make five more rounds.

5 Heat a griddle or frying pan until hot. Add one of the rounds and fry until the underside is beginning to brown and blister. Turn the round over and cook the other side briefly, until the colour is just beginning to change. Slide on to a plate and crimp the rim to form a raised edge. Fill with the spicy beef and keep hot while cooking and filling the remaining tartlets. Garnish with parsley.

COOK'S TIP
Take care that the dough for the *sopes* does not become dry. Wrap it in clear film (plastic wrap) while it is set aside.

Energy 441kcal/1840kJ; Protein 15.9g; Carbohydrate 45.3g, of which sugars 8.5g; Fat 10.3g, of which saturates 2.1g; Cholesterol 24mg; Calcium 28mg; Fibre 2.1g; Sodium 42mg

QUESADILLAS

THESE CHEESE-FILLED TORTILLAS ARE THE MEXICAN EQUIVALENT OF TOASTED SANDWICHES. SERVE THEM AS SOON AS THEY ARE COOKED, OR THEY WILL BECOME CHEWY. IF YOU ARE MAKING THEM FOR A CROWD, FILL AND FOLD THE TORTILLAS AHEAD OF TIME, BUT ONLY COOK THEM TO ORDER.

SERVES FOUR

INGREDIENTS

200g/7oz mozzarella, Monterey Jack or mild Cheddar cheese
1 fresh fresno chilli (optional)
8 wheat flour tortillas, about 15cm/6in across
Onion Relish or Classic Tomato Salsa, to serve

VARIATIONS

Try spreading a thin layer of your favourite Mexican salsa on the tortilla before adding the cheese, or adding a few pieces of cooked chicken or prawns before folding the tortilla in half.

1 If using mozzarella cheese, it must be drained thoroughly and then patted dry and sliced into thin strips. Monterey Jack and Cheddar cheese should both be coarsely grated, as finely grated cheese will melt and ooze away when cooking. Set the cheese aside in a bowl.

2 If using the chilli, spear it on a long-handled metal skewer and roast it over the flame of a gas burner until the skin blisters and darkens. Do not let the flesh burn. Alternatively, dry fry it in a griddle pan until the skin is scorched. Place the roasted chilli in a strong plastic bag and tie the top to keep the steam in. Set aside for 20 minutes.

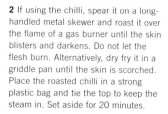

3 Remove the chilli from the bag and peel off the skin. Cut off the stalk, then slit the chilli and scrape out the seeds. Cut the flesh into eight thin strips.

4 Warm a large frying pan or griddle. Place one tortilla on the pan or griddle at a time, sprinkle about an eighth of the cheese on to one half and add a strip of chilli, if using. Fold the tortilla over the cheese and press the edges together gently to seal. Cook the filled tortilla for 1 minute, then turn over and cook the other side for 1 minute.

5 Remove the filled tortilla from the pan or griddle, cut it into three triangles or four strips and serve at once, with the onion relish or tomato salsa.

Energy 372kcal/1559kJ; Protein 17.2g; Carbohydrate 37.4g, of which sugars 0.8g; Fat 17g, of which saturates 10.9g; Cholesterol 49mg; Calcium 438mg; Fibre 1.5g; Sodium 537mg

MEXICAN RICE

VERSIONS OF THIS DISH – A RELATIVE OF SPANISH RICE – ARE POPULAR ALL OVER SOUTH AMERICA.
CLASSIFIED AS A SOPA SECA OR DRY SOUP, IT IS A DELICIOUS MEDLEY OF RICE, TOMATOES AND
AROMATIC FLAVOURINGS. THE STOCK IN WHICH THE RICE IS COOKED IS LARGELY ABSORBED BY THE
TIME THE DISH IS READY TO BE SERVED.

SERVES SIX

INGREDIENTS
   200g/7oz/1 cup long grain rice
   200g/7oz can chopped tomatoes in
      tomato juice
   ½ onion, roughly chopped
   2 garlic cloves, roughly chopped
   30ml/2 tbsp vegetable oil
   450ml/¾ pint/scant 2 cups chicken
      stock
   2.5ml/½ tsp salt
   3 fresh fresno chillies or other fresh
      green chillies, trimmed
   150g/5oz/1 cup frozen peas (optional)
   ground black pepper

1 Put the rice in a heatproof bowl and cover with boiling water. Stir once, then leave to stand for 10 minutes Tip into a strainer over the sink, rinse under cold water, then drain again. Set aside.

2 Meanwhile, pour the tomatoes and juice into a food processor or blender, add the onion and garlic and process until smooth.

3 Heat the oil in a large, heavy-based pan, add the rice and cook over a moderate heat until it becomes a delicate golden brown. Stir occasionally to ensure that the rice does not stick to the bottom of the pan.

4 Add the tomato mixture and stir over a moderate heat until all the liquid has been absorbed. Stir in the stock, salt, whole chillies and peas, if using. Continue to cook the mixture, stirring occasionally, until all the liquid has been absorbed and the rice is just tender.

5 Remove the pan from the heat, cover it with a tight-fitting lid and leave it to stand in a warm place for 5–10 minutes. Remove the chillies, fluff up the rice lightly and serve, sprinkled with black pepper. The chillies may be used as a garnish, if liked.

COOK'S TIP
Do not stir the rice too often after adding the stock or the grains will break down and the mixture will become starchy.

Energy 164kcal/685kJ; Protein 3g; Carbohydrate 28.6g, of which sugars 1.8g; Fat 4g, of which saturates 0.5g; Cholesterol 0mg; Calcium 25mg; Fibre 0.8g; Sodium 6mg

CHICKEN FLAUTAS

CRISP FRIED TORTILLAS WITH A CHICKEN AND CHEESE FILLING MAKE A DELICIOUS LIGHT MEAL, ESPECIALLY WHEN SERVED WITH A SPICY TOMATO SALSA. THE SECRET OF SUCCESS IS TO MAKE SURE THAT THE OIL IS SUFFICIENTLY HOT TO PREVENT THE FLUTES FROM ABSORBING TOO MUCH OF IT.

MAKES TWELVE

INGREDIENTS
    2 skinless, boneless chicken breasts
    1 onion
    2 garlic cloves
    15ml/1 tbsp vegetable oil
    90g/3½oz feta cheese, crumbled
    12 corn tortillas, freshly made or a
        few days old
    oil, for frying
    salt and ground black pepper
For the salsa
    3 tomatoes, peeled, seeded
        and chopped
    juice of ½ lime
    small bunch of coriander (cilantro),
        chopped
    ½ small onion, finely chopped
    3 fresh fresno chillies or similar
        fresh green chillies, seeded
        and chopped

1 Start by making the salsa. Mix the tomatoes, lime juice, coriander, onion and chillies in a bowl. Season with salt to taste and set aside.

COOK'S TIP
You might find it easier to keep the cocktail sticks (toothpicks) in place until after the flutes have been fried, in which case remove them before serving.

2 Put the chicken breasts in a large pan, add water to cover and bring to the boil. Lower the heat and simmer for 15–20 minutes or until the chicken is cooked. Remove the chicken from the pan and let it cool a little. Using two forks, shred the chicken into small pieces. Set it aside.

3 Chop the onion finely and crush the garlic. Heat the oil in a frying pan, add the onion and garlic and fry over a low heat for about 5 minutes, or until the onion has softened but not coloured. Add the shredded chicken, with salt and pepper to taste. Mix well, remove from the heat and stir in the feta.

4 Before they can be rolled, soften the tortillas by steaming three or four at a time on a plate over boiling water for a few moments until they are pliable. Alternatively, wrap them in microwave-safe film and then heat them in a microwave oven on full power for about 30 seconds.

5 Place a spoonful of the chicken filling on one of the tortillas. Roll the tortilla tightly around the filling to make a neat cylinder. Secure with a cocktail stick. Immediately cover the roll with clear film (plastic wrap) to prevent the tortilla from drying out and splitting. Fill and roll the remaining tortillas in the same way.

6 Pour oil into a frying pan to a depth of 2.5cm/1in. Heat it until a small cube of bread, added to the oil, rises to the surface and bubbles at the edges before turning golden. Remove the cocktail sticks (toothpicks), then add the flutes to the pan, a few at a time.

7 Fry the flutes for 2–3 minutes until golden, turning frequently. Drain on kitchen paper and serve at once, with the salsa.

Energy 131kcal/553kJ; Protein 9.6g; Carbohydrate 16.8g, of which sugars 1.9g; Fat 3.3g, of which saturates 1.4g; Cholesterol 23mg; Calcium 73mg; Fibre 1.2g; Sodium 209mg

EGGS WITH CHORIZO

IN MEXICO, THERE ARE TWO TYPES OF CHORIZO SAUSAGE. THE FIRST IS FRESHLY MADE AND SOLD LOOSE; THE SECOND IS PACKED IN SAUSAGE SKINS AND AIR-DRIED, LIKE SPANISH CHORIZO. THIS IS A RECIPE FOR THE FORMER. FRESHLY MADE CHORIZO CAN BE USED IN A NUMBER OF SAVOURY DISHES, BUT IS PARTICULARLY GOOD WITH SCRAMBLED EGG, AS HERE.

SERVES FOUR

INGREDIENTS

25g/1oz/2 tbsp lard
500g/1¼lb minced (ground) pork
3 garlic cloves, crushed
10ml/2 tsp dried oregano
5ml/1 tsp ground cinnamon
2.5ml/½ tsp ground cloves
2.5ml/½ tsp ground black pepper
30ml/2 tbsp dry sherry
5ml/1 tsp sugar
5ml/1 tsp salt
6 eggs
2 tomatoes, peeled, seeded and
  finely diced
½ small onion, finely chopped
60ml/4 tbsp milk or single (light)
  cream
fresh oregano sprigs, to garnish
warm corn or wheat flour tortillas,
  to serve

1 Melt the lard in a large frying pan over a moderate heat. Add the pork mince and cook until browned, stirring frequently. Stir in the garlic, dried oregano, cinnamon, cloves and black pepper. Cook for 3–4 minutes more.

2 Add the sherry, sugar and salt to the mince, stir well and cook for 3–4 minutes until the flavours are blended. Remove from the heat.

3 Put the eggs in a bowl. Beat lightly to mix, then stir in the finely diced tomatoes and chopped onion.

4 Return the chorizo mixture to the heat. Heat it through and pour in the egg mixture. Cook, stirring constantly, until the egg is almost firm.

5 Stir in the milk or cream and check the seasoning. Garnish with fresh oregano and serve with warm corn or wheat flour tortillas.

CHILLIES IN CHEESE SAUCE

THIS MAKES AN EXCELLENT APPETIZER, LIGHT LUNCH OR DIP TO SERVE WITH DRINKS. THE CHILLIES AND TEQUILA GIVE IT QUITE A KICK.

SERVES FOUR TO SIX

INGREDIENTS

4 fresh fresno chillies or other fresh
  green chillies
15ml/1 tbsp vegetable oil
½ red onion, finely chopped
500g/1¼lb/5 cups grated Monterey
  Jack cheese
30ml/2 tbsp crème fraîche
150ml/¼ pint/⅔ cup double (heavy)
  cream
2 firm tomatoes, peeled
15ml/1 tbsp reposada tequila

COOK'S TIP
Cross-cut the base of a tomato and cover with boiling water. Plunge into cold water and the skin will peel easily.

1 Place the chillies in a dry frying pan over a moderate heat, turning them frequently until the skin blisters and darkens. Place the chillies in a strong plastic bag and tie the top to keep the steam in. Set aside for 20 minutes, then carefully peel off the skins. Slit the chillies and scrape out the seeds, then cut the flesh into thin strips. Cut these in half lengthways.

2 Heat the oil in a frying pan and fry the onion over a moderate heat for 5 minutes, until it is beginning to soften. Add the cheese, crème fraîche and cream. Stir over a low heat until the cheese melts and the mixture becomes a rich, creamy sauce. Stir in the thick chilli strips.

3 Cut the tomatoes in half and scrape out the seeds. Cut the flesh into 1cm/½in pieces and stir these into the sauce.

4 Just before serving, stir in the tequila. Pour the sauce into a serving dish and serve warm, with the tortilla chips.

Energy 399kcal/1665kJ; Protein 41g; Carbohydrate 6.4g, of which sugars 2.7g; Fat 22.7g, of which saturates 7.5g; Cholesterol 380mg; Calcium 137mg; Fibre 2.9g; Sodium 256mg
Energy 402kcal/1668kJ; Protein 21.8g; Carbohydrate 3.1g, of which sugars 2.8g; Fat 31.3g, of which saturates 19.7g; Cholesterol 86mg; Calcium 625mg; Fibre 0.7g; Sodium 608mg

MOLETTES

THIS IS THE MEXICAN VERSION OF BEANS ON TOAST. SOLD BY STREET TRADERS AROUND MID-MORNING, THEY MAKE THE PERFECT SNACK FOR THOSE WHO HAVE MISSED BREAKFAST.

SERVES FOUR

INGREDIENTS
  4 crusty finger rolls
  50g/2oz/¼ cup butter, softened
  225g/8oz/1⅓ cups Refried Beans
  150g/5oz/1¼ cups grated medium
    Cheddar cheese
  green salad leaves, to garnish
  120ml/4fl oz/½ cup Classic Tomato
    Salsa, to serve

1 Cut the rolls in half, then take a sliver off the base so that they lie flat. Remove a little of the crumb. Spread them lightly with enough butter to crisp.

2 Arrange them on a baking sheet and grill (broil) for about 5 minutes, or until they are crisp and golden. Meanwhile, heat the refried beans over a low heat in a small pan.

3 Scoop the beans into the rolls, then sprinkle the grated cheese on top. Pop back under the grill (broiler) until the cheese melts. Serve with the tomato salsa and garnish with salad leaves.

EGGS MOTULENOS

A TASTY AND FILLING BREAKFAST OR MIDDAY SNACK, BLACK BEANS, WHICH ARE ALSO KNOWN AS TURTLE BEANS, ARE TOPPED WITH EGGS AND CHILLI SAUCE AND SURROUNDED BY PEAS AND HAM.

SERVES FOUR

INGREDIENTS
  225g/8oz/generous 1 cup black
    beans, soaked overnight in water
  1 small onion, finely chopped
  2 garlic cloves
  small bunch of coriander (cilantro),
    chopped
  150g/5oz/1 cup frozen peas
  4 corn tortillas
  30ml/2 tbsp oil
  4 eggs
  150g/5oz cooked ham, diced
  60ml/4 tbsp hot chilli sauce
  75g/3oz feta cheese, crumbled
  salt and ground black pepper
  Classic Tomato Salsa, to serve

1 Drain the beans, rinse them under cold water and drain again. Put them in a pan, add the onion and garlic and water to cover. Bring to the boil, then simmer for 40 minutes. Stir in the coriander, with salt and pepper to taste, and keep the beans hot.

2 Cook the peas in a small pan of boiling water until they are just tender. Drain and set aside. Wrap the tortillas in foil and place them on a plate. Stand the plate over a pan of boiling water and steam them for about 5 minutes. Alternatively, wrap them in microwave-safe film and heat them in a microwave on full power for about 30 seconds.

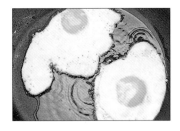

3 Heat the oil in a frying pan and fry the eggs until the whites are set. Lift them on to a plate and keep them warm while you quickly heat the ham and peas in the oil remaining in the pan.

4 Place the tortillas on warmed plates and top each one with some beans. Place an egg on each tortilla, spoon over 15ml/1 tbsp hot chilli sauce, then surround each egg with some peas and ham. Sprinkle feta over the peas and serve at once, with salsa on the side.

Energy 446kcal/1868kJ; Protein 20.9g; Carbohydrate 40.8g, of which sugars 7g; Fat 22.2g, of which saturates 13.8g; Cholesterol 59mg; Calcium 460mg; Fibre 4.4g; Sodium 1091mg
Energy 423kcal/1773kJ; Protein 31g; Carbohydrate 36.1g, of which sugars 4.9g; Fat 18.4g, of which saturates 5.8g; Cholesterol 223mg; Calcium 178mg; Fibre 7.4g; Sodium 779mg

EGGS RANCHEROS

THERE ARE MANY VARIATIONS ON THIS POPULAR DISH, WHICH IS GREAT FOR BREAKFAST OR BRUNCH.
THE COMBINATION OF CREAMY EGGS WITH ONION, CHILLI AND TOMATOES WORKS WONDERFULLY WELL.

SERVES FOUR FOR BREAKFAST

INGREDIENTS
   2 corn tortillas, several days old
   oil, for frying
   2 fresh green jalapeño chillies
   1 garlic clove
   4 spring onions (scallions)
   1 large tomato
   8 eggs, beaten
   150ml/¼ pint/⅔ cup single (light)
    cream
   small bunch of coriander (cilantro),
    finely chopped
   salt and ground black pepper

1 Cut the tortillas into long strips. Pour oil into a frying pan to a depth of 1cm/½in. Heat the oil until it is very hot, watching it closely all the time.

2 Fry the tortilla strips in batches for a minute or two until they are crisp and golden, turning them occasionally, then drain on kitchen paper.

COOK'S TIP
When cooking the tortilla strips it is important that the oil is the correct temperature. To test if the oil is ready to use, carefully add a strip of tortilla. If the strip floats and the oil immediately bubbles around its edges, the oil is ready.

3 Spear the chillies on a long-handled metal skewer and roast them over the flame of a gas burner until the skins blister and darken. Do not let the flesh burn. Alternatively, dry fry them in a griddle pan until the skins are scorched. Place them in a strong plastic bag and tie the top to keep the steam in. Set aside for 20 minutes.

4 Meanwhile, crush the garlic and chop the spring onions finely. Cut a cross in the base of the tomato. Place it in a heatproof bowl and pour over boiling water to cover. After 3 minutes lift the tomato out using a slotted spoon and plunge it into a bowl of cold water. Leave for a few minutes to cool.

5 Drain the tomato, remove the skin and cut it into four pieces. Using a teaspoon scoop out the seeds and the core, then dice the flesh finely.

6 Remove the chillies from the bag and peel off the skins. Cut off the stalks, then slit the chillies and scrape out the seeds. Chop the flesh finely. Put the eggs in a bowl, season with salt and pepper and beat lightly.

7 Heat 15ml/1 tbsp oil in a large frying pan. Add the garlic and spring onions and fry gently for 2–3 minutes until soft. Stir in the diced tomato and cook for 3–4 minutes more, then stir in the chillies and cook for 1 minute.

8 Pour the eggs into the pan and stir until they start to set. When only a small amount of uncooked egg remains visible, stir in the cream so that the cooking process is slowed down and the mixture cooks to a creamy mixture rather than a solid mass.

9 Stir the chopped coriander into the scrambled egg. Arrange the tortilla strips on four serving plates and spoon the eggs over. Serve at once.

Energy 307kcal/1281kJ; Protein 16.4g; Carbohydrate 17.2g, of which sugars 2.5g; Fat 20g, of which saturates 8.5g; Cholesterol 405mg; Calcium 151mg; Fibre 1.5g; Sodium 229mg

TORTILLA CHIPS

THESE ARE KNOWN AS TOTOPOS *IN* MEXICO, *AND THE TERM REFERS TO BOTH THE FRIED TORTILLA STRIPS USED TO GARNISH SOUPS AND THE TRIANGLES OF CORN TORTILLA USED FOR SCOOPING SALSA OR DIPS. USE TORTILLAS THAT ARE A FEW DAYS OLD; FRESH ONES WILL NOT CRISP UP SO WELL.*

SERVES FOUR

INGREDIENTS
4–8 corn tortillas
oil, for frying
salt

1 Cut each tortilla into six triangular wedges. Pour oil into a large frying pan to a depth of 1cm/½in, place the pan over a moderate heat and heat until very hot (see Cook's Tip).

2 Fry the tortilla wedges in the hot oil in small batches until they turn golden and are crisp. This will only take a few moments. Remove with a slotted spoon and drain on kitchen paper. Sprinkle with salt.

VARIATION
When fried, wheat flour tortillas do not crisp up as well as corn tortillas, but they make a delicious sweet treat when sprinkled with ground cinnamon and caster (superfine) sugar. Serve them hot with cream.

COOK'S TIP
The oil needs to be very hot for cooking the tortillas – test it by carefully adding one of the wedges. It should float and begin to bubble in the oil immediately.

3 *Totopos* should be served warm. They can be cooled completely and stored in an airtight container for a few days, but will need to be reheated in a microwave or a warm oven before being served.

PEPITAS

THESE LITTLE SNACKS ARE ABSOLUTELY IRRESISTIBLE, ESPECIALLY IF YOU INCLUDE CHIPOTLE CHILLIES. THEIR SMOKY FLAVOUR IS THE PERFECT FOIL FOR THE NUTTY TASTE OF THE PUMPKIN SEEDS AND THE SWEETNESS CONTRIBUTED BY THE SUGAR. SERVE THEM WITH PRE-DINNER DRINKS.

SERVES FOUR

INGREDIENTS
130g/4½oz/1 cup pumpkin seeds
4 garlic cloves, crushed
1.5ml/¼ tsp salt
10ml/2 tsp crushed dried chillies
5ml/1 tsp sugar
a wedge of lime

2 When all the seeds have swollen, add the garlic and cook for a few minutes more, stirring all the time. Add the salt and the crushed chillies and stir to mix. Turn off the heat, but keep the pan on the stove. Sprinkle sugar over the seeds and shake the pan to ensure that they are all coated.

COOK'S TIP
It is important to keep the pumpkin seeds moving as they cook. Watch them carefully and do not let them burn, or they will taste bitter.

1 Heat a small heavy-based frying pan, add the pumpkin seeds and dry fry for a few minutes, stirring constantly as they swell.

3 Tip the *pepitas* into a bowl and serve with the wedge of lime for squeezing over the seeds. If the lime is omitted, the seeds can be cooled and stored in an airtight container for reheating later, but they are best served fresh.

Energy 230kcal/964kJ; Protein 3.8g; Carbohydrate 30.1g, of which sugars 0.6g; Fat 11.3g, of which saturates 2g; Cholesterol 0mg; Calcium 75mg; Fibre 3g; Sodium 430mg
Energy 299kcal/1242kJ; Protein 10.3g; Carbohydrate 11.2g, of which sugars 2g; Fat 23.8g, of which saturates 2.3g; Cholesterol 0mg; Calcium 57mg; Fibre 3.2g; Sodium 2mg

SPICED PLANTAIN CHIPS

PLANTAINS ARE MORE STARCHY THAN THE BANANAS TO WHICH THEY ARE RELATED, AND MUST BE COOKED BEFORE BEING EATEN. IN LATIN AMERICA THE FRUIT IS USED MUCH AS A POTATO WOULD BE. THIS SNACK HAS A LOVELY SWEET TASTE, WHICH IS BALANCED BY THE HEAT FROM THE CHILLI POWDER AND SAUCE. COOK THE CHIPS JUST BEFORE YOU PLAN TO SERVE THEM.

SERVES FOUR AS AN APPETIZER
OR SNACK

INGREDIENTS
  2 large plantains
  oil, for shallow frying
  2.5ml/½ tsp chilli powder
  5ml/1 tsp ground cinnamon
  hot chilli sauce, to serve

COOK'S TIP
Plantain skins are very dark, almost black, when the fruit is ready to eat. If they are green when you buy them, allow them to ripen at room temperature for a few days before use.

1 Peel the plaintains. Cut off and throw away the ends, then slice the fruit into rounds, cutting slightly on the diagonal to give larger, flatter slices.

2 Pour the oil for frying into a small frying pan, to a depth of about 1cm/½in. Heat the oil until it is very hot, watching it closely all the time. Test by carefully adding a slice of plantain; it should float and the oil should immediately bubble up around it.

3 Fry the plantain slices in small batches or the temperature of the oil will drop. When they are golden brown remove from the oil with a slotted spoon and drain on kitchen paper.

4 Mix the chilli powder with the cinnamon. Put the plantain chips on a serving plate, sprinkle them with the chilli and cinnamon mixture and serve immediately, with a small bowl of hot chilli sauce for dipping.

Energy 193kcal/806kJ; Protein 1.1g; Carbohydrate 22.7g, of which sugars 4.3g; Fat 11.5g, of which saturates 1.4g; Cholesterol 0mg; Calcium 23mg; Fibre 1.6g; Sodium 14mg

POPCORN <u>WITH</u> LIME <u>AND</u> CHILLI

IF THE ONLY POPCORN YOU'VE HAD CAME OUT OF A CARTON AT THE CINEMA, TRY THIS MEXICAN SPECIALITY. THE LIME JUICE AND CHILLI POWDER ARE INSPIRED ADDITIONS, AND THE SNACK IS QUITE A HEALTHY CHOICE TO SERVE WITH DRINKS.

MAKES ONE LARGE BOWL

INGREDIENTS
  30ml/2 tbsp vegetable oil
  225g/8oz/1¼ cups corn kernels
    for popcorn
  10ml/2 tsp chilli powder
  juice of 2 limes

1 Heat the oil in a large, heavy-based frying pan until it is very hot. Add the popcorn and immediately cover the pan with a lid and reduce the heat.

2 After a few minutes the corn should start to pop. Resist the temptation to lift the lid to check. Shake the pan occasionally so that all corn will be cooked and browned.

3 When the sound of popping corn has stopped, quickly remove the pan from the heat and allow to cool slightly. Take off the lid and with a spoon lift out and discard any corn kernels that have not popped. The uncooked corn will have fallen to the bottom of the pan and is completely inedible.

4 Add the chilli powder. Shake the pan again and again to make sure that all of the corn is covered with a colourful dusting of chilli.

5 Tip the popcorn into a large bowl and keep warm. Add a squeeze of lime juice immediately before serving.

Energy 741kcal/3085kJ; Protein 7.8g; Carbohydrate 60.9g, of which sugars 1.4g; Fat 53.5g, of which saturates 5.4g; Cholesterol 0mg; Calcium 13mg; Fibre 0g; Sodium 5mg

MEAT DISHES

Pork is undoubtedly the most popular meat in Mexico. Every part of the animal is processed for food, so it represents terrific value for money; traditionally a family keeps its own pig and feeds it on scraps from their table. Turkey was popular in pre-Columbian times and still features on the menu today, although chicken is widely used for everyday dishes. Beef is popular in the north, where cattle are raised, and lamb and kid are also used.

This chapter includes a wide range of favourite Mexican meat dishes, from Chicken Fajitas and Tacos with Shredded Beef to the aptly named Drunken Chicken. Classics such as Turkey Mole and Pork in Green Sauce with Cactus are included, along with Albondigas, delicious meatballs that can be served for a main meal or — in miniature — as snacks.

BURRITOS WITH CHICKEN AND RICE

IN MEXICO, BURRITOS ARE A POPULAR STREET FOOD, EATEN ON THE HOOF. THE SECRET OF A SUCCESSFUL BURRITO IS TO HAVE ALL THE FILLING NEATLY PACKAGED INSIDE THE TORTILLA FOR EASY EATING, SO THESE SNACKS ARE SELDOM SERVED WITH A POUR-OVER SAUCE.

SERVES FOUR

INGREDIENTS
  90g/3½oz/½ cup long grain rice
  15ml/1 tbsp vegetable oil
  1 onion, chopped
  2.5ml/½ tsp ground cloves
  5ml/1 tsp dried, or fresh oregano
  200g/7oz can chopped tomatoes in
    tomato juice
  2 skinless, boneless chicken breasts
  150g/5oz/1¼ cups grated Monterey
    Jack or mild Cheddar cheese
  60ml/4 tbsp sour cream (optional)
  8 x 20–25cm/8–10in fresh wheat
    flour tortillas
  salt
  fresh oregano, to garnish (optional)

1 Bring a pan of lightly salted water to the boil. Add the rice and cook for 8 minutes. Drain, rinse and then drain again.

2 Heat the oil in a large pan. Add the onion, with the ground cloves and oregano, and fry for 2–3 minutes. Stir in the rice and tomatoes and cook over a low heat until all the tomato juice has been absorbed. Set the pan aside.

3 Put the chicken breasts in a large pan, pour in enough water to cover and bring to the boil. Lower the heat and simmer for about 10 minutes or until the chicken is cooked through. Lift the chicken out of the pan, put on a plate and cool slightly.

4 Preheat the oven to 160°C/325°F/ Gas 3. Shred the chicken by pulling the flesh apart with two forks, then add the chicken to the rice mixture, with the grated cheese. Stir in the sour cream, if using.

COOK'S TIP
If you use very fresh tortillas, you may be able to dispense with the cocktail sticks. Secure the tortilla parcels by damping the final fold with a little water. When you lay the burritos in the dish, place them with the folded surfaces down.

5 Wrap the tortillas in foil and place them on a plate. Stand the plate over boiling water for about 5 minutes. Alternatively, wrap in microwave-safe film and heat in a microwave on full power for 1 minute.

6 Spoon one-eighth of the filling into the centre of a tortilla and fold in both sides. Fold the bottom up and the top down to form a parcel. Secure with a cocktail stick (toothpick).

7 Put the filled burrito in a shallow dish or casserole, cover with foil and keep warm in the oven while you make seven more. Remove the cocktail sticks before serving, sprinkled with fresh oregano.

Energy 626kcal/2634kJ; Protein 37.1g; Carbohydrate 82.4g, of which sugars 3.5g; Fat 17.2g, of which saturates 8.7g; Cholesterol 89mg; Calcium 403mg; Fibre 3.1g; Sodium 601mg

CHICKEN AND TOMATILLO CHIMICHANGAS

THESE FRIED BURRITOS ARE A COMMON SIGHT ON STREET STALLS AND IN CAFÉS ALONG THE MEXICAN BORDER WITH TEXAS, BUT ARE NOT SO WELL KNOWN FURTHER SOUTH.

SERVES FOUR

INGREDIENTS

2 skinless, boneless chicken breasts
1 chipotle chilli, seeded
15ml/1 tbsp vegetable oil
2 onions, finely chopped
4 garlic cloves, crushed
2.5ml/½ tsp ground cumin
2.5ml/½ tsp ground coriander
2.5ml/½ tsp ground cinnamon
2.5ml/½ tsp ground cloves
300g/11oz/scant 2 cups drained
  canned tomatillos
400g/14oz/2⅓ cups cooked
  pinto beans
8 x 20–25cm/8–10in fresh wheat
  flour tortillas
oil, for frying
salt and ground black pepper

1 Put the chicken breasts in a large pan, pour over water to cover and add the chilli. Bring to the boil, lower the heat and simmer for 10 minutes or until the chicken is cooked through and the chilli has softened. Remove the chilli and chop it finely. Lift the chicken breasts out of the pan and put them on a plate. Leave to cool slightly, then shred with two forks.

2 Heat the oil in a frying pan. Fry the onions until translucent, then add the garlic and ground spices and cook for 3 minutes more. Add the tomatillos and pinto beans. Cook over a moderate heat for 5 minutes, stirring constantly to break up the tomatillos and some of the beans. Simmer gently for 5 minutes more. Add the chicken and seasoning.

3 Wrap the tortillas in foil and place them on a plate. Stand the plate over boiling water for about 5 minutes until they become pliable. Alternatively, wrap them in microwave-safe film and heat them in a microwave on full power for 1 minute.

4 Spoon one-eighth of the bean filling into the centre of a tortilla, fold in both sides, then fold the bottom of the tortilla up and the top down to form a neat parcel. Secure with a cocktail stick (toothpick).

5 Heat the oil in a large frying pan and fry the chimichangas in batches until crisp, turning once. Remove them from the oil with a slotted spoon and drain on kitchen paper. Serve hot.

COOK'S TIP

The word "pinto" means speckled, which aptly describes these attractive dried beans. If you prepare them yourself, they will need to be soaked overnight in water, then cooked in unsalted boiling water for 1–1¼ hours until tender.

Energy 626kcal/2634kJ; Protein 37.1g; Carbohydrate 82.4g, of which sugars 3.5g; Fat 17.2g, of which saturates 8.7g; Cholesterol 89mg; Calcium 403mg; Fibre 3.1g; Sodium 601mg

DRUNKEN CHICKEN

TEQUILA IS THIS CHICKEN'S TIPPLE, AND THE DISH HAS A DELICIOUS SWEET-AND-SOUR FLAVOUR.
SERVE IT WITH GREEN OR YELLOW RICE AND FLOUR TORTILLAS TO MOP UP THE SAUCE.

SERVES FOUR

INGREDIENTS
150g/5oz/scant 1 cup raisins
120ml/4fl oz/½ cup sherry
115g/4oz/1 cup plain (all-purpose)
  flour
2.5ml/½ tsp salt
2.5ml/½ tsp ground black pepper
45ml/3 tbsp vegetable oil
8 skinless chicken thighs, bone-in
1 onion, halved and thinly sliced
3 garlic cloves, crushed
2 tart eating apples, such as
  Granny Smith
115g/4oz/1 cup slivered almonds
1 ripe plantain, peeled and sliced
350ml/12fl oz/1½ cups well-flavoured
  chicken stock
250ml/8fl oz/1 cup tequila
fresh herbs, chopped, to garnish

2 Heat the remaining vegetable oil in a large, deep frying pan. Add the onion slices and crushed garlic and cook for 2–3 minutes. Meanwhile, peel, core and dice the apples.

3 Add the diced apple to the onion mixture with the almonds and plantain slices. Cook, stirring occasionally, for 3–4 minutes, then add the soaked raisins, with any free sherry. Add the chicken pieces to the pan.

4 Pour the stock and tequila over the chicken mixture. Cover the pan with a lid and cook for 15 minutes, then take off the lid and cook for 10 minutes more or until the sauce has reduced by about half.

1 Put the raisins in a bowl and pour the sherry over. Set aside to plump up. Season the flour with the salt and pepper and spread it out on a large, flat dish or soup plate. Heat 30ml/2 tbsp of the oil in a large frying pan. Dip each chicken thigh in turn in the seasoned flour, then fry in the hot oil until browned, turning occasionally. Drain on kitchen paper.

5 Check that the chicken thighs are cooked by lifting one out of the pan and piercing it in the thickest part with a sharp knife or skewer. Any juices that come out should be clear. If necessary, cook the chicken for a little longer before serving, sprinkled with chopped fresh herbs, if desired.

Energy 626kcal/2634kJ; Protein 37.1g; Carbohydrate 82.4g, of which sugars 3.5g; Fat 17.2g, of which saturates 8.7g; Cholesterol 89mg; Calcium 403mg; Fibre 3.1g; Sodium 601mg

CHICKEN FAJITAS

THE PERFECT DISH FOR CASUAL ENTERTAINING, FAJITAS ARE FLOUR TORTILLAS WHICH ARE BROUGHT TO THE TABLE FRESHLY COOKED. GUESTS ADD THEIR OWN FILLINGS BEFORE FOLDING THE TORTILLAS AND TUCKING IN.

SERVES SIX

INGREDIENTS

   3 skinless, boneless chicken breasts
   finely grated rind and juice of
     2 limes
   30ml/2 tbsp sugar
   10ml/2 tsp dried oregano
   2.5ml/½ tsp cayenne pepper
   5ml/1 tsp ground cinnamon
   2 onions
   3 (bell) peppers (1 red, 1 yellow or
     orange and 1 green)
   45ml/3 tbsp vegetable oil
   guacamole, salsa and sour cream,
     to serve
For the tortillas
   250g/9oz/2¼ cups plain (all-purpose)
     flour, sifted
   1.5ml/¼ tsp baking powder
   pinch of salt
   50g/2oz/¼ cup lard
   60ml/4 tbsp warm water

1 Slice the chicken breasts into 2cm/ ¾in wide strips and place these in a large bowl. Add the lime rind and juice, sugar, oregano, cayenne and cinnamon. Mix thoroughly. Set aside to marinate for at least 30 minutes.

COOK'S TIP
Tortilla dough can be very difficult to roll out thinly. If the dough is breaking up try placing each ball between two sheets of clean plastic (this can be cut from a new sandwich bag). Roll out, turning over, still inside the plastic, until the tortilla is the right size.

2 Meanwhile, make the tortillas. Mix the flour, baking powder and salt in a large bowl. Rub in the lard, then add the warm water, a little at a time, to make a stiff dough. Knead this on a lightly floured surface for 10–15 minutes until it is smooth and elastic.

3 Divide the dough into 12 small balls, then roll each ball to a 15cm/6in round. Cover the rounds with plastic or clear film (plastic wrap) to keep them from drying out while you prepare the vegetables.

4 Cut the onions in half and slice them thinly. Cut the peppers in half, remove the cores and seeds, then slice the flesh into 1cm/½in wide strips.

5 Heat a large frying pan or griddle and cook each tortilla in turn for about 1 minute on each side, or until the surface colours and begins to blister. Keep the cooked tortillas warm and pliable by wrapping them in a clean, dry dish towel.

6 Heat the oil in a large frying pan. Stir-fry the marinated chicken for 5–6 minutes, then add the peppers and onions and cook for 3–4 minutes more, until the chicken strips are cooked through and the vegetables are soft and tender, but still juicy.

7 Spoon the chicken mixture into a serving bowl and take it to the table with the cooked tortillas, guacamole, salsa and sour cream. Keep the tortillas wrapped and warm.

8 To serve, each guest takes a warm tortilla, spreads it with a little salsa, adds a spoonful of guacamole and piles some of the chicken mixture in the centre. The final touch is to add a small dollop of sour cream. The tortilla is then folded over the filling and eaten in the hand.

Energy 485kcal/2044kJ; Protein 26g; Carbohydrate 67.4g, of which sugars 15.3g; Fat 14.2g, of which saturates 3.8g; Cholesterol 60mg; Calcium 118mg; Fibre 4g; Sodium 53mg

CHICKEN WITH CHIPOTLE SAUCE

IT IS IMPORTANT TO SEEK OUT CHIPOTLE CHILLIES FOR THIS RECIPE, AS THEY IMPART A WONDERFULLY RICH AND SMOKY FLAVOUR TO THE CHICKEN BREASTS. THE PURÉE CAN BE MADE AHEAD OF TIME, MAKING THIS A VERY EASY RECIPE FOR ENTERTAINING.

SERVES SIX

INGREDIENTS
   6 chipotle chillies
   200ml/7fl oz/scant 1 cup water
   chicken stock (see method)
   3 onions
   6 boneless chicken breasts
   45ml/3 tbsp vegetable oil
   salt and ground black pepper
   fresh oregano to garnish

1 Put the dried chillies in a bowl and pour over hot water to cover. Leave to stand for about 30 minutes until very soft. Drain, reserving the soaking water in a measuring jug. Cut off the stalk from each chilli, then slit them lengthways and scrape out the seeds with a small sharp knife.

2 Preheat the oven to 180°C/350°F/ Gas 4. Chop the flesh of the chillies roughly and put it in a food processor or blender. Add enough chicken stock to the soaking water to make it up to 400ml/14fl oz/1⅔ cups. Pour it into the processor or blender and process at maximum power until smooth.

3 Peel the onions. Using a sharp knife, cut them in half, then slice them thinly. Separate the slices.

4 Remove the skin from the chicken breasts and trim off any stray pieces of fat or membrane.

5 Heat the oil in a large frying pan, add the onions and cook over a low to moderate heat for about 5 minutes, or until they have softened but not coloured, stirring occasionally.

6 Using a slotted spoon, transfer the onion slices to a casserole that is large enough to hold all the chicken breasts in a single layer. Sprinkle the onion slices with a little salt and ground black pepper.

COOK'S TIP
If you are a lover of chipotle chillies, you may wish to use more than six.

7 Arrange the chicken breasts on top of the onion slices. Sprinkle with a little salt and several grindings of black pepper.

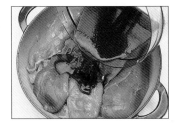

8 Pour the chipotle purée over the chicken breasts, making sure that each piece is evenly coated.

9 Place the casserole in the preheated oven and bake for 45 minutes–1 hour or until the chicken is cooked through, but is still moist and tender. Garnish with fresh oregano and serve with boiled white rice, and *Frijoles de Olla*.

Energy 234kcal/984kJ; Protein 37.1g; Carbohydrate 5.3g, of which sugars 3.8g; Fat 7.3g, of which saturates 1.1g; Cholesterol 105mg; Calcium 27mg; Fibre 0.9g; Sodium 93mg

TURKEY MOLE

A MOLE IS A RICH STEW, TRADITIONALLY SERVED ON A FESTIVE OCCASION. THE WORD COMES FROM THE AZTEC "MOLLI", MEANING A CHILLI-FLAVOURED SAUCE. THERE ARE MANY DIFFERENT TYPES, INCLUDING THE FAMOUS MOLE POBLANO DE GUAJALOTE. TOASTED NUTS, FRUIT AND CHOCOLATE ARE AMONG THE CLASSIC INGREDIENTS; THIS VERSION INCLUDES COCOA POWDER.

SERVES FOUR

INGREDIENTS

1 ancho chilli, seeded
1 guajillo chilli, seeded
115g/4oz/¾ cup sesame seeds
50g/2oz/½ cup whole blanched
  almonds
50g/2oz/½ cup shelled unsalted
  peanuts, skinned
1 small onion
2 garlic cloves
50g/2oz/¼ cup lard or 60ml/4 tbsp
  vegetable oil
50g/2oz/⅓ cup canned tomatoes in
  tomato juice
1 ripe plantain
50g/2oz/⅓ cup raisins
75g/3oz/½ cup ready-to-eat
  prunes, stoned
5ml/1 tsp dried oregano
2.5ml/½ tsp ground cloves
2.5ml/½ tsp crushed allspice berries
5ml/1 tsp ground cinnamon
25g/1oz/¼ cup cocoa powder
4 turkey breast steaks
fresh oregano, to garnish (optional)

1 Soak both types of dried chilli in a bowl of hot water for 30 minutes, then lift them out and chop them roughly. Reserve 250ml/8fl oz/1 cup of the soaking liquid.

COOK'S TIP
It is important to use good quality cocoa powder, which is unsweetened.

2 Spread out the sesame seeds in a heavy-based frying pan. Toast them over a moderate heat, shaking the pan lightly so that they turn golden all over. Do not let them burn, or the sauce will taste bitter. Set aside 45ml/3 tbsp of the toasted seeds for the garnish and tip the rest into a bowl. Toast the almonds and peanuts in the same way and add them to the bowl.

3 Chop the onion and garlic finely. Heat half the lard or oil in a frying pan, cook the chopped onion and garlic for 2–3 minutes, then add the chillies and tomatoes. Cook gently for 10 minutes.

4 Peel the plantain and slice it into short diagonal slices. Add it to the onion mixture with the raisins, prunes, dried oregano, spices and cocoa. Stir in the 250ml/8fl oz/1 cup of the reserved water in which the chillies were soaked. Bring to the boil, stirring, then add the toasted sesame seeds, almonds and peanuts. Cook for 10 minutes, stirring frequently, then remove from the heat and allow to cool slightly.

5 Blend the sauce in batches in a food processor or blender until smooth. The sauce should be fairly thick, but a little water may be added if necessary.

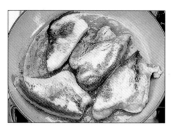

6 Heat the remaining lard or oil in a flameproof casserole. Add the turkey and brown over a moderate heat.

7 Pour the sauce over the steaks and cover the casserole with foil and a tight-fitting lid. Cook over a gentle heat for 20–25 minutes or until the turkey is cooked, and the sauce has thickened. Sprinkle with sesame seeds and chopped oregano, and serve with a rice dish and warm tortillas.

Energy 710kcal/2977kJ; Protein 63g; Carbohydrate 36.7g, of which sugars 26.1g; Fat 35.7g, of which saturates 5.5g; Cholesterol 111mg; Calcium 219mg; Fibre 6.4g; Sodium 232mg

ENCHILADAS WITH PORK AND GREEN SAUCE

THE GREEN TOMATILLO SAUCE PROVIDES A TART CONTRAST TO THE PORK FILLING IN THIS POPULAR DISH. CASCABELS ARE DRIED CHILLIES WHICH RATTLE WHEN SHAKEN.

SERVES THREE TO FOUR

INGREDIENTS
  500g/1¼lb pork shoulder, diced
  1 cascabel chilli
  30ml/2 tbsp oil
  2 garlic cloves, crushed
  1 onion, finely chopped
  300g/11oz/scant 2 cups drained
    canned tomatillos
  6 fresh corn tortillas
  75g/3oz/¾ cup grated Monterey Jack
    or mild Cheddar cheese

1 Put the diced pork in a pan and pour over water to cover. Bring to the boil, lower the heat and simmer for 40 minutes.

2 Meanwhile, soak the dried chilli in hot water for 30 minutes until softened. Drain, remove the stalk, then slit the chilli and scrape out the seeds.

3 Drain the pork and let it cool slightly, then shred it, using two forks. Put the pork in a bowl and set it aside.

4 Heat the oil in a frying pan and fry the garlic and onion for 3–4 minutes until translucent. Chop and add the chilli with the tomatillos. Cook, stirring constantly, until the tomatillos start to break up. Lower the heat and simmer the sauce for 10 minutes more. Cool slightly, then purée in a blender.

5 Preheat the oven to 180°C/350°F/Gas 4. Soften the tortillas by wrapping them in foil and steaming on a plate over boiling water for a few minutes until they are pliable. Alternatively, wrap them in microwave-safe film and heat in a microwave on full power for about 30 seconds.

6 Spoon one-sixth of the shredded pork on to the centre of a tortilla and roll it up to make an enchilada. Place it in a shallow baking dish which is large enough to hold all the enchiladas in a single layer. Fill and roll the remaining tortillas and add them to the dish.

7 Pour the sauce over the enchiladas to cover completely. Sprinkle evenly with cheese. Bake for 25–30 minutes or until the cheese bubbles. Serve at once. Tomato salad makes a good accompaniment for this dish.

Energy 522kcal/2194kJ; Protein 41g; Carbohydrate 49.5g, of which sugars 4.8g; Fat 18.6g, of which saturates 7g; Cholesterol 106mg; Calcium 251mg; Fibre 3.1g; Sodium 461mg

PORK IN GREEN SAUCE WITH CACTUS

CHILE VERDE IS A CLASSIC SAUCE. THE INCLUSION OF CACTUS PIECES — A POPULAR INGREDIENT IN MEXICAN COOKING — GIVES THIS DISH AN INTRIGUING FLAVOUR WHICH WILL DOUBTLESS PROVE A GOOD TALKING POINT AT THE DINNER TABLE.

SERVES FOUR

INGREDIENTS

30ml/2 tbsp vegetable oil
500g/1¼lb pork shoulder, cut in
 2.5cm/1in cubes
1 onion, finely chopped
2 garlic cloves, crushed
5ml/1 tsp dried oregano
3 fresh jalapeño chillies, seeded
 and chopped
300g/11oz/scant 2 cups drained
 canned tomatillos
150ml/¼ pint/⅔ cup vegetable stock
300g/11oz jar *nopalitos*, drained
salt and ground black pepper
warm fresh corn tortillas, to serve

COOK'S TIP

Nopalitos are cactus paddles which have been cut into strips and pickled in vinegar or packed in brine. Look for them in speciality food stores.

1 Heat the oil in a large pan. Add the pork cubes and cook over a high heat, turning several times until browned all over. Add the onion and garlic and fry gently until soft, then stir in the oregano and chopped jalapeños. Cook for 2 minutes more.

2 Tip the canned tomatillos into a blender, add the stock and process until smooth. Add to the pork mixture, cover and cook for 30 minutes.

3 Meanwhile, soak the *nopalitos* in cold water for 10 minutes. Drain, then add to the pork and continue cooking for about 10 minutes or until the pork is cooked through and tender.

4 Season the mixture with salt and plenty of ground black pepper. Serve with warm corn tortillas.

Energy 246kcal/1031kJ; Protein 31.1g; Carbohydrate 5g, of which sugars 4.7g; Fat 11.4g, of which saturates 2.7g; Cholesterol 87mg; Calcium 102mg; Fibre 2.4g; Sodium 108mg

STUFFED LOIN OF PORK

PORK FEATURES TWICE IN THIS DELICIOUS AND LUXURIOUS DISH, WHICH CONSISTS OF A ROAST LOIN STUFFED WITH A RICH MINCED PORK MIXTURE. THE PERFECT CENTREPIECE FOR A SPECIAL OCCASION DINNER, IT IS SERVED IN MEXICO AT WEDDINGS AND SIMILAR CELEBRATIONS.

SERVES SIX

INGREDIENTS

1.5kg/3–3½lb boneless pork loin,
   butterflied ready for stuffing
For the stuffing
   50g/2oz/⅓ cup raisins
   120ml/4fl oz/½ cup dry white wine
   15ml/1 tbsp vegetable oil
   1 onion, diced
   2 garlic cloves, crushed
   2.5ml/½ tsp ground cloves
   5ml/1 tsp ground cinnamon
   500g/1¼lb minced (ground) pork
   150ml/¼ pint/⅔ cup vegetable stock
   2 tomatoes
   50g/2oz/½ cup chopped almonds
   2.5ml/½ tsp each salt and ground
    black pepper

3 While the pork is simmering, peel the tomatoes. Cut a cross in the base of each tomato, then put them both in a heatproof bowl. Pour over boiling water to cover. Leave the tomatoes in the water for 3 minutes, then lift them out on a slotted spoon and plunge them into a bowl of cold water. Drain. The skins will have begun to peel back from the crosses.

6 Preheat the oven to 180°C/350°F/ Gas 4. Open out the pork loin and trim it neatly. Season the minced pork stuffing with salt and pepper to taste. Spread over the surface of the meat in a neat layer, taking it right to the edges and keeping it as even as possible.

1 Make the stuffing. Put the raisins and wine in a bowl. Set aside. Heat the oil in a large pan, add the onion and garlic and cook for 5 minutes over a low heat.

4 Remove the skins completely, then chop the flesh.

7 Roll up the pork loin carefully and tie it at intervals with kitchen string. Weigh the pork and calculate the cooking time at 30 minutes per lb/450g, plus another 30 minutes.

8 Put the stuffed pork joint in a roasting tin, season with salt and pepper and roast for the calculated time. When the joint is cooked, transfer it to a meat platter, place a tent of foil over it, and let it stand for 10 minutes before carving and serving with the roast vegetables of your choice.

2 Add the cloves and cinnamon, then the pork. Cook, stirring, until the pork has browned. Add the stock. Simmer, stirring frequently, for 20 minutes.

5 Stir the tomatoes and almonds into the mince mixture, add the raisins and wine. Cook until the mixture has reduced to a thick sauce. Leave to cool.

COOK'S TIP
Your butcher will prepare the pork loin for you.

Energy 569kcal/2383kJ; Protein 71.9g; Carbohydrate 11.2g, of which sugars 10.8g; Fat 24.7g, of which saturates 7.1g; Cholesterol 213mg; Calcium 56mg; Fibre 1.3g; Sodium 243mg

CARNITAS

Succulent little pieces of meat, usually pork, carnitas, literally "little meats", can be eaten as part of a main dish or used to fill tacos or burritos. They are also served with salsa as snacks or antojitos (nibbles).

SERVES EIGHT AS AN APPETIZER,
SIX AS A MAIN COURSE

INGREDIENTS
    2 dried bay leaves
    10ml/2 tsp dried thyme
    5ml/1 tsp dried marjoram
    1.5kg/3–3½lb mixed boneless pork
        (loin and leg)
    3 garlic cloves
    2.5ml/½ tsp salt
    200g/7oz/scant 1 cup lard
    1 orange, cut into 8 wedges
    1 small onion, thickly sliced
    warm wheat flour tortillas, to serve
For the salsa
    small bunch of coriander (cilantro)
    1 white onion
    8–10 pickled jalapeño chilli slices
    45ml/3 tbsp freshly squeezed
        orange juice

1 Crumble the bay leaves into a mortar. Add the dried thyme and dried marjoram and grind the mixture with a pestle to a fine powder.

2 Cut the pork into 5cm/2in cubes and place it in a non-metallic bowl. Add the herbs and salt. Using your fingers, rub the spice mixture into the meat. Cover and marinate for at least 2 hours, preferably overnight.

3 To make the salsa, remove the stems from the coriander and chop the leaves roughly. Cut the onion in half, then slice each half thinly. Finely chop the jalapeño chilli slices.

4 Mix all the salsa ingredients in a bowl, pour over the freshly squeezed orange juice and toss gently to mix. Cover and chill until required.

5 Heat the lard in a flame-proof casserole. Add the pork mixture, with the oranges, garlic cloves and onion. Brown the pork cubes on all sides.

6 Using a slotted spoon, lift out the onion and garlic and discard. Cover the casserole and continue to cook over a low heat for about 1½ hours.

7 Remove the lid and lift out and discard the orange wedges. Continue to cook the mixture, uncovered, until all the meat juices have been absorbed and the pork cubes are crisp on the outside and tender and moist inside. Serve with warm tortillas and the salsa.

COOK'S TIP
If the *carnitas* are to be served in tacos or burritos, shred or chop them. Make the chunks about half the given size if serving them as *antojitos*. Reduce the cooking time accordingly.

Energy 297kcal/1241kJ; Protein 40.8g; Carbohydrate 2.1g, of which sugars 1.9g; Fat 13.9g, of which saturates 5.1g; Cholesterol 124mg; Calcium 37mg; Fibre 0.7g; Sodium 135mg

TORTILLA PIE WITH CHORIZO

*THIS IS A POPULAR MEXICAN BREAKFAST DISH, KNOWN AS CHILAQUILES. THE FRIED TORTILLA STRIPS
STAY CRISP IN THE TOMATILLO, CREAM AND CHEESE SAUCE.*

SERVES SIX

INGREDIENTS

25g/1oz/2 tbsp lard or 30ml/2 tbsp
  vegetable oil
500g/1¼lb minced (ground) pork
3 garlic cloves, crushed
10ml/2 tsp dried oregano
5ml/1 tsp ground cinnamon
2.5ml/½ tsp ground cloves
2.5ml/½ tsp ground black pepper
30ml/2 tbsp dry sherry
5ml/1 tsp sugar
5ml/1 tsp salt
12 corn tortillas, freshly made or a
  few days old
oil, for frying
350g/12oz/3 cups grated Monterey
  Jack or mild Cheddar cheese
300ml/½ pint/1¼ cups crème fraîche
For the tomatillo sauce
300g/11oz/scant 2 cups drained
  canned tomatillos
60ml/4 tbsp stock or water
2 fresh serrano chillies, seeded and
  roughly chopped
2 garlic cloves
small bunch of coriander (cilantro)
120ml/4fl oz/½ cup sour cream

1 Preheat the oven to 180°C/350°F/
Gas 4. Heat the lard or oil in a large
pan. Add the minced pork and crushed
garlic. Stir over a moderate heat until
the meat has browned, then stir in the
oregano, cinnamon, cloves and pepper.
Cook for 3–4 minutes more, stirring all
the time, then add the sherry, sugar and
salt. Stir for 3–4 minutes until all the
flavours are blended, then remove the
pan from the heat.

2 Cut the tortillas into 2cm/¾in strips.
Pour oil into a frying pan to a depth of
2cm/¾in and heat to 190°C/375°F. Fry
the tortilla strips in batches until crisp
and golden brown all over.

3 Spread half the minced pork mixture
in a baking dish. Top with half the
tortilla strips and grated cheese, then
add dollops of crème fraîche. Repeat
the layers. Bake for 20–25 minutes, or
until bubbling.

4 To make the sauce, put all the
ingredients except the sour cream in a
food processor or blender. Reserve a
little coriander for sprinkling. Process
until smooth. Scrape into a pan, bring
to the boil, then lower the heat and
simmer for 5 minutes.

5 Stir the sour cream into the sauce,
with salt and pepper to taste. Pour the
mixture over the layer bake and serve
immediately, sprinkled with coriander.

Energy 874kcal/3636kJ; Protein 39.5g; Carbohydrate 40.5g, of which sugars 4.7g; Fat 60.9g, of which saturates 30.5g; Cholesterol 173mg; Calcium 565mg; Fibre 5.4g; Sodium 977mg

TOSTADAS WITH SHREDDED PORK AND SPICES

CRISP FRIED TORTILLAS TOPPED WITH REFRIED BEANS AND SPICED SHREDDED PORK MAKE A
DELECTABLE TREAT AND ARE OFTEN SOLD FROM STALLS IN MEXICAN CITY STREETS.

SERVES SIX

INGREDIENTS
   6 corn tortillas, freshly made or a few
      days old
   oil, for frying
For the topping
      500g/1¼lb pork shoulder, cut into
         2.5cm/1in cubes
      2.5ml/½ tsp salt
      15ml/1 tbsp oil
      1 small onion, halved and sliced
      1 garlic clove, crushed
      1 pasilla chilli, seeded and ground
      5ml/1 tsp ground cinnamon
      2.5ml/½ tsp ground cloves
      175g/6oz/1 cup Refried Beans
      90ml/6 tbsp sour cream
      2 tomatoes, seeded and diced
      115g/4oz feta cheese, crumbled
      fresh oregano sprigs, to garnish

COOK'S TIP
In Mexico, the local fresh goat's or cow's
cheese – *queso fresco* – would be used,
feta is the nearest equivalent.

1 Make the topping. Place the pork
cubes in a pan, pour over water to
cover and bring to the boil. Lower the
heat, cover and simmer for 40 minutes.
Drain, discarding the cooking liquid.
Shred the pork, using two forks. Put it
in a bowl and season with the salt.

2 Heat the oil in a large frying pan. Add
the onion, garlic, chilli and spices. Stir
over the heat for 2–3 minutes, then add
the shredded meat and cook until the
meat is thoroughly heated and has
absorbed the flavourings. Heat the
refried beans in a separate, small pan.

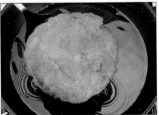

3 Meanwhile, cook the tortillas. Pour oil
into a large frying pan to a depth of
2cm/¾in. Heat the oil and fry one
tortilla at a time, pressing down with a
fish slice or a pair of tongs to keep it
flat. As soon as a tortilla is crisp, lift it
out and drain it on kitchen paper.

4 Place each tortilla on a plate. Top with
refried beans. Add a little of the meat
mixture, then spoon 15ml/1 tbsp of the
sour cream over each. Divide the
chopped tomato among the tostadas
and top with the crumbled feta. Serve at
once, garnished with fresh oregano.

Energy 525kcal/2195kJ; Protein 34.8g; Carbohydrate 37.2g, of which sugars 2.9g; Fat 27.3g, of which saturates 5.9g; Cholesterol 92mg; Calcium 104mg; Fibre 3.4g; Sodium 369mg

TAMALES FILLED WITH SPICED PORK

THESE TAMALES ARE AMONG THE MOST ANCIENT OF MEXICAN FOODS. AT ONE TIME THE NEAT LITTLE CORN HUSK PARCELS FILLED WITH PLAIN, SAVOURY OR SWEET MASA DOUGH WERE COOKED IN THE ASHES OF A WOOD FIRE. TODAY THEY ARE MORE LIKELY TO BE STEAMED, BUT THE THRILL OF UNWRAPPING THEM REMAINS THE SAME.

SERVES SIX

INGREDIENTS
  500g/1¼lb lean pork, cut into
    5cm/2in cubes
  750ml/1¼ pints/3 cups chicken stock
  600g/1lb 6oz/4½ cups *masa harina*
  450g/1lb/2 cups lard, softened
  30ml/2 tbsp salt
  12 large or 24 small dried corn husks
  2 ancho chillies, seeded
  15ml/1 tbsp vegetable oil
  ½ onion, finely chopped
  2–3 garlic cloves, crushed
  2.5ml/½ tsp allspice berries
  2 dried bay leaves
  2.5ml/½ tsp ground cumin
  lime wedges, to serve (optional)

1 Put the pork cubes in a large pan. Pour over water to cover. Bring to the boil, lower the heat and simmer for 40 minutes.

2 Meanwhile, heat the chicken stock in a separate pan. Put the *masa harina* in a large bowl and add the hot stock, a little at a time, to make a stiff dough.

3 Put the lard in another bowl and beat with an electric whisk until light and fluffy, as when beating butter for a cake. Test by dropping a small amount of the whipped lard into a cup of water. If it floats, it is ready for use.

4 Continue to beat the lard, gradually adding the *masa* dough. When all of it has been added and the mixture is light and spreadable, beat in the salt. Cover closely with clear film (plastic wrap) to prevent the mixture from drying out.

5 Put the corn husks in a bowl and pour over boiling water to cover. Leave to soak for 30 minutes. Soak the seeded chillies in a separate bowl of hot water for the same time. Drain the pork, reserving 105ml/7 tbsp of the cooking liquid, and chop the meat finely.

6 Heat the oil in a large pan and fry the onion and garlic over a moderate heat for 2–3 minutes. Drain the chillies, chop them finely and add them to the pan. Put the allspice berries and bay leaves in a mortar, grind them with a pestle, then work in the ground cumin. Add to the onion mixture and stir well. Cook for 2–3 minutes more. Add the chopped pork and reserved cooking liquid and continue cooking over a moderate heat until all the liquid is absorbed. Leave to cool slightly.

7 Drain the corn husks and pat them dry in a clean dish towel. Place one large corn husk (or overlap two smaller ones) on a board. Spoon about one-twelfth of the *masa* mixture on to the centre of the husk wrapping and spread it almost to the sides.

8 Place a spoonful of the meat mixture on top of the *masa*. Fold the two long sides of the corn husk over the filling, then bring up each of the two shorter sides in turn, to make a neat parcel. Slide one of the two short sides inside the other, if possible, to prevent the parcel from unravelling, or tie with string or strips of the corn husk.

9 Place the *tamales* in a steamer basket over a pan of steadily simmering water and steam for 1 hour, topping up the water as needed. To test if the *tamales* are ready, unwrap one. The filling should peel away from the husk cleanly. Pile the *tamales* on a plate, leave to stand for 10 minutes, then serve with lime wedges, if liked. Guests unwrap their own *tamales* at the table.

Energy 848kcal/3528kJ; Protein 38.1g; Carbohydrate 74g, of which sugars 0.6g; Fat 43.5g, of which saturates 15.5g; Cholesterol 114mg; Calcium 18mg; Fibre 2.3g; Sodium 94mg

LAMB STEW WITH CHILLI SAUCE

THE CHILLIES IN THIS STEW ADD DEPTH AND RICHNESS TO THE SAUCE, WHILE THE POTATO SLICES ENSURE THAT IT IS SUBSTANTIAL ENOUGH TO SERVE ON ITS OWN.

SERVES SIX

INGREDIENTS

6 guajillo chillies, seeded
2 pasilla chillies, seeded
250ml/8fl oz/1 cup hot water
3 garlic cloves, peeled
5ml/1 tsp ground cinnamon
2.5ml/½ tsp ground cloves
2.5ml/½ tsp ground black pepper
15ml/1 tbsp vegetable oil
1kg/2¼lb lean boneless lamb
    shoulder, cut into 2cm/¾in cubes
400g/14oz potatoes, scrubbed and
    cut into 1cm/½in thick slices
salt
strips of red (bell) pepper and fresh
    oregano to garnish

COOK'S TIP

When frying the lamb, don't be tempted to cook too many cubes at one time, as the meat will steam rather than fry.

1 Snap or tear the dried chillies into large pieces, put them in a bowl and pour over the hot water. Leave to soak for 30 minutes, then tip the contents of the bowl into a food processor or blender. Add the garlic and spices. Process until smooth.

2 Heat the oil in a large pan. Add the lamb cubes, in batches, and stir-fry over a high heat until the cubes are browned on all sides.

3 Return all the lamb cubes to the pan, spread them out, then cover them with a layer of potato slices. Add salt to taste. Put a lid on the pan and cook over a medium heat for 10 minutes.

4 Pour over the chilli mixture and mix well. Replace the lid and simmer over a low heat for about 1 hour or until the meat and the potato are tender. Serve with a rice dish, and garnish with strips of red pepper and fresh oregano.

Energy 370kcal/1547kJ; Protein 34.8g; Carbohydrate 10.8g, of which sugars 0.9g; Fat 21.2g, of which saturates 9.1g; Cholesterol 129mg; Calcium 21mg; Fibre 0.7g; Sodium 154mg

ALBONDIGAS

*DON'T BE DAUNTED BY THE LENGTH OF THE INGREDIENT LIST. THESE MEATBALLS ARE ABSOLUTELY
DELICIOUS AND THE CHIPOTLE CHILLI GIVES THE SAUCE A DISTINCTIVE, SLIGHTLY SMOKY FLAVOUR.*

SERVES FOUR

INGREDIENTS

   225g/8oz minced (ground) pork
   225g/8oz lean minced (ground) beef
   1 onion, finely chopped
   50g/2oz/1 cup fresh white breadcrumbs
   5ml/1 tsp dried oregano
   2.5ml/½ tsp ground cumin
   2.5ml/½ tsp salt
   2.5ml/½ tsp ground black pepper
   1 egg, beaten
   oil, for frying
   fresh oregano sprigs, to garnish
For the sauce
   1 chipotle chilli, seeded
   15ml/1 tbsp vegetable oil
   1 onion, finely chopped
   2 garlic cloves, crushed
   175ml/6fl oz/¾ cup beef stock
   400g/14oz can chopped tomatoes in
      tomato juice
   105ml/7 tbsp passata (bottled
      strained tomatoes)

1 Mix the pork and beef in a large
bowl. Add the onion, breadcrumbs,
oregano, cumin, salt and pepper. Mix
with clean hands until all the
ingredients are well combined.

2 Stir in the egg, mix well, then roll
into 4cm/1½in balls. Put these on a
baking sheet and chill while you
prepare the sauce.

3 Soak the dried chilli in hot water to
cover for 15 minutes. Heat the oil in a
pan and fry the onion and garlic for
3–4 minutes until softened.

4 Drain the chilli, reserving the soaking
water, then chop it and add it to the
onion mixture. Fry for 1 minute, then
stir in the beef stock, tomatoes, passata
and soaking water, with salt and pepper
to taste. Bring to the boil, lower the heat
and simmer, stirring occasionally, while
you cook the meatballs.

5 Heat the oil for frying in a frying pan
and fry the meatballs in batches for
about 5 minutes, turning them
occasionally, until browned.

6 Drain off the oil and transfer all the
meatballs to a shallow casserole.
Pour over the sauce and simmer for
10 minutes, stirring gently from time to
time so that the meatballs are coated
but do not disintegrate. Garnish with the
oregano and serve. Plain white rice
makes a good accompaniment.

COOK'S TIP
Dampen your hands before shaping the
meatballs and the mixture will be less
likely to stick.

Energy 420kcal/1759kJ; Protein 29g; Carbohydrate 33.5g, of which sugars 10.3g; Fat 19.9g, of which saturates 6.8g; Cholesterol 119mg; Calcium 88mg; Fibre 3.2g; Sodium 322mg

TACOS <u>WITH</u> SHREDDED BEEF

IN MEXICO TACOS ARE MOST OFTEN MADE WITH SOFT CORN TORTILLAS, WHICH ARE FILLED AND FOLDED IN HALF. IT IS UNUSUAL TO SEE THE CRISP SHELLS OF CORN WHICH ARE SO WIDELY USED IN TEX-MEX COOKING. TACOS ARE ALWAYS EATEN IN THE HAND.

SERVES SIX

INGREDIENTS
   450g/1lb rump steak, diced
   150g/5oz/1 cup *masa harina*
   2.5ml/½ tsp salt
   120ml/4fl oz/½ cup warm water
   10ml/2 tsp dried oregano
   5ml/1 tsp ground cumin
   30ml/2 tbsp oil
   1 onion, thinly sliced
   2 garlic cloves, crushed
   fresh coriander (cilantro), to garnish
   shredded lettuce, lime wedges and
      Classic Tomato Salsa, to serve

1 Put the steak in a deep frying pan and pour over water to cover. Bring to the boil, then lower the heat and simmer for 1–1½ hours.

2 Meanwhile, make the tortilla dough. Mix the *masa harina* and salt in a large mixing bowl. Add the warm water, a little at a time, to make a dough that can be worked into a ball. Knead the dough on a lightly floured surface for 3–4 minutes until smooth, then wrap the dough in clear film (plastic wrap) and leave to rest for 1 hour.

3 Put the meat on a board, let it cool slightly, then shred it, using two forks. Put the meat in a bowl. Divide the tortilla dough into six equal balls.

4 Open a tortilla press and line both sides with plastic (this can be cut from a new plastic sandwich bag). Put each ball on the press and flatten it into a 15–20cm/6–8in round.

5 Heat a griddle or frying pan until hot. Cook each tortilla for 15–20 seconds on each side, and then for a further 15 seconds on the first side. Keep the tortillas warm and soft by folding them inside a slightly damp dish towel.

6 Add the oregano and cumin to the shredded meat and mix well. Heat the oil in a frying pan and fry the onion and garlic for 3–4 minutes until softened. Add the spiced meat mixture and toss over the heat until heated through.

7 Place some shredded lettuce on a tortilla, top with shredded beef and salsa, fold in half and serve with lime wedges. Garnish with fresh coriander.

Energy 202kcal/846kJ; Protein 18.8g; Carbohydrate 14.9g, of which sugars 0.5g; Fat 7.4g, of which saturates 1.7g; Cholesterol 44mg; Calcium 6mg; Fibre 0.7g; Sodium 46mg

BEEF ENCHILADAS WITH RED SAUCE

ENCHILADAS ARE USUALLY MADE WITH CORN TORTILLAS, ALTHOUGH IN PARTS OF NORTHERN MEXICO FLOUR TORTILLAS ARE SOMETIMES USED.

SERVES THREE TO FOUR

INGREDIENTS
    500g/1¼lb rump steak, cut into
      5cm/2in cubes
    2 ancho chillies, seeded
    2 pasilla chillies, seeded
    2 garlic cloves, crushed
    10ml/2 tsp dried oregano
    2.5ml/½ tsp ground cumin
    30ml/2 tbsp vegetable oil
    7 fresh corn tortillas
    shredded onion and flat-leaved
      parsley to garnish
    Mango Salsa, to serve

1 Put the steak in a deep frying pan and cover with water. Bring to the boil, then lower the heat and simmer for 1–1½ hours, or until very tender.

2 Meanwhile, put the dried chillies in a bowl and pour over the hot water. Leave to soak for 30 minutes, then tip the contents of the bowl into a blender and whizz to a smooth paste.

3 Drain the steak and let it cool, reserving 250ml/8fl oz/1 cup of the cooking liquid. Meanwhile, fry the garlic, oregano and cumin in the oil for 2 minutes.

4 Stir in the chilli paste and the reserved cooking liquid from the beef. Tear one of the tortillas into small pieces and add it to the mixture. Bring to the boil, then lower the heat. Simmer for 10 minutes, stirring occasionally, until the sauce has thickened. Shred the steak, using two forks, and stir it into the sauce, heat through for a few minutes.

5 Spoon some of the meat mixture on to each tortilla and roll it up to make an enchilada. Keep the enchiladas in a warmed dish until you have rolled them all. Garnish with shreds of onion and fresh flat-leaved parsley and then serve immediately with the Mango Salsa.

VARIATION
For a richer version place the rolled enchiladas side by side in a gratin dish. Pour over 300ml/½ pint/1¼ cups sour cream and 75g/3oz/¾ cup grated Cheddar cheese. Place under a preheated grill (broiler) for 5 minutes or until the cheese melts and the sauce begins to bubble. Serve at once, with the salsa.

Energy 460kcal/1939kJ; Protein 38g; Carbohydrate 52.4g, of which sugars 1.1g; Fat 12.3g, of which saturates 3.1g; Cholesterol 84mg; Calcium 108mg; Fibre 2.1g; Sodium 331mg

STUFFED BUTTERFLY OF BEEF WITH CHEESE AND CHILLI SAUCE

THIS RECIPE HAD ITS ORIGINS IN NORTHERN MEXICO OR IN NEW MEXICO, WHICH IS BEEF COUNTRY. IT IS A GOOD WAY TO COOK STEAKS, EITHER UNDER THE GRILL OR ON THE BARBECUE.

SERVES FOUR

INGREDIENTS

    4 fresh serrano chillies
    115g/4oz/½ cup full-fat soft cheese
    30ml/2 tbsp reposada tequila
    30ml/2 tbsp oil
    1 onion
    2 garlic cloves
    5ml/1 tsp dried oregano
    2.5ml/½ tsp salt
    2.5ml/½ tsp ground black pepper
    175g/6oz/1½ cups grated medium
       Cheddar cheese
    4 fillet steaks, at least 2.5cm/
       1in thick

1 Dry roast the chillies in a griddle pan over a moderate heat, turning them frequently until the skins are blistered but not burnt. Put them in a strong plastic bag and tie the top to keep the steam in. Set aside for 20 minutes.

2 Remove the chillies from the bag, slit them and scrape out the seeds with a sharp knife. Cut the flesh into long narrow strips, then cut each strip into several shorter strips.

3 Put the full-fat soft cheese in a small heavy-based pan and stir over a low heat until it has melted. Add the chilli strips and the tequila and stir to make a smooth sauce. Keep warm over a very low heat.

4 Heat the oil in a frying pan and fry the onion, garlic and oregano for about 5 minutes over a moderate heat, stirring frequently until the onion has browned. Season with the salt and pepper.

5 Remove the pan from the heat and stir in the grated cheese so that it melts into the onion mixture.

6 Cut each steak almost but not quite in half across its width, so that it can be opened out, butterfly-fashion. Preheat the grill (broiler) to its highest setting.

7 Spoon a quarter of the cheese and onion filling on to one side of each steak and close the other side over it. Place the steaks in a grill (broiling) pan and grill (broil) for 3–5 minutes on each side, depending on how you like your steak. Serve on heated plates with the vegetables of your choice, and with the cheese and chilli sauce poured over.

COOK'S TIP
One of the easiest ways of testing whether a steak is cooked is by touch. A steak that is very rare or "blue" will feel soft to the touch; the meat will be relaxed. A rare steak will feel like a sponge, and will spring back when lightly pressed. A medium-rare steak offers more resistance, while a well-cooked steak will feel very firm.

Energy 640kcal/2659kJ; Protein 56.1g; Carbohydrate 1.3g, of which sugars 1g; Fat 44.8g, of which saturates 23.5g; Cholesterol 201mg; Calcium 329mg; Fibre 0.2g; Sodium 508mg

FISH AND SEAFOOD

Mexico's marvellous fish dishes are perhaps the country's best-kept secret. Asked to name the ten most popular Mexican dishes, few people would suggest seafood, yet the Pacific Ocean and the waters of the Gulf of Mexico are teeming with fish, and Mexican cooks put the bounty to excellent use. Tuna, swordfish, snapper and sea bass are just some of the varieties available in fish markets. Large succulent prawns (shrimp) are a speciality, and crabs, crayfish and lobster are also available.

Between Ceviche, which requires no cooking at all, and Escabeche, which involves frying fish and then marinating it for 24 hours, there are a host of easy-to-cook dishes that take very little time to prepare. Some of these, such as Crab with Green Rice and Scallops with Garlic, make simple but delicious after-work meals, while others, such as Baked Salmon with a Guava Sauce, are more elaborate and are perfect for entertaining.

ESCABECHE

A CLASSIC DISH THAT THE MEXICANS INHERITED FROM THE SPANISH, ESCABECHE IS OFTEN CONFUSED WITH CEVICHE, WHICH CONSISTS OF MARINATED RAW FISH. IN ESCABECHE, THE RAW FISH IS INITIALLY MARINATED IN LIME JUICE, BUT IS THEN COOKED BEFORE BEING PICKLED.

SERVES FOUR

INGREDIENTS

900g/2lb whole fish fillets
juice of 2 limes
300ml/½ pint/1¼ cups olive oil
6 peppercorns
3 garlic cloves, sliced
2.5ml/½ tsp ground cumin
2.5ml/½ tsp dried oregano
2 bay leaves
50g/2oz/⅓ cup pickled jalapeño chilli
  slices, chopped
1 onion, thinly sliced
250ml/8fl oz/1 cup white wine vinegar
150g/5oz/1¼ cups green olives
  stuffed with pimiento, to garnish

1 Place the fish fillets in a single layer in a shallow non-metallic dish. Pour the lime juice over, turn the fillets over once to ensure that they are completely coated, then cover the dish and leave to marinate for 15 minutes.

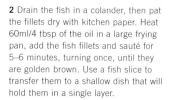

2 Drain the fish in a colander, then pat the fillets dry with kitchen paper. Heat 60ml/4 tbsp of the oil in a large frying pan, add the fish fillets and sauté for 5–6 minutes, turning once, until they are golden brown. Use a fish slice to transfer them to a shallow dish that will hold them in a single layer.

3 Heat 30ml/2 tbsp of the remaining oil in a frying pan. Add the peppercorns, garlic, ground cumin, oregano, bay leaves and jalapeños, and cook over a low heat for 2 minutes, then increase the heat, add the onion slices and vinegar and bring to the boil. Lower the heat and simmer for 4 minutes.

4 Remove the pan from the heat and carefully add the remaining oil. Stir well, then pour the mixture over the fish. Leave to cool, then cover the dish and marinate for 24 hours in the refrigerator.

5 When you are ready to serve, drain off the liquid and garnish the pickled fish with the stuffed olives. Salad leaves would make a good accompaniment.

COOK'S TIP
Use the largest frying pan you have when cooking the fish. If your pan is too small, it may be necessary to cook them in batches. Do not overcrowd the pan as they will cook unevenly.

Energy 414kcal/1720kJ; Protein 41.9g; Carbohydrate 1.3g, of which sugars 1g; Fat 26.7g, of which saturates 3.2g; Cholesterol 104mg; Calcium 30mg; Fibre 0.2g; Sodium 137mg

CEVICHE

THIS FAMOUS DISH IS PARTICULARLY POPULAR ALONG MEXICO'S WESTERN SEABOARD, IN PLACES SUCH AS ACAPULCO. IT CONSISTS OF VERY FRESH RAW FISH, "COOKED" BY THE ACTION OF LIME JUICE.

SERVES SIX

INGREDIENTS

200g/7oz raw peeled prawns (shrimp)
200g/7oz shelled scallops
200g/7oz squid, cleaned and cut
    into serving pieces
7 limes
3 tomatoes
1 small onion
1 ripe avocado
20ml/4 tbsp chopped fresh oregano,
    or 10ml/2 tsp dried
5ml/1 tsp salt
ground black pepper
fresh oregano sprigs, to garnish
crusty bread and lime wedges,
    to serve (optional)

1 Spread out the prawns, scallops and squid in a non-metallic bowl. Squeeze 6 of the limes and pour the juice over the mixed seafood to cover it completely. Cover the dish with clear film (plastic wrap) and set aside for 8 hours or overnight.

2 Drain the seafood in a colander to remove the excess lime juice, then pat it dry with kitchen paper. Place the prawns, scallops and squid in a bowl.

3 Cut the tomatoes in half, squeeze out the seeds, then dice the flesh. Cut the onion in half, then slice it thinly. Cut the avocado in half lengthways, remove the stone and peel, then cut the flesh into 1cm/½in dice.

4 Add the tomatoes, onion and avocado to the seafood with the oregano and seasoning. Squeeze the remaining lime and pour over the juice. Garnish with oregano and serve, with crusty bread and lime wedges, if liked.

Energy 147kcal/620kJ; Protein 21.9g; Carbohydrate 4.4g, of which sugars 2.2g; Fat 4.8g, of which saturates 1.1g; Cholesterol 175mg; Calcium 53mg; Fibre 1.2g; Sodium 186mg

SALT COD FOR CHRISTMAS EVE

THIS MEXICAN DISH IS MILDER THAN THE SIMILAR SPANISH DISH, BACALDO A LA VIZCAINA. IT IS EATEN ON CHRISTMAS EVE THROUGHOUT MEXICO.

SERVES SIX

INGREDIENTS
   450g/1lb dried salt cod
   105ml/7 tbsp extra virgin olive oil
   1 onion, halved and thinly sliced
   4 garlic cloves, crushed
   2 x 400g/14oz cans chopped
      tomatoes in tomato juice
   75g/3oz/¾ cup slivered almonds
   75g/3oz/½ cup pickled jalapeño
      chilli slices
   115g/4oz/1 cup green olives stuffed
      with pimiento
   small bunch of fresh parsley,
      finely chopped
   salt and ground black pepper
   fresh flat-leaved parsley, to garnish
   crusty bread, to serve

1 Put the cod in a large bowl and pour over enough cold water to cover. Soak for 24 hours, changing the water at least five times during this period.

2 Drain the cod and remove the skin using a large sharp knife. Shred the flesh finely using two forks, and put it into a bowl. Set it aside.

3 Heat half the oil in a large frying pan. Add the onion slices and fry over a moderate heat until the onion has softened and is translucent.

4 Remove the onion from the pan and set aside. Make sure you transfer the oil with the onion as it is an important flavouring in this dish and mustn't be discarded. In the same pan add the remaining olive oil. When the oil is hot but not smoking, add the crushed garlic and fry gently for 2 minutes.

5 Add the canned tomatoes and their juice to the pan with the garlic. Cook over a medium-high heat for about 20 minutes, stirring occasionally, until the mixture has reduced and thickened.

COOK'S TIPS
• Salt cod is available in specialist fishmongers, Spanish delicatessens and West Indian stores.
• Any leftovers can be used to fill burritos or empanadas.

6 Meanwhile, spread out the slivered almonds in a single layer in a large heavy-based frying pan. Toast them over a moderate heat for a few minutes, shaking the pan lightly throughout the process so that they turn golden brown all over. Do not let them burn.

7 Add the jalapeño chilli slices and stuffed olives to the toasted almonds.

8 Stir in the shredded fish, mixing it in thoroughly, and cook for 20 minutes more, stirring occasionally, until the mixture is almost dry.

9 Season to taste, add the parsley and cook for a further 2–3 minutes. Garnish with parsley leaves and serve in heated bowls, with crusty bread.

Energy 353kcal/1473kJ; Protein 29g; Carbohydrate 6.2g, of which sugars 5.5g; Fat 23.9g, of which saturates 2.8g; Cholesterol 44mg; Calcium 97mg; Fibre 3.6g; Sodium 881mg

RED SNAPPER WITH CORIANDER AND ALMONDS

THIS SIMPLE TREATMENT IS PERFECT FOR RED SNAPPER, A FISH THAT IS VERY POPULAR IN MEXICO.

SERVES FOUR

INGREDIENTS
  75g/3oz/¾ cup plain (all-purpose)
    flour
  4 red snapper fillets
  salt and ground black pepper
  75g/3oz/6 tbsp butter
  15ml/1 tbsp vegetable oil
  75g/3oz/¾ cup flaked almonds
  grated rind and juice of 1 lime
  small bunch of fresh coriander
    (cilantro), finely chopped
  warm wheat flour tortillas, to serve

COOK'S TIP
Warm the tortillas by wrapping them in
foil and steaming them on a plate over
boiling water for a few minutes.
Alternatively, wrap them in microwave-
safe film and heat them in a microwave
on full power for about 30 seconds.

1 Preheat the oven to 140°C/275°F/
Gas 1. Spread out the flour in a shallow
dish and add seasoning. Dry the fish
fillets with kitchen paper, then coat
each fillet in the seasoned flour.

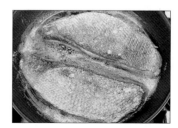

2 Heat the butter and oil in a frying
pan. Add the snapper fillets, in batches
if necessary, and cook for 2 minutes.
Turn the fillets over carefully and cook
the other side until golden.

3 Using a fish slice, carefully transfer
the fillets to a shallow dish and keep
them warm in the oven. Add the
almonds to the fat remaining and fry
them for 3–4 minutes, until golden.

4 Add the lime rind, juice and coriander
to the almonds in the frying pan and stir
well. Heat through for 1–2 minutes,
then pour the mixture over the fish.
Serve with warm wheat flour tortillas.

Energy 465kcal/1936kJ; Protein 25.8g; Carbohydrate 16.3g, of which sugars 1.5g; Fat 33.4g, of which saturates 13.2g; Cholesterol 85mg; Calcium 140mg; Fibre 2.6g; Sodium 221mg

VERACRUZ-STYLE RED SNAPPER

THIS IS A CLASSIC MEXICAN DISH WHICH BORROWS BAY LEAVES AND OLIVES FROM SPAIN TO GO WITH THE NATIVE CHILLIES.

SERVES FOUR

INGREDIENTS
4 whole red snapper, cleaned
juice of 2 limes
4 garlic cloves, crushed
5ml/1 tsp dried oregano
2.5ml/½ tsp salt
drained bottled capers, to garnish
lime wedges, to serve (optional)
For the sauce
120ml/4fl oz/½ cup olive oil
2 bay leaves
2 garlic cloves, sliced
4 fresh jalapeño chillies, seeded and
cut in strips
1 onion, thinly sliced
8 fresh tomatoes
75g/3oz/½ cup pickled jalapeño
chilli slices
15ml/1 tbsp soft dark brown sugar
2.5ml/½ tsp ground cloves
2.5ml/½ tsp ground cinnamon
150g/5oz/1¼ cups green olives
stuffed with pimiento

1 Preheat the oven to 180°C/350°F/ Gas 4. Rinse the fish inside and out, then pat dry with kitchen paper. Place in a large roasting tin in a single layer.

2 Mix the lime juice, garlic, oregano and salt in a small bowl. Pour the mixture over the fish. Bake for about 30 minutes, or until the flesh flakes easily when tested with the tip of a sharp knife.

3 Meanwhile, make the sauce. Heat the olive oil in a pan, add the bay leaves, garlic and chilli strips; fry over a low heat for 3–4 minutes.

4 Add the onion slices to the oil in the pan and cook for 3–4 minutes more, until all the onion is softened and translucent.

5 Cut a cross in the base of each tomato. Place them in a heatproof bowl and pour over boiling water to cover. After 3 minutes, lift the tomatoes out on a slotted spoon and plunge them into a bowl of cold water. Drain. The skins will have begun to peel back from the crosses.

6 Skin the tomatoes completely, then cut them in half and squeeze out the seeds. Chop the flesh finely and add it to the onion mixture. Cook for 3–4 minutes, until the tomato is starting to soften.

7 Add the pickled jalapeños, brown sugar, ground cloves and cinnamon to the sauce. Cook for 10 minutes, stirring frequently, then stir the olives into the sauce and pour a little over each fish. Garnish with the capers and serve with lime wedges, if liked. A rice dish would make a good accompaniment.

Energy 421kcal/1757kJ; Protein 31.7g; Carbohydrate 11.4g, of which sugars 11.1g; Fat 28g, of which saturates 4.3g; Cholesterol 56mg; Calcium 106mg; Fibre 3.3g; Sodium 979mg

RED SNAPPER BURRITOS

FISH MAKES A GREAT FILLING FOR A TORTILLA, ESPECIALLY WHEN IT IS SUCCULENT RED SNAPPER MIXED WITH RICE, CHILLI AND TOMATOES.

SERVES SIX

INGREDIENTS

3 red snapper fillets
90g/3½ oz/½ cup long grain white rice
30ml/2 tbsp vegetable oil
1 small onion, finely chopped
5ml/1 tsp ground achiote seed
   (annatto powder)
1 pasilla or similar dried chilli,
   seeded and ground
75g/3oz/¾ cup slivered almonds
200g/7oz can chopped tomatoes in
   tomato juice
150g/5oz/1¼ cups grated Monterey
   Jack or mild Cheddar cheese
8 x 20cm/8in wheat flour tortillas
fresh flat-leaved parsley to garnish
lime wedges (optional)

1 Preheat the grill (broiler). Grill (broil) the fish on an oiled rack for about 5 minutes, turning once. When cool, remove the skin and flake the fish into a bowl. Set it aside.

2 Meanwhile, put the rice in a pan, cover with cold water, cover and bring to the boil. Drain, rinse and drain again.

3 Heat the oil in a pan and fry the onion until soft and translucent. Stir in the ground achiote (annatto powder) and the chilli and cook for 5 minutes.

4 Add the rice, stir well, then stir in the fish and almonds. Add the tomatoes, with their juice. Cook over a moderate heat until the juice is absorbed and the rice is tender. Stir in the cheese and remove from the heat. Warm the tortillas.

5 Divide the filling among the tortillas and fold them as shown, to make neat parcels. Garnish with fresh parsley and serve with lime wedges, if liked. A green salad makes a good accompaniment.

Energy 484kcal/2033kJ; Protein 31.9g; Carbohydrate 54.7g, of which sugars 2.1g; Fat 15.9g, of which saturates 4.8g; Cholesterol 53mg; Calcium 262mg; Fibre 2.6g; Sodium 388mg

SEA BASS WITH ORANGE CHILLI SALSA

THE CITRUS SALSA HAS A FRESHNESS WHICH PROVIDES THE PERFECT CONTRAST TO THE WONDERFUL FLAVOUR OF FRESH SEA BASS.

SERVES FOUR

INGREDIENTS
   4 sea bass fillets
   salt and ground black pepper
   fresh coriander (cilantro), to garnish
For the salsa
   2 fresh green chillies
   2 oranges or pink grapefruit
   1 small onion

1 Make the salsa. Roast the chillies in a dry griddle pan until the skins are blistered, being careful not to let the flesh burn. Put them in a strong plastic bag and tie the top to keep the steam in. Set aside for 20 minutes.

COOK'S TIP
If the fish has not been scaled, do this by running the back of a small filleting knife against the grain of the scales. They should come away cleanly. Rinse and pat dry with kitchen paper.

2 Slice the top and bottom off each orange or grapefruit and cut off all the peel and pith. Cut between the membranes and put each segment in a bowl.

3 Remove the chillies from the bag and peel off the skins. Cut off the stalks, then slit the chillies and scrape out the seeds. Chop the flesh finely. Cut the onion in half and slice it thinly. Add the onion and chillies to the orange pieces and mix lightly. Season and chill.

4 Season the sea bass fillets. Line a steamer with baking parchment, allowing extra to hang over the sides to enable the fish to be lifted out after cooking. Place the empty steamer over a pan of water and bring to the boil.

5 Place the fish in a single layer in the steamer. Cover with a lid and steam for about 8 minutes or until just cooked. Garnish with fresh coriander and serve with the salsa and a vegetable side dish of your choice.

Energy 186kcal/783kJ; Protein 30.3g; Carbohydrate 7.7g, of which sugars 7.3g; Fat 3.9g, of which saturates 0.6g; Cholesterol 120mg; Calcium 238mg; Fibre 1.5g; Sodium 109mg

FRIED SOLE WITH LIME

SIMPLE FISH DISHES LIKE THIS ONE CAPITALIZE ON THE DELICIOUS FLAVOUR OF GOOD FRESH FISH.

SERVES FOUR

INGREDIENTS

   75g/3oz/¾ cup plain (all-purpose)
     flour
   10ml/2 tsp garlic salt
   5ml/1 tsp ground black pepper
   4 sole fillets
   oil, for frying
   juice of 2 limes
   small bunch of fresh parsley,
     chopped, plus extra sprigs,
     to garnish
   fresh salsa, to serve

COOK'S TIP

Make sure the oil is hot enough when
you add the fish, or it will be absorbed
by the fish and the dish will be
too greasy.

1 Mix the flour, garlic salt and pepper
together. Spread out the seasoned flour
mixture in a shallow dish. Pat the sole
fillets dry with kitchen paper, then turn
them in the seasoned flour until they
are evenly coated.

2 Pour oil into a wide frying pan to a
depth of 2.5cm/1in. Heat it until a cube
of bread added to the oil rises to the
surface and browns in 45–60 seconds.

3 Add the fish, in batches if necessary,
and fry for 3–4 minutes. Lift each fillet
out and drain it on kitchen paper.
Transfer to a heated serving dish.

4 Squeeze the juice of half a lime over
each piece of fish and sprinkle with the
chopped parsley. Serve immediately,
with a fresh salsa to complement the
fish. Garnish with parsley sprigs. New
potatoes would also go well.

BAKED SALMON WITH A GUAVA SAUCE

*GUAVAS HAVE A CREAMY FLESH WITH A SLIGHT CITRUS TANG, WHICH MAKES THEM THE PERFECT FRUIT
FOR A SAUCE TO SERVE WITH SALMON. THE SAUCE WORKS WELL WITH OTHER GRILLED FISH AND IS
ALSO GOOD WITH CHICKEN OR TURKEY.*

SERVES FOUR

INGREDIENTS

   6 ripe guavas
   45ml/3 tbsp vegetable oil
   1 small onion, finely chopped
   120ml/4fl oz/½ cup well-flavoured
     chicken stock
   10ml/2 tsp hot pepper sauce
   4 salmon steaks
   salt and ground black pepper
   strips of red (bell) pepper to garnish

COOK'S TIP

Ripe guavas have yellow skin and
succulent flesh that ranges in colour
from white to deep pink or salmon red.
They are exceptionally rich in vitamin C.
Ripe fruit will keep in the refrigerator for
a few days; green guavas will need to be
placed in a warm spot until they ripen.

1 Cut each guava in half. Scoop the
seeded soft flesh into a sieve (strainer)
placed over a bowl. Press it through the
sieve, discard the seeds and skin and
set the pulp aside.

2 Heat 30ml/2 tbsp of the oil in a frying
pan. Fry the chopped onion for about
4 minutes over a moderate heat until
softened and turned translucent.

3 Stir in the guava pulp, with the
chicken stock and hot pepper sauce.
Cook, stirring constantly, until the sauce
thickens. Keep it warm until needed.

4 Brush the salmon steaks on one side
with a little of the remaining oil. Season
them with salt and pepper. Heat a
griddle or ridged grill (broiling) pan until
very hot and add the salmon steaks,
oiled side down. Cook for 2–3 minutes,
until the underside is golden, then brush
the surface with oil, turn each salmon
steak over and cook the other side until
the fish is cooked and flakes easily when
tested with the tip of a sharp knife.

5 Transfer each steak to a warmed
plate. Serve, garnished with strips of red
pepper on a pool of sauce. A fresh
green salad is a good accompaniment.

Energy 254kcal/1066kJ; Protein 21.5g; Carbohydrate 25.6g, of which sugars 0.8g; Fat 7.9g, of which saturates 0.7g; Cholesterol 50mg; Calcium 100mg; Fibre 1.6g; Sodium 105mg
Energy 1060kcal/4378kJ; Protein 31.5g; Carbohydrate 7.9g, of which sugars 7.5g; Fat 100.5g, of which saturates 12.6g; Cholesterol 75mg; Calcium 53mg; Fibre 5.2g; Sodium 76mg

SALMON WITH TEQUILA CREAM SAUCE

*USE REPOSADA TEQUILA, WHICH IS LIGHTLY AGED, FOR THIS SAUCE. IT HAS A SMOOTHER, MORE
ROUNDED FLAVOUR, WHICH GOES WELL WITH THE CREAM.*

SERVES FOUR

INGREDIENTS

   3 fresh jalapeño chillies
   45ml/3 tbsp olive oil
   1 small onion, finely chopped
   150ml/¼ pint/⅔ cup fish stock
   grated rind and juice of 1 lime
   120ml/4fl oz/½ cup single (heavy)
    cream
   30ml/2 tbsp reposada tequila
   1 firm avocado
   4 salmon fillets
   salt and ground white pepper
   green (bell) pepper, to garnish

1 Roast the chillies in a frying pan until
the skins are blistered, being careful
not to let the flesh burn. Put them in
a strong plastic bag and tie the top
to keep the steam in. Set aside for
20 minutes.

2 Heat 15ml/1 tbsp of the oil in a pan.
Add the onion and fry for 3–4 minutes,
then add the stock, lime rind and juice.
Cook for 10 minutes, until the stock
starts to reduce. Remove the chillies
from the bag and peel off the skins, slit
and scrape out the seeds.

3 Stir the cream into the onion and
stock mixture. Slice the chilli flesh into
strips and add to the pan. Cook over a
gentle heat, stirring constantly, for
2–3 minutes. Season to taste with salt
and white pepper.

4 Stir the tequila into the onion and
chilli mixture. Leave the pan over a very
low heat. Peel the avocado, remove the
stone and slice the flesh. Brush the
salmon fillets on one side with a little of
the remaining oil.

5 Heat a frying pan or ridged grill
(broiling) pan until very hot and add the
salmon, oiled side down. Cook for 2–3
minutes, until the underside is golden,
then brush the top with oil, turn each
fillet over and cook the other side until
the fish is cooked and flakes easily when
tested with the tip of a sharp knife.

6 Serve on a pool of sauce, with the
avocado slices. Garnish with strips of
green pepper and fresh parsley. This is
good with Fried Potatoes.

Energy 2895kcal/12052kJ; Protein 304.5g; Carbohydrate 2.3g, of which sugars 1.6g; Fat 183.1g, of which saturates 33.7g; Cholesterol 764mg; Calcium 345mg; Fibre 1.1g; Sodium 685mg

YUCATAN-STYLE SHARK STEAK

A FIRM-FLESHED FISH, SHARK IS WIDELY AVAILABLE, EITHER FRESH OR FROZEN. IT NEEDS CAREFUL WATCHING, AS OVERCOOKING WILL MAKE IT DRY AND TOUGH, BUT THE FLAVOUR IS EXCELLENT.

<u>SERVES FOUR</u>

INGREDIENTS
  grated rind and juice of 1 orange
  juice of 1 small lime
  45ml/3 tbsp white wine
  30ml/2 tbsp olive oil
  2 garlic cloves, crushed
  10ml/2 tsp ground achiote seed
  (annatto powder)
  2.5ml/½ tsp cayenne pepper
  2.5ml/½ tsp dried marjoram
  5ml/1 tsp salt
  4 shark steaks
  fresh oregano leaves, to garnish
  4 wheat flour tortillas and any
  suitable salsa, to serve

COOK'S TIP
Shark freezes successfully, with little or no loss of flavour on thawing, so use frozen steaks if you can't find fresh.

1 Put the orange rind and juice in a shallow non-metallic dish which is large enough to hold all the shark steaks in a single layer. Add the lime juice, white wine, olive oil, garlic, ground achiote, cayenne, marjoram and salt. Mix well.

2 Add the shark steaks to the dish and spoon the marinade over them. Cover and set aside for 1 hour, turning once.

3 Heat a griddle pan until very hot and cook the marinated shark steaks for 2–3 minutes on each side. Alternatively, they are very good cooked on the barbecue, so long as they are cooked after the coals have lost their fierce initial heat. Do not overcook.

4 Garnish the shark steaks with oregano and serve with the tortillas and salsa. A green vegetable would also go well.

Energy 222kcal/931kJ; Protein 35g; Carbohydrate 1.4g, of which sugars 0.1g; Fat 7.7g, of which saturates 1g; Cholesterol 66mg; Calcium 60mg; Fibre 1.2g; Sodium 233mg

SWORDFISH TACOS

IT IS IMPORTANT NOT TO OVERCOOK SWORDFISH, OR IT CAN BE TOUGH AND DRY. COOKED CORRECTLY, HOWEVER, IT IS ABSOLUTELY DELICIOUS AND MAKES A GREAT CHANGE FROM BEEF OR CHICKEN AS A TACO FILLING.

SERVES SIX

INGREDIENTS
3 swordfish steaks
30ml/2 tbsp vegetable oil
2 garlic cloves, crushed
1 small onion, chopped
3 fresh green chillies, seeded
  and chopped
3 tomatoes
small bunch of coriander (cilantro),
  chopped
6 fresh corn tortillas
½ iceberg lettuce, shredded
salt and ground black pepper
lemon wedges, to serve (optional)

1 Preheat the grill (broiler). Put the swordfish on an oiled rack over a grill (broiling) pan and grill (broil) for 2–3 minutes on each side. When cool enough to handle, remove the skin and flake the fish into a bowl.

2 Heat the oil in a pan. Add the garlic, onion and chillies and fry for 5 minutes or until the onion is soft and translucent.

3 Cut a cross in the base of each tomato and pour over boiling water. After 3 minutes plunge into cold water. Remove the skins and seeds and chop the flesh into 1cm/½in dice.

4 Add the tomatoes and swordfish to the onion mixture. Cook for 5 minutes over a low heat. Add the coriander and cook for 1–2 minutes. Season to taste.

5 Wrap the tortillas in foil and steam on a plate over boiling water until pliable. Place some shredded lettuce and fish mixture on each tortilla. Fold in half and serve with lemon wedges, if liked.

CHARGRILLED SWORDFISH WITH CHILLI AND LIME SAUCE

SWORDFISH IS A PRIME CANDIDATE FOR THE BARBECUE, AS LONG AS IT IS NOT OVERCOOKED. IT TASTES WONDERFUL WITH A SPICY SAUCE WHOSE FIRE IS TEMPERED WITH CRÈME FRAÎCHE.

SERVES FOUR

INGREDIENTS
2 fresh serrano chillies
4 tomatoes
45ml/3 tbsp olive oil
grated rind and juice of 1 lime
4 swordfish steaks
2.5ml/½ tsp salt
2.5ml/½ tsp ground black pepper
175ml/6fl oz/¾ cup crème fraîche
chargrilled vegetables, to serve

1 Roast the chillies in a dry griddle pan until the skins blister. Put in a plastic bag and set aside for 20 minutes, then peel off the skins. Cut off the stalks, remove the seeds and slice the flesh.

2 Cut a cross in the base of each tomato. Place them in a heatproof bowl and pour over boiling water to cover. After 3 minutes, lift the tomatoes out on a slotted spoon and plunge them into a bowl of cold water. Drain. The skins will have begun to peel back from the crosses. Remove all the skin from the tomatoes, then cut them in half and squeeze out the seeds. Chop the flesh into 1cm/½in pieces.

3 Heat 15ml/1 tbsp of the oil in a small pan and add the strips of chilli, with the lime rind and juice. Cook for 2–3 minutes, then stir in the tomatoes. Cook for 10 minutes, stirring the mixture occasionally, until the tomato is pulpy.

4 Brush the swordfish with olive oil and season. Grill (broil) for 3–4 minutes or until just cooked, turning once. Stir the crème fraîche into the sauce, heat it through and pour over the swordfish steaks. Garnish with fresh parsley and serve with chargrilled vegetables.

Energy 293kcal/1236kJ; Protein 22.7g; Carbohydrate 33.2g, of which sugars 3.7g; Fat 8.6g, of which saturates 1.4g; Cholesterol 41mg; Calcium 77mg; Fibre 2.1g; Sodium 276mg
Energy 444kcal/1843kJ; Protein 28.8g; Carbohydrate 4.3g, of which sugars 4.2g; Fat 34.7g, of which saturates 16.2g; Cholesterol 118mg; Calcium 42mg; Fibre 1g; Sodium 215mg

PRAWNS WITH ALMOND SAUCE

GROUND ALMONDS ADD AN INTERESTING TEXTURE TO THE CREAMY, PIQUANT SAUCE THAT ACCOMPANIES THESE PRAWNS.

SERVES SIX

INGREDIENTS

1 ancho or similar dried chilli
30ml/2 tbsp vegetable oil
1 onion, chopped
3 garlic cloves, roughly chopped
8 tomatoes
5ml/1 tsp ground cumin
120ml/4fl oz/½ cup chicken stock
130g/4½ oz/generous 1 cup
  ground almonds
175ml/6fl oz/¾ cup crème fraîche
½ lime
900g/2lb cooked peeled prawns
  (shrimp)
salt
coriander (cilantro) and spring onion
  (scallion) strips, to garnish
rice and warm tortillas, to serve

1 Place the dried chilli in a heatproof bowl and pour over boiling water to cover. Leave to soak for 30 minutes until softened. Drain, remove the stalk, then slit the chilli and scrape out the seeds with a small sharp knife. Chop the flesh roughly and set it aside.

2 Heat the oil in a frying pan and fry the onion and garlic until soft.

VARIATIONS
Try this sauce with other types of fish, too. Adding just a few prawns and serving it over steamed sole would make a very luxurious dish. The sauce is also very good with chicken.

3 Cut a cross in the base of each tomato. Place them in a heatproof bowl and pour over boiling water to cover. After 3 minutes, lift the tomatoes out on a slotted spoon and plunge them into a bowl of cold water. Drain. The skins will have begun to peel back.

4 Skin the tomatoes completely, then cut them in half and scoop out the seeds. Chop the flesh into 1cm/½in cubes and add it to the onion mixture, with the chopped chilli. Stir in the ground cumin and cook for 10 minutes, stirring occasionally.

5 Tip the mixture into a food processor or blender. Add the stock and process on high speed until smooth.

6 Pour the mixture into a large pan, add the ground almonds and stir over a low heat for 2–3 minutes. Stir in the crème fraîche until is has been incorporated completely.

7 Squeeze the juice from the lime and stir it into the sauce. Season with salt to taste, then increase the heat and bring the sauce to simmering point.

8 Add the prawns and heat for 2–3 minutes, depending on size, until warmed through. Serve on a bed of rice and offer warm tortillas separately.

Energy 236kcal/989kJ; Protein 27.8g; Carbohydrate 5.3g, of which sugars 5.1g; Fat 11.7g, of which saturates 5.2g; Cholesterol 311mg; Calcium 140mg; Fibre 1.5g; Sodium 301mg

PRAWNS IN GARLIC BUTTER

THIS QUICK AND EASY DISH IS PERFECT FOR SERVING TO FRIENDS WHO DON'T MIND GETTING THEIR
HANDS DIRTY. PROVIDE A PLATE FOR THE PRAWN SHELLS AND OFFER WARM TORTILLAS FOR MOPPING
UP THE DELECTABLE JUICES.

SERVES SIX

INGREDIENTS
 900g/2lb large raw tiger prawns
  (jumbo shrimp), in their shells,
 115g/4oz/½ cup butter
 15ml/1 tbsp vegetable oil
 6 garlic cloves, crushed
 grated rind and juice of 2 limes
 small bunch of coriander (cilantro),
  chopped
 warm tortillas, to serve
 lemon slices, for the finger bowls

1 Rinse the prawns in a colander,
remove their heads and leave them to
drain. Heat the butter and oil in a large
frying pan, add the garlic and fry over a
low heat for 2–3 minutes.

2 Add the lime rind and juice. Cook,
stirring constantly, for 1 minute more.

COOK'S TIP
Cook the prawns in a large frying pan or
cast iron flameproof dish that can be
taken directly to the table, so that they
retain their heat until they are served.

3 Add the prawns and cook them for
2–3 minutes until they turn pink.
Remove from the heat, sprinkle with
coriander and serve with the warm
tortillas. Give each guest a finger bowl
filled with water and a slice of lemon,
for cleaning their fingers after shelling
the prawns, and provide paper napkins.

Energy 156kcal/645kJ; Protein 13.7g; Carbohydrate 1.4g, of which sugars 0.4g; Fat 10.6g, of which saturates 5.3g; Cholesterol 66mg; Calcium 102mg; Fibre 0.7g; Sodium 974mg

PRAWN SALAD

IN MEXICO, THIS SALAD WOULD FORM THE FISH COURSE IN A FORMAL MEAL, BUT IT IS SO GOOD THAT YOU'LL WANT TO SERVE IT ON ALL SORTS OF OCCASIONS. IT IS PERFECT FOR A BUFFET LUNCH.

SERVES FOUR

INGREDIENTS

450g/1lb cooked peeled prawns
  (shrimp)
juice of 1 lime
3 tomatoes
1 ripe but firm avocado
30ml/2 tbsp hot chilli sauce
5ml/1 tsp sugar
150ml/¼ pint/⅔ cup sour cream
2 Little Gem lettuces
salt and ground black pepper
basil leaves and green (bell) pepper,
  to garnish

1 Put the prawns in a large bowl, add the lime juice and salt and pepper. Toss lightly, then leave to marinate.

2 Cut a cross in the base of each tomato. Place them in a heatproof bowl and pour over boiling water to cover.

3 After 3 minutes, lift the tomatoes out on a slotted spoon and plunge them into a bowl of cold water. Drain. The skins will have begun to peel back easily from the crosses.

4 Skin the tomatoes completely, then cut them in half and squeeze out the seeds. Chop the flesh into 1cm/½in cubes and add it to the prawns.

5 Cut the avocado in half, remove the skin and seed, then slice the flesh into 1cm/½in chunks. Add it to the prawn and tomato mixture.

6 Mix the hot chilli sauce, sugar and sour cream in a bowl. Fold into the prawn mixture. Line a bowl with lettuce leaves, then top with the prawn mixture. Cover and chill for at least 1 hour, then garnish with fresh basil and strips of green pepper. Crusty bread makes a perfect accompaniment.

Energy 240kcal/1001kJ; Protein 24.3g; Carbohydrate 5.7g, of which sugars 5.4g; Fat 13.4g, of which saturates 6g; Cholesterol 266mg; Calcium 149mg; Fibre 1.8g; Sodium 262mg

CRAB WITH GREEN RICE

THIS IS A POPULAR DISH IN THE WESTERN COASTAL AREAS OF MEXICO. PRAWNS CAN BE USED INSTEAD OF CRAB MEAT IF YOU PREFER AND THE DISH ALSO WORKS WELL WITH WARM CORN TORTILLAS.

SERVES FOUR

INGREDIENTS

225g/8oz/generous 1 cup long grain white rice
500g/1¼lb/3⅓ cups drained canned tomatillos
large bunch of coriander (cilantro)
1 onion, roughly chopped
3 poblano or other fresh green chillies, seeded and chopped
3 garlic cloves
45ml/3 tbsp olive oil
500g/1¼lb crab meat
300ml/½ pint/1¼ cups fish stock
60ml/4 tbsp dry white wine
salt
spring onions (scallions), to garnish

1 Put the rice in a heatproof bowl, pour over boiling water to cover and leave to stand for 20 minutes. Drain thoroughly.

2 Put the tomatillos in a food processor or blender and process until smooth. Chop half the coriander and add to the tomatillo purée, with the onion, chillies and garlic. Process again until smooth.

3 Heat the oil in a large pan. Add the rice and fry over a moderate heat for 5 minutes, until all the oil has been absorbed. Stir occasionally to prevent the rice from sticking.

4 Stir in the tomatillo mixture, with the crab meat, stock and wine. Cover and cook over a low heat for about 20 minutes or until all the liquid has been absorbed. Stir occasionally and add a little more liquid if the rice starts to stick to the pan. Add salt as required, then spoon into a dish and garnish with the remaining coriander and sliced spring onions. Green salad and lime wedges make good accompaniments.

Energy 336kcal/1403kJ; Protein 16.3g; Carbohydrate 44.4g, of which sugars 4.1g; Fat 9.2g, of which saturates 1.4g; Cholesterol 45mg; Calcium 100mg; Fibre 1.2g; Sodium 355mg

SCALLOPS WITH GARLIC AND CORIANDER

SHELLFISH IS OFTEN COOKED VERY SIMPLY IN MEXICO, HOT CHILLI SAUCE AND LIME BEING POPULAR INGREDIENTS IN MANY FISH RECIPES.

SERVES FOUR

INGREDIENTS
- 20 scallops
- 2 courgettes (zucchini)
- 75g/3oz/6 tbsp butter
- 15ml/1 tbsp vegetable oil
- 4 garlic cloves, chopped
- 30ml/2 tbsp hot chilli sauce
- juice of 1 lime
- small bunch of coriander (cilantro), finely chopped

COOK'S TIP
Oil can withstand higher temperatures than butter, but butter gives fried food added flavour. Using a mixture, as here, provides the perfect compromise.

1 If you have bought scallops in their shells, open them. Hold a scallop shell in the palm of your hand, with the flat side uppermost. Insert the blade of a knife close to the hinge that joins the shells and prise them apart. Run the blade of the knife across the inside of the flat shell to cut away the scallop, Only the white adductor muscle and the orange coral are eaten, so pull away and discard all other parts. Rinse the scallops under cold running water.

2 Cut the courgettes in half, then into four pieces. Melt the butter in the oil in a large frying pan. Add the courgettes and fry until soft. Remove from the pan. Add the garlic and fry until golden. Stir in the hot chilli sauce.

3 Add the scallops to the sauce. Cook, stirring constantly, for 1–2 minutes only. Stir in the lime juice, chopped coriander and the courgette pieces. Serve immediately on heated plates.

Energy 278kcal/1151kJ; Protein 13.7g; Carbohydrate 5.8g, of which sugars 3.9g; Fat 22.4g, of which saturates 12.4g; Cholesterol 71mg; Calcium 45mg; Fibre 1g; Sodium 350mg

PUEBLO FISH BAKE

*THE LIME JUICE IS A PERFECT PARTNER FOR THE TROUT, WHICH IS AN OILY FISH. MARINATING MEANS
THAT THE FISH IS BEAUTIFULLY TENDER WHEN COOKED.*

SERVES FOUR

INGREDIENTS
2 fresh pasilla chillies
4 rainbow trout, cleaned
4 garlic cloves
10ml/2 tsp dried oregano
juice of 2 limes
50g/2oz/½ cup slivered almonds
salt and ground black pepper

1 Roast the chillies in a dry frying pan
or griddle pan until the skins are
blistered, being careful not to let the
flesh burn. Put them in a strong plastic
bag and tie the top to keep the steam
in. Set aside for 20 minutes.

2 Meanwhile, rub a little salt into the
cavities in the trout, to ensure they are
completely clean, then rinse them
under cold running water. Drain and pat
dry with kitchen paper.

COOK'S TIP
Cooking fish in a paper parcel means
that it stays very moist. Trout cooks
perfectly by this method, but you could
use other fish; try tuna steaks, small
mackerel or salmon fillets.

3 Remove the chillies from the bag and
peel off the skins. Cut off the stalks,
then slit the chillies and scrape out the
seeds. Chop the flesh roughly and put it
in a mortar. Crush with a pestle until the
mixture forms a paste.

4 Place the chilli paste in a shallow
dish that will hold all the trout in a
single layer. Slice the garlic lengthways
and add to the dish.

5 Add the oregano and 10ml/2 tsp salt,
then stir in the lime juice and pepper
to taste. Add the trout, turning to coat
them in the mixture. Cover the dish
and set aside for at least 30 minutes,
turning the trout again halfway through.

6 Preheat the oven to 200°C/400°F/
Gas 6. Have ready four pieces of
kitchen foil, each large enough to wrap
a trout. Top each sheet with a piece of
baking parchment of the same size.

7 Place one of the trout on one of the
pieces of paper, moisten with the
marinade, then sprinkle about a quarter
of the almonds over the top.

8 Bring up the sides of the paper and
fold over to seal in the fish, then fold
the foil over to make a neat parcel.
Make three more parcels in the same
way, then place them side by side in a
large roasting tin.

9 Transfer the parcels to the oven and
bake for 25 minutes. Put each parcel
on an individual plate, or open them in
the kitchen and serve unwrapped if you
prefer. This dish goes well with new
potatoes and cooked fresh vegetables.

Energy 236kcal/989kJ; Protein 27.2g; Carbohydrate 1.1g, of which sugars 0.8g; Fat 13.7g, of which saturates 1.8g; Cholesterol 77mg; Calcium 63mg; Fibre 1g; Sodium 64mg

FISHERMAN'S STEW

THIS IS JUST THE SORT OF ONE-POT MEAL YOU CAN IMAGINE FISHERMEN COOKING FOR THEMSELVES, USING FRESHLY CAUGHT FISH AND A FEW VEGETABLES.

SERVES SIX

INGREDIENTS

500g/1¼lb mussels
3 onions
2 garlic cloves, sliced
300ml/½ pint/1¼ cups fish stock
12 scallops
450g/1lb cod fillet
30ml/2 tbsp olive oil
1 large potato, about 200g/7oz
few sprigs of fresh thyme, chopped
1 red and 1 green (bell) pepper
120ml/4fl oz/½ cup dry white wine
250ml/8fl oz/1 cup crème fraîche
275g/10oz raw prawns (shrimp)
75g/3oz/¾ cup grated mature (sharp)
  Cheddar cheese
salt and ground black pepper
fresh thyme sprigs, to garnish

1 Clean the mussel shells, removing any beards. Discard any that stay open when tapped. Rinse in cold water.

2 Pour water to a depth of 2.5cm/1in into a large, deep frying pan. Chop one onion and add it to the pan, with the sliced garlic. Bring to the boil, then add the mussels and cover the pan tightly.

3 Cook the mussels for 5–6 minutes, shaking the pan occasionally. Remove them as they open, discarding any that remain shut. Remove the mussels from their shells and set them aside.

4 Strain the cooking liquid from the mussels through a muslin- (cheesecloth-) lined sieve (strainer) to remove any remaining sand. Make up the liquid with fish stock to 300ml/½ pint/1¼ cups.

5 If you have bought scallops in their shells, open them: hold a scallop shell in the palm of your hand, with the flat side uppermost. Insert the blade of a knife close to the hinge that joins the shells and prise apart. Run the blade of the knife across the inside of the flat shell to cut away the scallop. Only the white adductor muscle and the orange coral are eaten, so pull away and discard all other parts. Rinse the scallops under cold running water to remove any grit or sand, then put them in a bowl and set them aside.

6 Cut the cod into large cubes and put it in a bowl. Season with salt and pepper and set aside.

7 Cut the remaining onions into small wedges. Heat the olive oil in a large pan and fry the onion wedges for 2–3 minutes. Slice the potato about 1cm/½in thick and add to the pan, with the fresh chopped thyme. Cover and cook for about 15 minutes, until the potato has softened.

8 Core the peppers, remove the cores and seeds, then dice the flesh. Add to the onion and potato mixture and cook for a few minutes. Stir in the mixed mussel and fish stock, with the wine and crème fraîche.

9 Bring to just below boiling point, then add the cod and scallops. Lower the heat and simmer for 5 minutes, then add the prawns. Simmer for a further 3–4 minutes more, until all the seafood is cooked. Stir in the mussels and warm through for 1–2 minutes. Season the sauce if necessary. Spoon into bowls, garnish with the thyme sprigs and sprinkle with the cheese. Crusty bread would be an ideal accompaniment.

Energy 450kcal/1876kJ; Protein 39g; Carbohydrate 16.2g, of which sugars 6.2g; Fat 24.2g, of which saturates 13.4g; Cholesterol 206mg; Calcium 273mg; Fibre 1.7g; Sodium 370mg

VEGETABLES

When the Spaniards arrived in Mexico they discovered that the indigenous people cultivated a wide range of vegetables including corn, several varieties of squash and pumpkin, avocados, (bell) peppers and green beans. Many of these vegetables have since been introduced into our diets – French (green) beans were brought to England during the reign of Queen Elizabeth 1, others, such as jicama, the crisp textured vegetable which can be eaten raw or cooked, have been introduced to our diets through other cuisines such as Chinese. Many of these dishes could form the basis of a meal on their own, while side dishes such as green and yellow rice, fried potatoes, and Mexican-style green peas will add flavour and colour to any meal. The wide range of recipes in this chapter is testimony to the great variety of vegetables that are still being eaten in Mexico today.

MEXICAN-STYLE GREEN PEAS

THIS IS A DELICIOUS WAY OF COOKING FRESH PEAS, AND MAKES AN EXCELLENT ACCOMPANIMENT TO ANY MEAL. THE FLAVOUR COMES FROM THE VEGETABLES THEMSELVES, SO USE VINE-RIPENED TOMATOES AND THE FRESHEST ORGANIC PEAS IF POSSIBLE.

SERVES FOUR

INGREDIENTS
2 tomatoes
50g/2oz/¼ cup butter
2 garlic cloves, halved
1 medium onion, halved and
    thinly sliced
400g/14oz/scant 3 cups shelled
    fresh peas
30ml/2 tbsp water
salt and ground black pepper
fresh chives, to garnish

1 Cut a cross in the base of each tomato. Place the tomatoes in a heatproof bowl and pour over boiling water to cover. Leave them in the water for 3 minutes, then lift the tomatoes out on a slotted spoon and plunge them into a bowl of cold water. Drain. The skins will have begun to peel back.

2 Remove the skins completely, then cut the tomatoes in half and squeeze out the seeds. Chop the flesh into 1cm/½in dice.

3 Melt the butter in a pan. Cook the garlic until golden. Do not overcook or it will add a bitter taste. Lift it out on a slotted spoon and discard it. Add the onion slices to the pan and fry until transparent.

4 Add the tomato to the onion, mix well, then stir in the peas. Pour over the water, lower the heat and cover the pan tightly. Cook for 10 minutes, shaking the pan occasionally to stop the mixture from sticking to the bottom.

5 Check that the peas are cooked, then season with plenty of salt and pepper. Transfer the mixture to a heated dish and serve, garnished with fresh chives.

MUSHROOMS WITH CHIPOTLE CHILLIES

CHIPOTLE CHILLIES ARE JALAPENOS THAT HAVE BEEN SMOKE-DRIED. THEIR SMOKY FLAVOUR IS THE PERFECT FOIL FOR THE MUSHROOMS IN THIS SIMPLE SALAD.

SERVES SIX

INGREDIENTS
2 chipotle chillies
450g/1lb/6 cups button (white)
    mushrooms
60ml/4 tbsp vegetable oil
1 onion, finely chopped
2 garlic cloves, crushed or chopped
salt
small bunch of fresh coriander
    (cilantro), to garnish

COOK'S TIP
Baby button (white) mushrooms are perfect for this dish, if you can get them. You can, of course, use any white mushrooms, but larger ones may be better halved or quartered.

1 Soak the dried chillies in a bowl of hot water for about 10 minutes until they are softened. Drain, cut off the stalks, then slit the chillies and scrape out the seeds. Chop the flesh finely.

2 Trim the mushrooms, then clean them with a damp cloth or kitchen paper. If they are large, cut them in half.

3 Heat the oil in a large frying pan. Add the onion, garlic, chillies and mushrooms and stir until evenly coated in the oil. Fry for 6–8 minutes, stirring occasionally, until the onion and mushrooms are tender. Season to taste and spoon into a serving dish. Chop some of the coriander, leaving some whole leaves, and use to garnish. Serve hot.

Energy 232kcal/958kJ; Protein 11g; Carbohydrate 19.8g, of which sugars 5.9g; Fat 12.7g, of which saturates 7g; Cholesterol 27mg; Calcium 41mg; Fibre 7.8g; Sodium 82mg
Energy 69kcal/287kJ; Protein 2.4g; Carbohydrate 1.3g, of which sugars 0.9g; Fat 6.1g, of which saturates 0.8g; Cholesterol 0mg; Calcium 14mg; Fibre 1.2g; Sodium 7mg

STUFFED CHILLIES ᴵᴺ ᴬ WALNUT SAUCE

THE POTATO AND MEAT FILLING IN THESE CHILLIES IS A GOOD PARTNER FOR THE RICH, CREAMY SAUCE THAT COVERS THEM.

SERVES FOUR

INGREDIENTS

   8 ancho chillies
   1 large potato, about 200g/7oz
   45ml/3 tbsp vegetable oil
   115g/4oz lean minced (ground) pork
   1 onion, chopped
   5ml/1 tsp ground cinnamon
   115g/4oz/1 cup walnuts, chopped
   50g/2oz/½ cup chopped almonds
   150g/5oz/⅔ cup cream cheese
   50g/2oz/½ cup soft goat's cheese
   120ml/4fl oz/½ cup single (light)
     cream
   120ml/4fl oz/½ cup dry sherry
   50g/2oz/½ cup plain (all-purpose)
     flour
   2.5ml/½ tsp ground white pepper
   2 eggs, separated
   oil, for deep frying
   salt
   chopped fresh herbs to garnish

1 Soak the dried chillies in a bowl of hot water for 30 minutes until softened. Drain, slit them down one side, and scrape out the seeds with a small sharp knife, keeping the chillies intact.

2 Peel the potato and cut it into 1cm/½in cubes. Heat 15ml/1 tbsp of the oil in a large frying pan, add the pork mince and cook, stirring, until it has browned evenly.

COOK'S TIP
The potatoes must not break or become too floury. Do not overcook. For the best results buy waxy potatoes.

3 Add the potato cubes and mix well. Cover and cook over a low heat for 25–30 minutes, stirring occasionally. Do not worry if the potato sticks to the bottom of the pan. Season with salt, remove from the heat and set aside.

4 Heat the remaining oil in a separate frying pan and fry the onion with the cinnamon for 3–4 minutes or until softened. Stir in the nuts and fry for 3–4 minutes more.

5 Add both types of cheese to the pan, with the cream and sherry. Mix well. Reduce the heat to the lowest setting and cook until the cheese melts and the sauce starts to thicken. Taste and season if necessary.

6 Spread out the flour on a plate or in a shallow dish. Season with the white pepper. Beat the egg yolks in a bowl until they are pale and thick.

7 In a separate, grease-free bowl, whisk the whites until they form soft peaks. Add a generous pinch of salt, then fold in the yolks, a little at a time.

8 Spoon some of the filling into each chilli. Pat the outside dry with kitchen paper. Heat the oil for deep frying to a temperature of 180°C/350°F.

9 Coat a chilli in flour, then dip it in the egg batter, covering it completely. Drain for a few seconds, then add to the hot oil. Add several more battered chillies, but do not overcrowd the pan. Fry the chillies until golden, then drain on kitchen paper and keep hot while cooking successive batches.

10 Reheat the sauce over a low heat, if necessary. Arrange the chillies on individual plates, spoon a little sauce over each and serve immediately, sprinkled with chopped fresh herbs. A green salad goes well with this dish.

Energy 989kcal/4098kJ; Protein 29.2g; Carbohydrate 27.3g, of which sugars 4.7g; Fat 84g, of which saturates 28g; Cholesterol 202mg; Calcium 238mg; Fibre 3.2g; Sodium 415mg

POTATOES WITH CHORIZO AND GREEN CHILLIES

MEXICANS MAKE THEIR OWN CHORIZO SAUSAGE, SOMETIMES USING IT FRESH, BUT ALSO PUTTING IT INTO CASINGS TO DRY, WHEN IT RESEMBLES THE SPANISH VERSION WHICH IS NOW POPULAR THE WORLD OVER. THIS RECIPE MAKES A DELICIOUS BRUNCH DISH. TYPICAL OF PEASANT FOOD, IT IS BASED ON THE COMBINATION OF PLENTY OF POTATO MIXED WITH STRONGLY FLAVOURED MEAT TO HELP IT GO FURTHER.

SERVES FOUR TO SIX

INGREDIENTS

900g/2lb potatoes, peeled and diced
30ml/2 tbsp vegetable oil
2 garlic cloves, crushed
4 spring onions (scallions), chopped
2 fresh jalapeño chillies, seeded
 and diced
300g/11oz chorizo sausage, skinned
150g/5oz/1¼ cups grated Monterey
 Jack or Cheddar cheese
salt (optional)

1 Bring a large pan of water to the boil and add the potatoes. When the water returns to the boil, lower the heat and simmer the potatoes for 5 minutes. Tip the potatoes into a colander and drain thoroughly.

COOK'S TIP
Use firm-textured potatoes such as Desiree, Pentland Dell and Estima for this dish. If you can't locate Monterey Jack, look out for a mature (sharp) Gouda, or use a medium mature Cheddar.

2 Heat the oil in a large frying pan, add the garlic, spring onions and chillies and cook for 3–4 minutes. Add the diced potato and cook until the cubes begin to brown a little.

3 Cut the chorizo into small cubes and add these to the pan. Cook the mixture for 5 minutes more, until the sausage has heated through.

4 Season with salt if necessary, then add the cheese. Mix quickly and carefully, trying not to break up the cubes of potato. Serve immediately, while the cheese is still melting.

Energy 443kcal/1847kJ; Protein 16g; Carbohydrate 32.4g, of which sugars 3.6g; Fat 28.1g, of which saturates 12.3g; Cholesterol 49mg; Calcium 226mg; Fibre 1.9g; Sodium 728mg

RED CAULIFLOWER

VEGETABLES ARE SELDOM SERVED PLAIN IN MEXICO. THE CAULIFLOWER HERE IS FLAVOURED WITH A SIMPLE TOMATO SALSA AND FRESH CHEESE. THE SALSA COULD BE ANY TABLE SALSA; TOMATILLO IS PARTICULARLY GOOD. THE CONTRAST WITH THE TEXTURE AND MILD FLAVOUR OF THE CAULIFLOWER MAKES FOR A TASTY DISH.

SERVES SIX

INGREDIENTS

1 small onion
1 lime
1 medium cauliflower
400g/14oz can chopped tomatoes
4 fresh serrano chillies, seeded and
  finely chopped
1.5ml/¼ tsp sugar
75g/3oz feta cheese, crumbled
salt
chopped fresh flat-leaved parsley,
  to garnish

COOK'S TIP
Use a zester for the lime, if have you
have one. This handy little tool enables
you to pare off tiny strips of the rind,
leaving the pith behind.

1 Chop the onion very finely and place in a bowl. With a zester peel away the zest of the lime in thin strips. Add to the chopped onion.

2 Cut the lime in half and add the juice from both halves to the onions and lime zest mixture. Set aside so that the lime juice can soften the onion. Cut the cauliflower into florets.

3 Tip the tomatoes into a pan and add the chillies and sugar. Heat gently. Meanwhile, place the cauliflower in a pan of boiling water and cook gently for 5–8 minutes until tender.

4 Add the onions to the tomato salsa, with salt to taste, stir in and heat through, then spoon about a third of the salsa into a serving dish.

5 Arrange the drained cauliflower florets on top of the salsa and spoon the remaining salsa on top.

6 Sprinkle with the feta, which should soften a little on contact. Serve immediately, sprinkled with chopped fresh flat-leaved parsley.

Energy 81kcal/338kJ; Protein 5.9g; Carbohydrate 5.6g, of which sugars 4.9g; Fat 4g, of which saturates 2.3g; Cholesterol 11mg; Calcium 79mg; Fibre 2.3g; Sodium 230mg

GREEN LIMA BEANS <small>IN A</small> SAUCE

MAKE THE MOST OF LIMA BEANS OR BROAD BEANS BY TEAMING THEM WITH TOMATOES AND FRESH CHILLIES IN THIS SIMPLE ACCOMPANIMENT.

SERVES FOUR

INGREDIENTS
   450g/1lb fresh lima beans or
      broad (fava) beans
   30ml/2 tbsp olive oil
   1 onion, finely chopped
   2 garlic cloves, crushed
   400g/14oz can plum tomatoes,
      drained and chopped
   25g/1oz/about 3 tbsp drained pickled
      jalapeño chilli slices, chopped
   salt
   fresh coriander (cilantro) and lemon
      slices, to garnish

COOK'S TIP
Pickled chillies are often hotter than
roasted chillies – taste one before adding
to the recipe and adjust the quantity to
suit your taste.

1 Bring a pan of lightly salted water to
the boil. Add the lima beans or broad
beans and cook for 15 minutes, or until
just tender.

2 Meanwhile, heat the olive oil in a
frying pan, add the onion and garlic and
sauté until the onion is translucent. Tip
in the tomatoes and continue to cook,
stirring, until the mixture thickens.

3 Add the chilli slices and cook for
1–2 minutes. Season with salt to taste.

4 Drain the beans and return them to
the pan. Pour over the tomato mixture
and stir over the heat for a few minutes.
If the sauce thickens too quickly add a
little water. Spoon into a serving dish,
garnish with the coriander and lemon
slices and serve.

GREEN BEANS <small>WITH</small> EGGS

THIS IS AN UNUSUAL WAY OF COOKING GREEN BEANS, BUT TASTES DELICIOUS. TRY THIS DISH FOR A LIGHT SUPPER OR AS AN ACCOMPANIMENT TO A SIMPLE ROAST.

SERVES SIX

INGREDIENTS
   300g/11oz runner (string) beans,
      topped, tailed and halved
   30ml/2 tbsp vegetable oil
   1 onion, halved and thinly sliced
   3 eggs
   salt and ground black pepper
   50g/2oz/½ cup grated Monterey Jack
      or mild Cheddar cheese
   strips of lemon rind, to garnish

VARIATION
Freshly grated Parmesan can be used
instead of the Monterey Jack or Cheddar
cheese for a sharper flavour.

1 Bring a pan of water to the boil, add
the beans and cook for 5–6 minutes or
until tender. Drain in a colander, rinse
under cold water to preserve the bright
colour, then drain the beans once more.

2 Heat the oil in a frying pan and fry the
onion slices for 3–4 minutes until soft
and translucent. Break the eggs into a
bowl and beat them with seasoning.

3 Add the egg mixture to the onion.
Cook slowly over a moderate heat,
stirring constantly so that the egg is
lightly scrambled. The egg should be
moist throughout. Do not overcook.

4 Add the beans to the pan and cook
for a few minutes until warmed through.
Tip the mixture into a heated serving
dish, sprinkle with the grated cheese
and lemon rind and serve.

Energy 168kcal/707kJ; Protein 10.5g; Carbohydrate 17.6g, of which sugars 5.6g; Fat 6.7g, of which saturates 1g; Cholesterol 0mg; Calcium 81mg; Fibre 8.5g; Sodium 20mg
Energy 126kcal/519kJ; Protein 6.7g; Carbohydrate 2.7g, of which sugars 1.9g; Fat 9.8g, of which saturates 3.3g; Cholesterol 104mg; Calcium 106mg; Fibre 1.4g; Sodium 102mg

COURGETTES <u>WITH</u> CHEESE <u>AND</u> GREEN CHILLIES

THIS IS A VERY TASTY WAY TO SERVE COURGETTES, OFTEN A RATHER BLAND VEGETABLE, AND THE DISH LOOKS GOOD TOO. SERVE IT AS A VEGETARIAN MAIN DISH OR AN UNUSUAL SIDE DISH.

SERVES SIX AS AN ACCOMPANIMENT

INGREDIENTS
30ml/2 tbsp vegetable oil
½ onion, thinly sliced
2 garlic cloves, crushed
5ml/1 tsp dried oregano
2 tomatoes
50g/2oz/⅓ cup drained pickled
  jalapeño chilli slices, chopped
500g/1¼lb courgettes (zucchini)
115g/4oz/½ cup cream cheese,
  cubed
salt and ground black pepper
fresh oregano sprigs, to garnish

1 Heat the oil in a frying pan. Add the onion, garlic and dried oregano. Fry for 3–4 minutes, until the onion is soft and translucent.

2 Cut a cross in the base of each tomato. Place in a heatproof bowl and cover with boiling water. Leave in the water for 3 minutes, then lift out on a slotted spoon and plunge into a bowl of cold water. Drain. The skins will have begun to peel back from the crosses. Remove the skins and cut the tomatoes in half and squeeze out the seeds. Chop the flesh into strips.

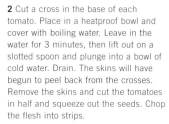

3 Top and tail the courgettes, then cut them lengthways into 1cm/½in wide strips. Slice the strips into matchsticks.

4 Stir the courgettes into the onion mixture and fry for 10 minutes, stirring occasionally, until just tender. Add the tomatoes and chopped jalapeños and cook for 2–3 minutes more.

5 Add the cream cheese. Reduce the heat to the lowest setting. As the cheese melts, stir gently to coat the courgettes. Season with salt, pile into a heated dish and serve, garnished with fresh oregano. If serving as a main dish, rustic bread makes a good accompaniment.

Energy 167kcal/687kJ; Protein 3g; Carbohydrate 2.7g, of which sugars 2.6g; Fat 16.1g, of which saturates 8g; Cholesterol 24mg; Calcium 53mg; Fibre 1.1g; Sodium 80mg

COURGETTE TORTE

THIS DISH LOOKS RATHER LIKE A SPANISH OMELETTE, WHICH IS TRADITIONALLY SERVED AT ROOM TEMPERATURE. SERVE WARM OR PREPARE IT IN ADVANCE AND LEAVE TO COOL, BUT DO NOT REFRIGERATE.

2 Slice the onion and add it to the oil remaining in the pan, with most of the jalapeño strips, reserving some for the garnish. Fry until the onions have softened and are golden. Using a slotted spoon, add the onions and jalapeños to the courgettes.

3 Beat the eggs in a large bowl. Add the self-raising flour, cheese and cayenne. Mix well, then stir in the courgette mixture, with salt to taste.

4 Grease a 23cm/9in round shallow ovenproof dish with the butter. Pour in the courgette mixture and bake for 30 minutes until risen, firm to the touch and golden. Allow to cool.

5 Serve the courgette torte in thick wedges, garnished with the remaining jalapeño strips. A tomato salad, sprinkled with chives, makes a colourful accompaniment.

SERVES FOUR TO SIX

INGREDIENTS
500g/1¼lb courgettes (zucchini)
60ml/4 tbsp vegetable oil
1 small onion
3 fresh jalapeño chillies, seeded and cut in strips
3 large eggs
50g/2oz/½ cup self-raising (rising) flour
115g/4oz/1 cup grated Monterey Jack or mild Cheddar cheese
2.5ml/½ tsp cayenne pepper
15g/½oz/1 tbsp butter
salt

1 Preheat the oven to 180°C/350°F/ Gas 4. Top and tail the courgettes, then slice them thinly. Heat the oil in a large frying pan. Add the courgettes and cook for a few minutes, turning them over at least once, until they are soft and beginning to brown. Using a slotted spoon, transfer them to a bowl.

Energy 252kcal/1050kJ; Protein 10.9g; Carbohydrate 15.4g, of which sugars 2.7g; Fat 16.4g, of which saturates 6.5g; Cholesterol 117mg; Calcium 226mg; Fibre 1.6g; Sodium 232mg

PUMPKIN <u>WITH</u> SPICES

ROASTED PUMPKIN HAS A WONDERFUL, RICH FLAVOUR. EAT IT STRAIGHT FROM THE SKIN, EAT THE SKIN TOO, OR SCOOP OUT THE COOKED FLESH, ADD A SPOONFUL OF SALSA AND WRAP IT IN A WARM TORTILLA. IT ALSO MAKES FLAVOURSOME SOUPS AND SAUCES.

SERVES SIX

INGREDIENTS
    1kg/2¼lb pumpkin
    50g/2oz/¼ cup butter, melted
    10ml/2 tsp hot chilli sauce
    2.5ml/½ tsp salt
    2.5ml/½ tsp ground allspice
    5ml/1 tsp ground cinnamon
    chopped fresh herbs, to garnish
    Classic Tomato Salsa and crème
        fraîche, to serve

COOK'S TIP
Green, grey or orange-skinned pumpkins all roast well. The orange-fleshed varieties are the most colourful when it comes to cooking.

1 Preheat the oven to 220°C/425°F/ Gas 7. Cut the pumpkin into large pieces. Scoop out and discard the fibre and seeds, then put the pumpkin pieces in a roasting tin.

2 Mix the melted butter and chilli sauce and drizzle the mixture evenly over the pumpkin pieces.

3 Put the salt in a small bowl and add the ground allspice and cinnamon. Sprinkle the mixture over the pumpkin.

4 Roast for 25 minutes or until the pumpkin flesh yields when pressed gently. Serve on a heated platter and offer the tomato salsa and crème fraîche separately.

Energy 68kcal/284kJ; Protein 1.8g; Carbohydrate 5.4g, of which sugars 2.9g; Fat 4.5g, of which saturates 2.3g; Cholesterol 9mg; Calcium 92mg; Fibre 3.2g; Sodium 55mg

POTATO CAKES

QUICK AND EASY TO MAKE, THESE POTATO CAKES ARE VERY MOREISH. SERVE THEM WITH SALSA AS A LIGHT MEAL, OR AS AN ACCOMPANIMENT TO ROAST OR PAN-FRIED MEATS.

MAKES TEN

INGREDIENTS
  600g/1lb 6oz potatoes
  115g/4oz/1 cup grated Cheddar
  cheese
  2.5ml/½ tsp salt
  50g/2oz/⅓ cup drained pickled
  jalapeño chilli slices, finely
  chopped (optional)
  1 egg, beaten
  small bunch of fresh coriander
  (cilantro), finely chopped
  plain (all-purpose) flour, for shaping
  oil, for shallow frying
  fresh citrus salsa, to serve

1 Peel the potatoes and halve them if large. Add them to a pan of cold water. Bring to the boil and cook for about 30 minutes, until tender. Drain, return to the pan and mash. The mash should not be smooth.

2 Scrape the potato into a bowl and stir in the grated cheese, with the salt and the chopped jalapeños, if using. Stir in the beaten egg and most of the chopped coriander and mix to a dough.

3 When the dough is cool enough to handle, put it on a board. With floured hands, divide it into ten pieces of equal size. Shape each piece into a ball, then flatten to a cake.

4 Heat the oil in a large frying pan. Fry the potato cakes, in batches if necessary, for 2–3 minutes over a moderate heat. Turn them over and cook until both sides are golden. Pile on a platter, sprinkle with salt and the remaining chopped coriander and serve with salsa.

Energy 137kcal/573kJ; Protein 4.8g; Carbohydrate 12.2g, of which sugars 1.1g; Fat 7.7g, of which saturates 3g; Cholesterol 30mg; Calcium 99mg; Fibre 1g; Sodium 96mg

FRIED PLANTAIN

THESE ARE THE PERFECT ACCOMPANIMENT TO HIGHLY SPICED AND SEASONED FOODS. THEIR SWEET FLAVOUR PROVIDES AN INTERESTING CONTRAST.

SERVES FOUR

INGREDIENTS

4 ripe plantains
75g/3oz/6 tbsp butter
10ml/2 tsp vegetable oil
strips of spring onion (scallions) and
red (bell) pepper, to garnish

COOK'S TIP

Ripe plantains have dark, almost black skins. Do not use under-ripe plantains, which are very hard and do not soften on cooking.

1 Peel the plantains, cut them in half lengthways, then cut them in half again. Melt the butter with the oil in a large frying pan.

2 Add the plantains to the pan in a single layer and fry for 8–10 minutes, turning halfway through. Spoon into a heated dish and serve, garnished with strips of spring onion and red pepper.

FRIED POTATOES

THESE MAKE THE PERFECT ACCOMPANIMENT FOR CHORIZO, AND ALSO GO VERY WELL WITH EGGS AND BACON.

SERVES FOUR

INGREDIENTS

6 fresh jalapeño chillies
60ml/4 tbsp vegetable oil
1 onion, finely chopped
450g/1lb waxy potatoes, scrubbed
and cut in 1cm/½in cubes
few sprigs of fresh oregano, chopped
plus extra sprigs, to garnish
75g/3oz/1 cup freshly grated
Parmesan cheese (optional)

1 Dry roast the jalapeños in a griddle pan, turning them frequently so that the skins blacken but do not burn. Place them in a strong plastic bag and tie the top to keep the steam in. Set aside for 20 minutes.

2 Remove the jalapeños from the bag, peel off the skins and remove any stems. Cut them in half, scrape out the seeds, then chop the flesh finely.

COOK'S TIP

If your frying pan does not have a lid, use foil instead.

3 Meanwhile, heat half the oil in a large heavy-based frying pan which has a lid. Add the onion and fry, stirring occasionally, for 3–4 minutes, until translucent, then add the potato cubes.

4 Stir to coat the potato cubes in oil, then cover the pan and cook over a moderate heat for 20–25 minutes, until the potatoes are tender. Shake the pan occasionally to stop them from sticking to the bottom.

5 When the potatoes are tender, push them to the side of the frying pan, then add the remaining oil.

6 When the oil is hot, spread out the potatoes again and add the chopped jalapeños. Cook over a high heat for 5–10 minutes, stirring carefully so that the potatoes turn golden brown all over but do not break up.

7 Add the chopped oregano, with the grated Parmesan, if using. Mix gently, spoon on to a heated serving dish and garnish with extra oregano sprigs. Serve as part of a cooked breakfast or brunch.

Energy 301kcal/1264kJ; Protein 1.8g; Carbohydrate 44.2g, of which sugars 8.7g; Fat 14.3g, of which saturates 8.2g; Cholesterol 32mg; Calcium 16mg; Fibre 2g; Sodium 97mg
Energy 186kcal/777kJ; Protein 2.5g; Carbohydrate 19.4g, of which sugars 2.4g; Fat 11.5g, of which saturates 1.4g; Cholesterol 0mg; Calcium 15mg; Fibre 1.3g; Sodium 14mg

CORN WITH CREAM

*IN MEXICO, THIS WOULD BE MADE WITH "HEAVY CREAM", THE AMERICAN EQUIVALENT OF DOUBLE
CREAM, BUT THE SAUCE HAS A BETTER CONSISTENCY WHEN MADE WITH FULL-FAT SOFT CHEESE.*

SERVES SIX AS A SIDE DISH

INGREDIENTS
  4 corn cobs
  50g/2oz/¼ cup butter
  1 small onion, finely chopped
  115g/4oz/⅔ cup drained pickled
    jalapeño chilli slices
  130g/4½oz/⅔ cup full-fat soft cheese
  25g/1oz/⅓ cup freshly grated
    Parmesan cheese, plus shavings,
    to garnish
  salt and ground black pepper

1 Strip off the husks from the corn and pull off the silks. Place the cobs in a bowl of water and use a vegetable brush to remove any remaining silks. Stand each cob in turn on a board and slice off the kernels, cutting as close to the cob as possible.

2 Melt the butter in a pan, add the chopped onion and fry for 4–5 minutes, stirring occasionally, until the onion has softened and is translucent.

3 Add the corn kernels and cook for 4–5 minutes, until they are just tender. Chop the jalapeños finely and stir them into the corn mixture.

4 Stir in the soft cheese and the grated Parmesan. Cook over a low heat until both cheeses have melted and the corn kernels are coated in the mixture. Season to taste, tip into a heated dish and serve, topped with shredded Parmesan.

VARIATION
A simplified version of this dish is sold on street stalls in Mexico. Whole cooked corn cobs are dipped in cream, then sprinkled with crumbled fresh cheese. Next time you barbecue, try this as an appetizer. Alternatively, put whole corn cobs in a shallow baking dish and bake them in an oven preheated to 200°C/400°F/Gas 6 for 30 minutes, until tender and golden. Pour over 120ml/4fl oz/½ cup sour cream or crème fraîche, then sprinkle the cobs with 30ml/2 tbsp freshly grated Parmesan cheese and serve. The corn can also be brushed with butter and grilled (broiled), but it must have plenty of room below the heat, or it will burn.

Energy 328kcal/1367kJ; Protein 7.6g; Carbohydrate 27.7g, of which sugars 10.4g; Fat 21.6g, of which saturates 12.8g; Cholesterol 45mg; Calcium 126mg; Fibre 1.5g; Sodium 463mg

FRIJOLES DE OLLA

TRAVELLERS OFTEN SAY THAT "BEANS IN A POT", AS IT IS TRANSLATED, TASTE DIFFERENT IN MEXICO FROM THOSE COOKED ANYWHERE ELSE. THE SECRET IS, QUITE LITERALLY, IN THE POT. TRADITIONALLY, CLAY POTS ARE USED, WHICH GIVE THE BEANS A WONDERFUL, SLIGHTLY EARTHY FLAVOUR. THIS DISH WOULD BE SERVED AS JUST ONE OF THE COURSES IN A FORMAL MEXICAN MEAL.

3 While the beans are cooking, prepare the toppings. Spear the chillies on a long-handled metal skewer and roast them over the flame of a gas burner until the skins blister and darken. Do not let the flesh burn. Alternatively, dry fry them in a griddle pan until the skins are scorched. Put the roasted chillies in a strong plastic bag and tie the top immediately to keep the steam in. Set aside for 20 minutes.

4 Remove the chillies from the bag and peel off the skins. Cut off the stalks, then slit the chillies and scrape out the seeds. Cut the flesh into thin strips and put it in a bowl. Spoon all the other toppings into separate bowls.

5 Ladle about 250ml/8fl oz/1 cup of the beans and liquid into a food processor or blender. Process to a smooth purée. If you prefer, simply mash the beans with a potato masher.

6 Return the bean purée to the pan, and stir it in. Chop the coriander, reserving some leaves to garnish, season with salt and mix well. Ladle the beans into warmed individual bowls and take them to the table with the toppings.

SERVES FOUR

INGREDIENTS
 250g/9oz/1¼ cups dried pinto beans, soaked overnight in water to cover
 1.75 litres/3 pints/7½ cups water
 2 onions
 10 garlic cloves, peeled and left whole
 small bunch of coriander (cilantro)
 salt
For the toppings
 2 fresh red fresno chillies
 1 tomato, peeled and chopped
 2 spring onions (scallions), chopped
 60ml/4 tbsp sour cream
 50g/2oz feta cheese

COOK'S TIP
In Mexico, the local fresh cheese – *queso fresco* – would be used as the topping, but feta makes an acceptable substitute.

1 Drain the beans, rinse them under cold water and drain again. Put the water in a large pan, bring to the boil and add the beans.

2 Cut the onions in half and add them to the pan, with the whole garlic cloves. Bring to the boil again, then lower the heat and simmer for 1½ hours, until the beans are tender and there is only a little liquid remaining.

7 Serve the beans with the toppings and add coriander to garnish. Traditionally, each guest spoons a little of the chillies, tomatoes and spring onions over the beans, then adds a spoonful of sour cream. The finishing touch is a little feta cheese, crumbled over each portion.

Energy 255kcal/1074kJ; Protein 17.9g; Carbohydrate 32.7g, of which sugars 4.4g; Fat 6.7g, of which saturates 3.8g; Cholesterol 18mg; Calcium 154mg; Fibre 11.4g; Sodium 205mg

REFRIED BEANS

THESE ARE NOT ACTUALLY FRIED TWICE, BUT THEY ARE COOKED TWICE, FIRST AS FRIJOLES DE OLLA *AND THEN BY FRYING IN LARD. IF THE ONLY REFRIED BEANS YOU'VE TRIED HAVE BEEN THE CANNED ONES, YOU MAY HAVE FOUND THEM RATHER BLAND. THESE, HOWEVER, ARE SUPERB.*

SERVES FOUR

INGREDIENTS

25g/1oz/2 tbsp lard
2 onions, finely chopped
5ml/1 tsp ground cumin
5ml/1 tsp ground coriander
1 quantity *Frijoles de Olla*, without
  the toppings
3 garlic cloves, crushed
small bunch of fresh coriander
  (cilantro)
50g/2oz feta cheese
salt

1 Melt the lard in a large frying pan. Add the onions, cumin and ground coriander. Cook gently over a low heat for about 30 minutes or until the onions caramelize and become soft.

2 Add a ladleful of the soft, cooked beans. Fry them for only a few minutes simply to heat. Mash the beans into the onions as they cook, using a fork or a potato masher. Continue until all the beans have been added, a little at a time, then stir in the crushed garlic.

3 Lower the heat and cook the beans to form a thick paste. Season with salt and spoon into a warmed serving dish. Chop the coriander or crumble the avocado leaves, and sprinkle most of them over the beans. Crumble the feta cheese over the top, then garnish with the reserved sprigs or leaves.

Energy 193kcal/806kJ; Protein 10g; Carbohydrate 19g, of which sugars 5g; Fat.9g, of which saturates 4g; Cholesterol 15mg; Calcium 101mg; Fibre 8g; Sodium 189mg

FRIJOLES CHARROS

THESE "COWBOY BEANS" TASTE RATHER LIKE BOSTON BAKED BEANS, BUT WITH RATHER MORE PUNCH.
THE FLAVOUR IMPROVES ON KEEPING, SO MAKE IT THE DAY BEFORE YOU INTEND TO SERVE IT.

SERVES SIX

INGREDIENTS
    2 x 400g/14oz cans pinto beans
    120ml/4fl oz/½ cup Mexican beer
    115g/4oz/⅔ cups drained pickled
      jalapeño chilli slices
    2 tomatoes, peeled and chopped
    5ml/1 tsp ground cinnamon
    175g/6oz bacon fat
    1 onion, chopped
    2 garlic cloves, crushed
    175g/6oz rindless smoked lean
      bacon, diced
    45ml/3 tbsp soft dark brown sugar
    wheat flour tortillas, to serve

1 Put the drained pinto beans in a pan. Stir in the beer and cook over a high heat for 5 minutes, until some of the beer has been absorbed.

2 Lower the heat slightly and stir in the chopped jalapeños chilli, then add the tomatoes and cinnamon. Continue to cook, stirring occasionally, for about 10 minutes.

3 Meanwhile, heat the fat bacon in a frying pan until the fat runs. The quantity suggested should yield about 45ml/3 tbsp bacon fat.

4 Discard the bacon, then add the onion and garlic to the pan and fry for about 5 minutes, until browned. Using a slotted spoon, lift out the garlic and onions and stir them into the beans.

5 Add the diced smoked bacon to the fat remaining in the frying pan and fry until crisp. Add the bacon and any remaining fat to the beans and mix well.

6 Stir in the sugar. Cook the bean and bacon mixture over a low heat, stirring constantly, until the sugar is dissolved. Serve immediately or spoon into a bowl, leave to cool, cover, then chill for reheating next day. Serve with warmed wheat flour tortillas.

Energy 303kcal/1281kJ; Protein 18g; Carbohydrate 42g, of which sugars 14g; Fat 8g, of which saturates 2g; Cholesterol 17mg; Calcium 152mg; Fibre 14.1g; Sodium 498mg

GREEN RICE

THIS RICE SELDOM FEATURES ON MENUS IN MEXICAN RESTAURANTS, BUT IS OFTEN MADE IN THE HOME.
EXTRA CHILLIES AND GREEN PEPPER CAN BE DICED AND ADDED AT THE END, IF YOU LIKE.

SERVES FOUR

INGREDIENTS

2 fresh green chillies, preferably
  poblanos
1 small green (bell) pepper
200g/7oz/1 cup long grain white rice
1 garlic clove, roughly chopped
large bunch of coriander (cilantro)
small bunch of fresh flat leaf parsley
475ml/16fl oz/2 cups chicken stock
30ml/2 tbsp vegetable oil
1 small onion, finely chopped
salt

1 Dry roast the chillies and green pepper in a griddle pan, turning them frequently so that the skins blacken but the flesh does not burn. Place them in a strong plastic bag, tie the top securely and set aside for 20 minutes.

2 Put the rice in a heatproof bowl, pour over boiling water to cover and leave to stand for 20 minutes.

3 Drain the rice, rinse well under cold water and drain again. Remove the chillies and peppers from the bag and peel off the skins. Remove any stalks, then slit the vegetables and scrape out the seeds with a sharp knife.

4 Put the roasted vegetables in a food processor, with the garlic. Strip off the leaves from the coriander and parsley stalks, reserve some for the garnish and add the rest to the processor. Pour in half the chicken stock and process until smooth. Add the rest of the stock and process the purée again.

5 Heat the oil in a pan, add the onion and rice and fry for 5 minutes over a moderate heat until the rice is golden and the onion translucent. Stir in the purée. Lower the heat, cover and cook for 25–30 minutes or until all the liquid is absorbed and the rice is just tender. Add salt and garnish with the reserved herbs. Served with lime wedges, this rice goes extremely well with fish.

YELLOW RICE

THIS RICE DISH OWES ITS STRIKING COLOUR AND DISTINCTIVE FLAVOUR TO GROUND ACHIOTE SEED,
WHICH IS DERIVED FROM ANNATTO.

SERVES SIX

INGREDIENTS

200g/7oz/1 cup long grain white rice
30ml/2 tbsp vegetable oil
5ml/1 tsp ground achiote seed
  (annatto powder)
1 small onion, finely chopped
2 garlic cloves, crushed
475ml/16fl oz/2 cups chicken stock
50g/2oz/⅓ cup drained pickled
  jalapeño chilli slices, chopped
salt
coriander (cilantro) leaves, to garnish

COOK'S TIP

Achiote, the seed of the annatto tree, is used as a food colouring and flavouring throughout Latin America. You can buy it in specialist spice shops and ethnic food stores. It is sometimes labelled as annatto powder.

1 Put the rice in a heatproof bowl, pour over boiling water to cover and leave to stand for 20 minutes. Drain, rinse under cold water and drain again.

2 Heat the oil in a pan, add the ground achiote seed and cook for 2–3 minutes. Add the onion and garlic and cook for 3–4 minutes more until the onion is translucent. Stir in the rice and cook for 5 minutes.

3 Pour in the stock, mix well and bring to the boil. Lower the heat, cover the pan with a tight-fitting lid and simmer for 25–30 minutes, until all the liquid has been absorbed.

4 Add the chopped jalapeños to the pan and stir to distribute them evenly. Add salt to taste, then spoon into a heated serving dish and garnish with the fresh coriander leaves. Serve at once.

Energy 257kcal/1069kJ; Protein 5.4g; Carbohydrate 44.2g, of which sugars 3.6g; Fat 6.3g, of which saturates 0.7g; Cholesterol 0mg; Calcium 49mg; Fibre 1.4g; Sodium 8mg
Energy 163kcal/679kJ; Protein 3.6g; Carbohydrate 27.6g, of which sugars 0.8g; Fat 4.1g, of which saturates 0.4g; Cholesterol 0mg; Calcium 19mg; Fibre 0.1g; Sodium 3mg

CHAYOTES WITH CORN AND CHILLIES

SHAPED LIKE PEARS OR AVOCADOS, CHAYOTES ARE MEMBERS OF THE SQUASH FAMILY AND HAVE RATHER A BLAND TASTE. HOWEVER, THEY MARRY EXTREMELY WELL WITH OTHER INGREDIENTS, SUCH AS THE CORN AND ROASTED JALAPEÑOS IN THIS MEDLEY.

SERVES SIX

INGREDIENTS
    4 fresh jalapeño chillies
    3 *chayotes*
    oil, for frying
    1 red onion, finely chopped
    3 garlic cloves, crushed
    225g/8oz/1⅓ cups corn kernels,
        thawed if frozen
    150g/5oz/⅔ cup cream cheese
    5ml/1 tsp salt (optional)
    25g/1oz/⅓ cup freshly grated
        Parmesan cheese

1 Dry roast the fresh jalapeño chillies in a griddle pan, turning them frequently so that the skins blacken but do not burn. Place them in a plastic bag, tie the top securely, and set them aside for 20 minutes.

2 Meanwhile, peel the *chayotes*, cut them in half and remove the seed from each of them. Cut the flesh into 1cm/ ½in cubes.

COOK'S TIP
Chayotes go by several names, including *christophene* and *choko*. Store them in a plastic bag in the refrigerator and they will keep for up to 1 month.

3 Heat the oil in a frying pan. Add the onion, garlic, *chayote* cubes and corn. Fry over a moderate heat for 10 minutes, stirring occasionally.

4 Remove the jalapeños from the bag, peel off the skins and remove any stems. Cut them in half, scrape out the seeds, then cut the flesh into strips.

5 Add the chillies and cream cheese to the pan, stirring gently, until the cheese melts. Place in a serving dish.

6 Stir in salt, if needed, then spoon into a warmed dish. Sprinkle with Parmesan cheese and serve. This makes a good accompaniment for cold roast meats.

Energy 251kcal/1044kJ; Protein 6.9g; Carbohydrate 13.8g, of which sugars 6.1g; Fat 19.1g, of which saturates 9.7g; Cholesterol 32mg; Calcium 161mg; Fibre 1.5g; Sodium 281mg

SPINACH SALAD

YOUNG SPINACH LEAVES MAKE A WELCOME CHANGE FROM LETTUCE AND ARE EXCELLENT IN SALADS.
THE ROASTED GARLIC IS AN INSPIRED ADDITION TO THE DRESSING.

SERVES SIX

INGREDIENTS
   500g/1¼lb baby spinach leaves
   50g/2oz/⅓ cup sesame seeds
   50g/2oz/¼ cup butter
   30ml/2 tbsp olive oil
   6 shallots, sliced
   8 fresh serrano chillies, seeded and
     cut into strips
   4 tomatoes, sliced
For the dressing
   6 roasted garlic cloves
   120ml/4fl oz/½ cup white
     wine vinegar
   2.5ml/½ tsp ground white pepper
   1 bay leaf
   2.5ml/½ tsp ground allspice
   30ml/2 tbsp chopped fresh thyme,
     plus extra sprigs, to garnish

COOK'S TIP
To roast individual garlic cloves simply
place in a roasting tray in a moderate
oven for about 15 minutes until soft.

1 Make the dressing. Remove the skins
from the garlic when cool, then chop
and combine with the vinegar, pepper,
bay leaf, allspice and chopped thyme in
a jar with a screw-top lid. Close the lid
tightly, shake well, then put the dressing
in the refrigerator until needed.

2 Wash the spinach leaves and dry
them in a salad spinner or clean dish
towel. Put them in a plastic bag in
the refrigerator.

3 Toast the sesame seeds in a dry frying
pan, shaking frequently over a moderate
heat until golden. Set aside.

4 Heat the butter and oil in a frying
pan. Fry the shallots for 4–5 minutes,
until softened, then stir in the chilli
strips and fry for 2–3 minutes more.

5 In a large bowl, layer the spinach with
the shallot and chilli mixture, and the
tomato slices. Pour over the dressing.
Sprinkle with sesame seeds and serve,
garnished with thyme sprigs.

Energy 209kcal/866kJ; Protein 7.2g; Carbohydrate 9.2g, of which sugars 6.7g; Fat 16.2g, of which saturates 5.5g; Cholesterol 18mg; Calcium 218mg; Fibre 3.9g; Sodium 170mg

NOPALITOS SALAD

NOPALITOS — STRIPS OF PICKLED CACTUS PADDLES — ARE SOLD IN CANS OR JARS, AND ARE VERY USEFUL FOR MAKING QUICK AND EASY SALADS LIKE THIS ONE.

SERVES FOUR

INGREDIENTS

    300g/11oz/scant 2 cups drained
      canned *nopalitos*
    1 red (bell) pepper, deseeded and
      halved
    30ml/2 tbsp olive oil
    2 garlic cloves, sliced
    ½ red onion, thinly sliced
    120ml/4fl oz/½ cup cider vinegar
    small bunch of coriander (cilantro),
      chopped
    salt

1 Preheat the grill (broiler). Put the *nopalitos* in a bowl. Pour over water to cover and set aside for 30 minutes. Drain, replace with fresh water and leave to soak for a further 30 minutes.

2 Place the red peppers cut side down in a grill (broiling) pan. Grill (broil) them until the skins blister and char, then put the pepper halves in a strong plastic bag, tie the top securely to keep the steam in, and set aside for 20 minutes.

3 Heat the oil in a small frying pan and fry the garlic over a low heat until the slices start to turn golden. Using a slotted spoon, transfer them to a salad bowl. Pour the garlic-flavoured oil into a jug (pitcher) and set it aside to cool.

4 Add the red onion slices to the salad bowl, then pour over the vinegar. Remove the red pepper from the bag, peel off the skins, then cut the flesh into thin strips. Add to the salad bowl.

5 Drain the *nopalitos* thoroughly and add them to the salad, with the cool garlic-flavoured oil and a little salt, to taste. Toss lightly, then chill until needed. Sprinkle the chopped coriander over just before serving. This is delicious served with crusty bread.

Energy 101kcal/419kJ; Protein 1.6g; Carbohydrate 10.4g, of which sugars 9.6g; Fat 6.1g, of which saturates 0.8g; Cholesterol 0mg; Calcium 15mg; Fibre 2.5g; Sodium 6mg.

JICAMA, CHILLI ᴬᴺᴰ LIME SALAD

A VERY TASTY, CRISP VEGETABLE, THE JICAMA IS SOMETIMES CALLED THE MEXICAN POTATO. UNLIKE POTATO, HOWEVER, IT CAN BE EATEN RAW AS WELL AS COOKED. THIS MAKES A GOOD SALAD OR AN APPETIZER TO SERVE WITH DRINKS.

SERVES FOUR

INGREDIENTS
1 *jicama*
2.5ml/½ tsp salt
2 fresh serrano chillies
2 limes

COOK'S TIP
Look for *jicama* in Oriental supermarkets, as it is widely used in Chinese cooking. It goes by several names and you may find it labelled as either yam bean or Chinese turnip.

1 Peel the *jicama* with a potato peeler or knife, then cut it into 2cm/¾in cubes. Put these in a large bowl, add the salt and toss well.

2 Cut the chillies in half, scrape out the seeds with a sharp knife, then cut the flesh into fine strips. Grate one of the limes thinly, removing only the coloured part of the skin, then cut the lime in half and squeeze the juice.

3 Add the chillies, lime rind and juice to the *jicama* and mix thoroughly to ensure that all the *jicama* cubes are coated. Cut the other lime into wedges.

4 Cover and chill for at least 1 hour before serving with lime wedges. If the salad is to be served as an appetizer with drinks, transfer the *jicama* cubes to little bowls and offer them with cocktail sticks (toothpicks) for spearing.

Energy 73kcal/309kJ; Protein 2.1g; Carbohydrate 16.2g, of which sugars 1.4g; Fat 0.4g, of which saturates 0.1g; Cholesterol 0mg; Calcium 10mg; Fibre 1g; Sodium 12mg

CHAYOTE SALAD

COOL AND REFRESHING, THIS SALAD IS IDEAL ON ITS OWN OR WITH FISH OR CHICKEN DISHES. THE SOFT FLESH OF THE CHAYOTES ABSORBS THE FLAVOUR OF THE DRESSING BEAUTIFULLY.

SERVES FOUR

INGREDIENTS
  2 *chayotes*
  2 firm tomatoes
  1 small onion, finely chopped
  finely sliced strips of fresh red and
    green chilli, to garnish
For the dressing
  2.5ml/½ tsp Dijon mustard
  2.5ml/½ tsp ground anise
  90ml/6 tbsp white wine vinegar
  60ml/4 tbsp olive oil
  salt and ground black pepper

1 Bring a pan of water to the boil. Peel the *chayotes*, cut them in half and remove the seeds. Add them to the boiling water. Lower the heat and simmer for 20 minutes or until the *chayotes* are tender. Drain and set them aside to cool.

2 Meanwhile, peel the tomatoes. Cut a cross in the base of each tomato. Place them in a heatproof bowl and pour over boiling water to cover. After 3 minutes, lift the tomatoes out on a slotted spoon and plunge them into a bowl of cold water. Drain. The skins will have begun to peel back from the crosses. Remove the skins completely and cut the tomatoes into wedges.

3 Make the dressing by combining all the ingredients in a screw top jar. Close the lid tightly and shake the jar vigorously.

4 Cut the *chayotes* into wedges and place in a bowl with the tomato and onion. Pour over the dressing and serve garnished with strips of fresh red and green chilli.

Energy 104kcal/430kJ; Protein 1.4g; Carbohydrate 5.3g, of which sugars 4.4g; Fat 8.7g, of which saturates 1.4g; Cholesterol 0mg; Calcium 40mg; Fibre 1.8g; Sodium 24mg

CAESAR SALAD

ALTHOUGH THIS IS WIDELY REGARDED AS AN AMERICAN CLASSIC, CAESAR SALAD ACTUALLY ORIGINATED IN MEXICO, AND TAKES ITS NAME FROM THE CHEF, CAESAR CARDINI, WHO INVENTED IT IN HIS RESTAURANT IN TIJUANA IN 1924. PREGNANT WOMEN AND YOUNG CHILDREN ARE ADVISED TO AVOID EATING RAW EGG.

SERVES FOUR

INGREDIENTS
   2 large garlic cloves, peeled and
     left whole
   60ml/4 tbsp extra virgin olive oil
   4 slices of bread, crusts
     removed, cubed
   1 cos or Romaine lettuce, separated
     into leaves
   6 drained canned anchovy fillets
   shavings of Parmesan cheese,
     to garnish
For the dressing
   1 egg
   10ml/2 tsp Dijon mustard
   generous dash of Worcestershire
     sauce
   30ml/2 tbsp lemon juice
   30ml/2 tbsp extra virgin olive oil
   salt and ground black pepper

1 Cut one garlic clove in half and rub it around the inside of a salad bowl. Put the remaining garlic in a large frying pan. Add the oil and heat gently for 5 minutes, then discard the garlic. Add the bread cubes to the hot oil, in batches if necessary, and fry them until they are crisp on all sides. Drain on kitchen paper.

2 Line the salad bowl with the cos or Romaine leaves. Carefully cut the anchovy fillets in half lengthways and distribute them among the lettuce leaves. Toss the leaves to spread the flavour of the anchovies.

3 Crack the egg into a food processor or blender, with the Dijon mustard, Worcestershire sauce and lemon juice. Season and process to blend briefly, then add the oil with the motor running.

4 Pour the dressing over the salad in the bowl and toss lightly. Add the garlic croûtons. Transfer to individual bowls or carry to the table in the salad bowl. Scatter with Parmesan shavings and serve.

Energy 198kcal/824kJ; Protein 5.6g; Carbohydrate 13.8g, of which sugars 1.7g; Fat 13.8g, of which saturates 2.1g; Cholesterol 50mg; Calcium 64mg; Fibre 0.9g; Sodium 400mg

DESSERTS AND SWEETMEATS

Mexicans love sweet things. Ever since Hernàn Cortèz introduced sugar cane to the country, sweetmeats have been very much on the menu and the array of cakes and pastries in a Mexican pasterìa would rival any display in a European cake store. Special cakes and cookies are made for feast days and festivals, like the Day of the Dead or Twelfth Night. Kings' Day Bread is traditionally served to celebrate Epiphany, on January 6th, while Mexican Wedding Cookies, with their generous sugar coating, are served at marriage celebrations.

The most famous Mexican dessert is Flan, a caramel custard which is also very popular in Spain. Rice puddings of various types are often served, and rich, sticky puddings made from pumpkin or plantains go down very well, especially with children. However, with the wonderful produce at their disposal, Mexicans often opt to end a meal with a simple platter of colourful fresh fruit, served with salt, chilli powder and fresh lime juice, as they did in the days before Spanish and French cooks introduced them to puddings and pastries.

CHURROS

THESE DELECTABLE TREATS ARE TRADITIONALLY MADE BY FORCING DOUGH THROUGH A CHURRERA, WHICH IS A UTENSIL FITTED WITH A WOODEN PLUNGER. AN ICING BAG FITTED WITH A LARGE STAR NOZZLE MAKES A GOOD SUBSTITUTE. CHURROS ARE USUALLY SERVED WITH CAFE DE OLLA OR MEXICAN HOT CHOCOLATE AND ARE PERFECT FOR DIPPING.

MAKES ABOUT TWENTY-FOUR

INGREDIENTS
350g/12oz/3 cups plain (all-purpose) flour
5ml/1 tsp baking powder
600ml/1 pint/2½ cups water
2.5ml/½ tsp salt
25g/1oz/3 tbsp soft dark brown sugar
2 egg yolks
oil, for deep frying
2 limes, cut in wedges
caster (superfine) sugar, for dusting

1 Sift the flour and baking powder into a bowl and set aside. Bring the measured water to the boil in a pan, add the salt and brown sugar, stirring all the time until both have dissolved. Remove from the heat, tip in all the flour and baking powder and beat the mixture continuously until smooth.

2 Beat in the egg yolks, one at a time, until the mixture is smooth and glossy. Set the batter aside to cool. Have ready a piping bag fitted with a large star nozzle which will give the *churros* their traditional shape.

3 Pour oil into a deep fryer or suitable pan to a depth of about 5cm/2in. Heat to 190°C/375°F, or until a cube of dried bread, added to the oil, floats and turns golden after 1 minute.

4 Spoon the batter into the piping bag. Pipe five or six 10cm/4in lengths of the mixture into the hot oil, using a knife to slice off each length as it emerges from the nozzle. Fry for 3–4 minutes or until they are golden brown. Drain the *churros* on kitchen paper while cooking successive batches, then arrange on a plate with the lime wedges, dust them with caster sugar and serve warm.

SOPAIPILLAS

THESE GOLDEN PILLOWS OF PUFF PASTRY CAN BE SERVED AS A DESSERT, WITH HONEY, OR PLAIN WITH SOUPS. THEY ARE ALSO IDEAL FOR FINGER BUFFETS.

MAKES ABOUT THIRTY

INGREDIENTS
225g/8oz/2 cups plain (all-purpose) flour
15ml/1 tsp baking powder
5ml/1 tsp salt
25g/1oz/2 tbsp white cooking fat
175ml/6fl oz/¾ cup warm water
oil, for deep frying
clear honey, for drizzling
ground cinnamon for sprinkling
crème fraîche or thick double (heavy) cream, to serve

1 Sift the flour, baking powder and salt into a bowl. Rub in the cooking fat or margarine until the mixture resembles fine breadcrumbs. Gradually add enough of the water to form a dough. Wrap the dough in clear film (plastic wrap) and leave for 1 hour.

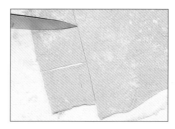

3 Heat the oil for deep frying to 190°C/375°F, or until a cube of dried bread, added to the oil, floats and turns golden after 1 minute. Add a few pastry squares, using tongs to push them down into the oil. Cook in batches until golden on both sides, turning them once, and drain on kitchen paper.

VARIATION
Instead of drizzling honey over the *sopaipillas*, use a mixture of 50g/2oz/¼ cup caster (superfine) sugar and 10ml/2 tsp ground cinnamon.

2 Working with half the dough at a time, roll it out to a square, keeping it as even and as thin as possible. Cut into 7.5cm/3in squares. When both pieces of the dough have been rolled and cut, set the squares aside.

4 When all the *sopaipillas* have been cooked, arrange on a large serving plate, drizzle with honey and sprinkle with ground cinnamon Serve warm, with crème fraîche or thick double cream.

Energy 122kcal/517kJ; Protein 2.6g; Carbohydrate 21.4g, of which sugars 2.3g; Fat 3.5g, of which saturates 0.5g; Cholesterol 17mg; Calcium 38mg; Fibre 0.8g; Sodium 2mg
Energy 79kcal/332kJ; Protein 1.3g; Carbohydrate 12.9g, of which sugars 2.8g; Fat 2.8g, of which saturates 0.2g; Cholesterol 0mg; Calcium 19mg; Fibre 0.4g; Sodium 9mg

CARAMEL CUSTARD

IF YOU ORDER "FLAN" FROM THE MENU IN MEXICO YOU MIGHT BE DISCONCERTED IF YOU WERE EXPECTING A SPONGE CASE FILLED WITH FRUIT. THIS HUGELY POPULAR PUDDING IS ACTUALLY A CARAMEL CUSTARD, AND HAS ITS ORIGINS IN SPAIN, WHERE THE SAME NAME IS USED. IT IS SIMILAR TO THE FRENCH CRÈME CARAMEL.

SERVES SIX

INGREDIENTS
    1 litre/1¾ pints/4 cups milk
    1 vanilla pod (bean), split
    6 eggs
    115g/4oz/½ cup sugar
    5ml/1 tsp natural vanilla extract
For the caramel
    175g/6oz/¾ cup sugar

1 Put six ramekins or dariole moulds in a sink of hot water. Make the caramel. Spread out the sugar evenly on the bottom of a large pan. Heat it slowly, without stirring, tilting the pan backwards and forwards on the heat until the sugar melts.

2 Lift the heated ramekins or moulds out of the water and dry them quickly. Watch the melted sugar closely, and when it turns a rich golden colour, pour the mixture into the dishes and simply turn until they are coated, or brush the caramel over the insides of the dishes. Set them aside.

3 Preheat the oven to 180°C/350°F/ Gas 4. Pour the milk into a pan, add the vanilla pod and bring the milk to just below boiling point. Pour it into a jug (pitcher) and set it aside to cool.

4 Put the eggs in a bowl, beat them lightly, then gradually beat in the sugar. Remove the vanilla from the milk, then gradually mix the milk into the egg.

5 Strain the egg mixture into the caramel-lined ramekins or moulds and stand them in a roasting tin. Pour boiling water into the roasting tin until it comes halfway up the sides of the dishes, then carefully put the tin in the oven.

6 Bake the caramel custards for about 40 minutes. The custards are done when a slender knife blade, inserted in one of them, comes out clean.

7 Lift the dishes out of the water, let them cool, then chill them for several hours in the refrigerator.

8 To serve, run a round-bladed knife around the edge of each custard, place a dessert plate upside down on top of the dish and turn the dish and plate over together. Lift off the dish. Some of the caramel will settle in a puddle around the custard, so it is important not to choose dessert dishes that are too shallow. Try serving these custards with fresh fruit.

VARIATIONS
Flavour the custard with cinnamon, cocoa or rum instead of vanilla. In the Tabasco region, where chestnuts grow, chestnut purée is sometimes added.

Energy 272kcal/1152kJ; Protein 10.7g; Carbohydrate 43.3g, of which sugars 43.3g; Fat 7.7g, of which saturates 2.9g; Cholesterol 198mg; Calcium 198mg; Fibre 0g; Sodium 126mg

RICE PUDDING

Rice is a popular dessert ingredient in Mexico. One way of serving it is to cook it in milk until soft and thick, then shape it into balls. These are coated in egg and breadcrumbs, fried in oil, then rolled in cinnamon sugar to make sweet treats. This is a light, easy-to-make rice pudding, which is full of flavour.

SERVES FOUR

INGREDIENTS

75g/3oz/½ cup raisins
75ml/5 tbsp dry sherry
90g/3½oz/½ cup short grain
   (pudding) rice
3 or 4 strips of pared lemon peel
250ml/8fl oz/1 cup water
475ml/16fl oz/2 cups milk
225g/8oz/1 cup sugar
pinch of salt
1 cinnamon stick, about 7.5cm/3in
   in length, plus 3 more, to decorate
2 egg yolks
15g/½oz/1 tbsp butter, diced
toasted flaked (sliced) almonds,
   to decorate
chilled orange segments, to serve

1 Put the raisins and sherry in a small pan. Heat gently until warm, then set the pan aside, which will allow the raisins to swell.

2 Mix the rice, lemon peel and water in a heavy-based pan and bring to the boil. Lower the heat, cover the pan and simmer for about 20 minutes. Remove the lemon peel.

3 Add the milk and the cinnamon stick to the pan, then stir until the rice has absorbed the milk. Stir in the sugar and salt. Add the egg yolks and butter. Stir constantly until the butter has melted.

4 Drain the raisins and stir into the rice mixture. Cook for 2–3 minutes, top with the toasted flaked almonds and serve with the orange segments. Place a cinnamon stick in each bowl.

Energy 433kcal/1829kJ; Protein 5.8g; Carbohydrate 85.6g, of which sugars 65.7g; Fat 6.9g, of which saturates 3.3g; Cholesterol 112mg; Calcium 113mg; Fibre 0.5g; Sodium 68mg

ALMOND PUDDING WITH CUSTARD

THIS DISH MAY WELL DATE FROM THE TIME OF THE FRENCH OCCUPATION OF MEXICO, FOR IT BEARS A CLOSE RESEMBLANCE TO ÎLE FLOTTANTE — FLOATING ISLANDS — ALTHOUGH IN THAT RECIPE THE MERINGUES ARE ACTUALLY POACHED IN THE CUSTARD. DELICIOUS AND VERY LIGHT, IT MAKES THE PERFECT DESSERT TO FOLLOW A SUBSTANTIAL MAIN COURSE.

SERVES SIX

INGREDIENTS
250ml/8fl oz/1 cup water
15g/½oz sachet powdered gelatine
275g/10oz/1¼ cups sugar
2.5ml/½ tsp almond extract
6 eggs, separated
pinch of salt
475ml/16fl oz/2 cups single (light) cream
2.5ml/½ tsp natural vanilla extract
ground cinnamon, for dusting

1 Pour the water into a pan and sprinkle the gelatine over the surface. When it has softened, add 225g/8oz/ 1 cup of the sugar and place the pan over a low heat. Stir until both the gelatine and the sugar have dissolved, then stir in the almond extract. Pour the mixture into a bowl and chill in the refrigerator until it starts to thicken.

2 Whisk the egg whites until they are stiff. Whisk the gelatine mixture until is frothy, then fold in the egg whites carefully. Chill until firm.

3 Meanwhile, make the custard. Put the egg yolks, remaining sugar and salt in a heavy-based pan. Stir in the cream and vanilla extract. Cook over a very low heat, stirring constantly until the custard thickens to a soft dropping consistency, enough to coat the back of a wooden spoon.

4 Pour the custard into dessert bowls. Cover each with a piece of dampened baking parchment until ready to serve to prevent the formation of a skin.

5 Serve each custard topped with a few spoonfuls of the meringue mixture and a sprinkle of ground cinnamon.

Energy 360kcal/1507kJ; Protein 8.9g; Carbohydrate 39.1g, of which sugars 39.1g; Fat 19.9g, of which saturates 10.7g; Cholesterol 232mg; Calcium 114mg; Fibre 0g; Sodium 94mg

PUMPKIN <u>IN</u> BROWN SUGAR

RICH, STICKY AND SWEET, THIS WARMING DESSERT LOOKS VERY ATTRACTIVE AND IS NOT AT ALL DIFFICULT TO PREPARE.

SERVES SIX

INGREDIENTS

  1 small pumpkin, about 800g/1¾lb
  350g/12oz/1½ cups soft dark
    brown sugar
  120ml/4fl oz/½ cup water
  5ml/1 tsp ground cloves
  12 cinnamon sticks, each about
    10cm/4in in length
  fresh mint sprigs, to decorate
  thick yogurt or crème fraîche, to serve

1 Halve the pumpkin, remove the seeds and fibres and cut into wedges. Arrange in a single layer in a shallow, flameproof casserole or heavy-based pan. Fill the hollows with the sugar.

2 Pour the water carefully into the pan, taking care not to wash all the sugar to the bottom. Make sure that some of the water trickles down to the bottom to prevent the pumpkin from burning. Sprinkle on the ground cloves and add two of the cinnamon sticks.

3 Cover the pan tightly and cook over a low heat for about 30 minutes, or until the pumpkin is tender and the sugar and water have formed a syrup. Check the casserole or pan occasionally to make sure that the pumpkin does not dry out or catch on the bottom.

4 Transfer the pumpkin to a platter and pour the hot syrup over. Decorate each portion with mint and cinnamon sticks and serve with thick yogurt or crème fraîche.

COOK'S TIP
Pumpkin cooked in this way can be used to fill sweet empanadas, so cook all of it and use the rest as filling.

Energy 184kcal/783kJ; Protein 1.3g; Carbohydrate 46.9g, of which sugars 46.1g; Fat 0.3g, of which saturates 0.2g; Cholesterol 0mg; Calcium 66mg; Fibre 1.5g; Sodium 3mg

COCONUT CUSTARD

LIGHT AND CREAMY, THIS IS THE PERFECT PUDDING FOR SERVING AFTER A SPICY MAIN COURSE.
CHILDREN LIKE IT, AND IT IS IDEAL FOR ENTERTAINING AS IT CAN BE MADE AHEAD OF TIME AND
KEPT IN THE REFRIGERATOR OVERNIGHT.

2 Add the coconut and cook over a low heat, stirring occasionally, for 5 minutes. Stir in the milk until the mixture has thickened slightly. Remove the cinnamon stick. Remove from the heat.

3 Whisk the eggs until light and fluffy. Gradually incorporate the coconut mixture, then scrape into a clean pan.

SERVES SIX

INGREDIENTS
225g/8oz/1 cup sugar
250ml/8fl oz/1 cup water
1 cinnamon stick, about 7.5cm/3in
   in length
175g/6oz/2 cups desiccated (dry
   unsweetened shredded) coconut
750ml/1¼ pints/3 cups milk
4 eggs
175ml/6fl oz/¾ cup whipping cream
50g/2oz/½ cup chopped almonds,
   toasted
strips of orange rind, to decorate

VARIATION
Use about 115g/4oz/1 cup fresh coconut, grated, instead, if you can find it.

1 To make the cinnamon syrup, place the sugar and water in a very large pan, add the cinnamon stick and bring to the boil. Lower the heat and simmer, uncovered, for 5 minutes.

4 Cook over a low heat, stirring constantly, until the mixture becomes a thick custard. Cool, then chill. Just before serving, whip the cream. Transfer to individual bowls, top with the cream, chopped almonds and orange rind and serve. Toasted flaked almonds also go well with this.

Energy 433kcal/1792kJ; Protein 10.2g; Carbohydrate 7.8g, of which sugars 7.8g; Fat 40.5g, of which saturates 29g; Cholesterol 170mg; Calcium 168mg; Fibre 4.6g; Sodium 108mg

BUÑUELOS

THESE LOVELY LITTLE PUFFS LOOK LIKE MINIATURE DOUGHNUTS AND TASTE SO GOOD IT IS HARD NOT TO OVER-INDULGE. MAKE THEM FOR BRUNCH, OR SIMPLY SERVE THEM WITH A CUP OF CAFE CON LECHE OR CAFE DE OLLA.

MAKES TWELVE

INGREDIENTS
225g/8oz/2 cups plain (all-purpose)
    flour
pinch of salt
5ml/1 tsp baking powder
2.5ml/½ tsp ground anise
115g/4oz/½ cup caster (superfine)
    sugar
1 large egg
120ml/4fl oz/½ cup milk
50g/2oz/¼ cup butter
oil, for deep frying
10ml/2 tsp ground cinnamon
cinnamon sticks, to decorate

1 Sift the flour, salt, baking powder and ground anise into a mixing bowl. Add 30ml/2 tbsp of the caster sugar.

2 Place the egg and milk in a small jug (pitcher) and whisk well with a fork. Melt the butter in a small pan.

COOK'S TIP
Buñuelos are sometimes served with syrup for dunking, although they are perfectly delicious without. To make the syrup, mix 175g/6oz/¾ cup soft dark brown sugar and 450ml/¾ pint/scant 2 cups water in a small pan. Add a cinnamon stick and heat, stirring until the sugar has dissolved. Bring to the boil, then lower the heat and simmer for 15 minutes without stirring. Cool slightly before serving with the *buñuelos*.

3 Pour the egg mixture and milk gradually into the flour, stirring all the time, until well blended, then add the melted butter. Mix first with a wooden spoon and then with your hands to make a soft dough.

4 Lightly flour a work surface, tip out the dough on to it and knead for about 10 minutes, until smooth.

5 Divide the dough into 12 pieces and roll into balls. Slightly flatten each ball with your hand and then make a hole in the centre with the floured handle of a wooden spoon.

6 Heat the oil for deep frying to a temperature of 190°C/375°F, or until a cube of dried bread, added to the oil, floats and then turns a golden colour in 30–60 seconds. Fry the *buñuelos* in small batches until they are puffy and golden brown, turning them once or twice during cooking. As soon as they are golden, lift them out of the oil using a slotted spoon and lie them on a double layer of kitchen paper to drain.

7 Mix the remaining caster sugar with the ground cinnamon in a small bowl. Add the *buñuelos*, one at a time, while they are still warm, toss them in the mixture until they are lightly coated and either serve at once or leave to cool. Decorate with cinnamon sticks.

Energy 169kcal/715kJ; Protein 4g; Carbohydrate 34.1g, of which sugars 8.7g; Fat 2.8g, of which saturates 1.4g; Cholesterol 21mg; Calcium 63mg; Fibre 1g; Sodium 24mg

CAPIROTADA

*MEXICAN COOKS BELIEVE IN MAKING GOOD USE OF EVERYTHING AVAILABLE TO THEM. THIS PUDDING
WAS INVENTED AS A WAY OF USING UP FOOD BEFORE THE LENTEN FAST, BUT IS NOW EATEN AT OTHER
TIMES TOO.*

SERVES SIX

INGREDIENTS
1 small baguette, a few days old
75–115g/3–4oz/⅓–½ cup butter,
  softened, plus extra for greasing
200g/7oz/scant 1 cup soft dark
  brown sugar
1 cinnamon stick, about 15cm/
  6in long
400ml/14fl oz/1⅔ cups water
45ml/3 tbsp dry sherry
75g/3oz/¾ cup flaked (sliced)
  almonds, plus extra, to decorate
75g/3oz/½ cup raisins
115g/4oz/1 cup grated Monterey Jack
  or mild Cheddar cheese
single (light) cream, for pouring

1 Slice the bread into about 30 rounds,
each 1cm/½in thick. Lightly butter on
both sides. Cook in batches in a warm
frying pan until browned, turning over
once. Set the slices aside.

2 Place the sugar, cinnamon stick and
water in a pan. Heat gently, stirring all
the time, until the sugar has dissolved.
Bring to the boil, then lower the heat
and simmer for 15 minutes without
stirring. Remove the cinnamon stick,
then stir in the sherry.

COOK'S TIP
This recipe works well with older bread
that is quite dry. If you only have fresh
bread, slice it and dry it out for a few
minutes in a low oven.

3 Preheat the oven to 180°C/350°F/
Gas 4. Grease a 20cm/8in square
baking dish with butter. Layer the bread
rounds, almonds, raisins and cheese in
the dish, pour the syrup over, letting it
soak into the bread. Bake the pudding
for about 30 minutes until golden brown.

4 Remove from the oven, leave to stand
for 5 minutes, then cut into squares.
Serve cold, with single cream poured
over and decorated with the extra
flaked almonds.

DRUNKEN PLANTAIN

*MEXICANS ENJOY THEIR NATIVE FRUITS AND UNTIL THEIR CUISINE WAS INFLUENCED BY THE SPANISH
AND THE FRENCH, THEY HAD NO PASTRIES OR CAKES, PREFERRING TO END THEIR MEALS WITH FRUIT,
WHICH WAS ABUNDANT. THIS DESSERT IS QUICK AND EASY TO PREPARE, AND TASTES DELICIOUS.*

SERVES SIX

INGREDIENTS
3 ripe plantains
50g/2oz/¼ cup butter, diced
45ml/3 tbsp rum
grated rind and juice of
  1 small orange
5ml/1 tsp ground cinnamon
50g/2oz/¼ cup soft dark brown sugar
50g/2oz/½ cup whole almonds, in
  their skins
fresh mint sprigs, to decorate
Crème fraîche or thick double (heavy)
  cream, to serve

1 Preheat the oven to 180°C/350°F/
Gas 4. Peel the plantains and cut them
in half lengthways. Put the pieces in a
shallow baking dish, dot them all over
with butter, then spoon over the rum
and orange juice.

2 Mix the orange rind, cinnamon and
brown sugar in a bowl. Sprinkle the
mixture over the plantains.

3 Bake for 25–30 minutes, until the
plantains are soft and the sugar has
melted into the rum and orange juice
to form a sauce.

4 Meanwhile, slice the almonds and dry
fry them in a heavy-based frying pan
until the cut sides are golden. Serve the
plantains in individual bowls, with some
of the sauce spooned over. Sprinkle the
almonds on top, decorate with the fresh
mint sprigs and offer crème fraîche or
double cream separately.

Energy 498kcal/2085kJ; Protein 13.7g; Carbohydrate 47.7g, of which sugars 11.9g; Fat 28g, of which saturates 13.4g; Cholesterol 53mg; Calcium 256mg; Fibre 2.8g; Sodium 655mg
Energy 240kcal/1006kJ; Protein 2.8g; Carbohydrate 27.5g, of which sugars 15.4g; Fat 12.1g, of which saturates 4.8g; Cholesterol 18mg; Calcium 43mg; Fibre 1.7g; Sodium 55mg

FRUIT PLATTER

MEXICANS LIKE TO EAT FRUIT WITH CHILLI AND LIME AS AN APPETIZER OR HORS D'OEUVRE, BUT THE COMBINATION ALSO MAKES A REFRESHING END TO A MEAL. THE SELECTION OF FRUIT BELOW IS JUST A SUGGESTION; USE ANY FRUIT IN SEASON, BEARING IN MIND THAT THE AIM IS TO PRODUCE A COLOURFUL PLATTER WITH PLENTY OF FLAVOUR.

SERVES SIX

INGREDIENTS
½ small watermelon
2 mangoes
2 papayas
1 small pineapple
1 fresh coconut
1 jicama
juice of 2 limes, plus lime wedges,
   to serve
sea salt
mild red chilli powder

1 Slice the watermelon thinly, then cut each slice into bite-size triangles, removing as many of the seeds as possible. Take a large slice off the stone on either side of each mango, then cross-hatch the mango flesh on each slice. Turn the slices inside out so that the cubes of mango flesh stand proud. Slice these off and put them in a bowl.

2 Cut the payayas in half, scoop out the seeds, then cut each half into wedges, leaving the skin on. Cut the leafy green top off the pineapple, then slice off the base. With a sharp knife, remove the skin, using a spiral action and cutting deeply enough to remove most of the "eyes". Use a small knife to take out any remaining "eyes". Cut the pineapple lengthways in quarters and remove the core from the centre of each piece. Slice each of the pieces into bite-size wedges.

3 Make a hole in two of the "eyes" at the top of the coconut, using a nail and hammer. Pour out the liquid. Tap the coconut with a hammer until it breaks into pieces. Remove the hard outer shell, then use a potato peeler to remove the thin brown layer. Cut the coconut into neat pieces.

4 Peel and slice the jicama. Arrange all the fruits on a platter, sprinkle them with lime juice and serve with lime wedges and small bowls of sea salt and chilli powder for sprinkling.

COOK'S TIP
Cut all the fruit into bite-size pieces, so that it can be speared on cocktail sticks (toothpicks) and eaten.

ICE CREAM WITH MEXICAN CHOCOLATE

THIS RICH, CREAMY ICE CREAM HAS A WONDERFULLY COMPLEX FLAVOUR, THANKS TO THE CINNAMON AND ALMONDS IN THE MEXICAN CHOCOLATE.

SERVES FOUR

INGREDIENTS
2 large eggs
115g/4oz/½ cup caster (superfine)
   sugar
2 bars Mexican chocolate, total
   weight about 115g/4oz
400ml/14fl oz/1⅔ cups double
   (heavy) cream
200ml/7fl oz/scant 1 cup milk
chocolate curls, to decorate

1 Put the eggs in a bowl and whisk them with an electric whisk until they are thick, pale and fluffy. Gradually whisk in the sugar.

2 Melt the chocolate in a heavy-based pan over a low heat, then add it to the egg mixture and mix thoroughly. Whisk in the cream, then stir in the milk, a little at a time. Cool the mixture, then chill. Pour the mixture into an ice cream maker and churn until thick.

3 Alternatively freeze it in a shallow plastic box in the fast-freeze section of the freezer for several hours, until ice crystals have begun to form around the edges. Process to break up the ice crystals, then freeze again. To serve, decorate with chocolate curls.

Energy 232kcal/975kJ; Protein 2.6g; Carbohydrate 32.9g, of which sugars 32.8g; Fat 11g, of which saturates 9g; Cholesterol 0mg; Calcium 54mg; Fibre 7.4g; Sodium 15mg
Energy 710kcal/2949kJ; Protein 7.6g; Carbohydrate 43.2g, of which sugars 43g; Fat 57.6g, of which saturates 34.7g; Cholesterol 220mg; Calcium 137mg; Fibre 0.6g; Sodium 79mg

GARBANZO CAKE

THIS IS A MOIST CAKE, WITH A TEXTURE LIKE THAT OF CHRISTMAS PUDDING. IT IS FLAVOURED WITH ORANGE AND CINNAMON AND TASTES WONDERFUL IN THIN SLICES, WITH FRESH MANGO OR PINEAPPLE AND A SPOONFUL OF NATURAL YOGURT. AS IT CONTAINS NO FLOUR, IT IS A GOOD CHOICE FOR ANYONE ON A WHEAT-FREE DIET.

SERVES SIX

INGREDIENTS

   2 x 275g/10oz cans chickpeas,
     drained
   4 eggs, beaten
   225g/8oz/1 cup caster (superfine)
     sugar
   5ml/1 tsp baking powder
   10ml/2 tsp ground cinnamon
   grated rind and juice of 1 orange
   cinnamon sugar (see Cook's Tip),
     for sprinkling

COOK'S TIP

To make the cinnamon sugar, mix
50g/2oz/¼ cup caster sugar with 5ml/
1 tsp ground cinnamon.

1 Preheat the oven to 180°C/350°F/ Gas 4. Tip the chick-peas into a colander, drain them thoroughly, then rub them between the palms of your hands to loosen and remove the skins. Put the skinned chick-peas in a food processor and process until smooth.

2 Spoon the purée into a bowl and stir in the eggs, sugar, baking powder, cinnamon, orange rind and juice. Grease and line a 450g/1lb loaf tin.

3 Pour the cake mixture into the loaf tin, level the surface and bake for about 1½ hours or until a skewer inserted into the centre comes out clean.

4 Remove the cake from the oven and leave to stand, in the tin, for about 10 minutes. Remove from the tin, place on a wire rack and sprinkle with the cinnamon sugar. Leave to cool completely before serving. Try serving this with sliced fresh pineapple.

Energy 344kcal/1455kJ; Protein 14.1g; Carbohydrate 57.9g, of which sugars 39.1g; Fat 7.9g, of which saturates 1.6g; Cholesterol 152mg; Calcium 104mg; Fibre 5.3g; Sodium 323mg

PECAN CAKE

This cake is an example of the French influence on Mexican cooking. It is traditionally served with cajeta — sweetened boiled milk — but whipped cream or crème fraîche can be used instead. Try serving the cake with a few redcurrants for a splash of colour.

SERVES EIGHT TO TEN

INGREDIENTS
115g/4oz/1 cup pecan nuts
115g/4oz/½ cup butter, softened
115g/4oz/½ cup soft light
  brown sugar
5ml/1 tsp natural vanilla extract
4 large eggs, separated
75g/3oz/¾ cup plain (all-purpose)
  flour
pinch of salt
12 whole pecan nuts, to decorate
cajeta, whipped cream or crème
  fraîche, to serve
50g/2oz/¼ cup butter and 120ml/4fl
  oz/scant ½ cup honey, to drizzle

1 Preheat the oven to 180°C/350°F/Gas 4. Grease a 20cm/8in round spring-form cake tin (pan). Toast the pecan nuts in a dry frying pan for 5 minutes, shaking frequently. Grind finely into a blender or food processor. Place in a bowl.

2 Cream the butter with the sugar in a mixing bowl, then beat in the vanilla extract and egg yolks.

3 Add the flour to the ground nuts and mix well. Whisk the egg whites with the salt in a grease-free bowl until soft peaks form. Fold the whites into the butter mixture, then gently fold in the flour and nut mixture. Spoon the mixture into the prepared cake tin and bake for 30 minutes or until a skewer inserted in the centre comes out clean.

4 Cool the cake in the tin for 5 minutes, then remove the sides of the tin. Stand the cake on a wire rack until cold.

5 Remove the cake from the base of the tin if necessary, then return it to the rack and arrange the pecans on top. Transfer to a plate. Melt the butter in a small pan, add the honey and bring to the boil, stirring. Lower the heat and simmer for 3 minutes. Pour over the cake. Serve with *cajeta*, whipped cream or crème fraîche.

Energy 404kcal/1684kJ; Protein 5.9g; Carbohydrate 37g, of which sugars 23.5g; Fat 26.8g, of which saturates 9.5g; Cholesterol 108mg; Calcium 55mg; Fibre 1.4g; Sodium 122mg

KINGS' DAY BREAD

ON TWELFTH NIGHT, JANUARY 6TH, MEXICAN CHILDREN RECEIVE GIFTS TO MARK THE DAY THE THREE KINGS BROUGHT GIFTS TO THE INFANT JESUS. THIS SWEETENED RICH BREAD, DECORATED WITH CANDIED FRUIT, IS AN IMPORTANT PART OF THE CELEBRATIONS. A DOLL AND A BEAN ARE HIDDEN INSIDE THE CAKE, AND THE PERSON WHO GETS THE DOLL HAS TO HOST A PARTY ON FEBRUARY 2ND, ANOTHER FEAST DAY. THE PERSON WHO FINDS THE BEAN BRINGS THE DRINKS.

SERVES EIGHT

INGREDIENTS
   120ml/4fl oz/½ cup lukewarm water
   6 eggs
   10ml/2 tsp active dried yeast
   275g/10oz/2½ cups plain (all-
     purpose) flour
   2.5ml/½ tsp salt
   50g/2oz/¼ cup sugar
   115g/4oz/½ cup butter, plus 25g/1oz/
     2 tbsp melted butter, for glazing
   225g/8oz/1½ cups crystallized fruit
     and candied peel
   175g/6oz/1½ cups icing
     (confectioners') sugar, plus extra,
     for dusting
   30ml/2 tbsp single (light) cream
   crystallized fruit and glacé cherries,
     to decorate

1 Pour the water into a small bowl, stir in the dried yeast and leave in a warm place until frothy Crack four of the eggs and place the four yolks in a small bowl. Use the whites in another recipe.

2 Put 150g/5oz/1¼ cups of the flour in a mixing bowl. Add the salt and sugar. Break the remaining two eggs into the bowl, then add the four egg yolks.

3 Add 115g/4oz/½ cup of the butter to the bowl together with the yeast and water mixture. Mix all the ingredients together well.

4 Put the crystallized fruit and peel into a separate bowl. Add 50g/2oz/½ cup of the remaining flour and toss the fruit with the flour to coat it.

5 Add the floured fruit to the egg mixture, with the rest of the flour. Mix to a soft, non-sticky dough. Knead the dough on a lightly floured surface for about 10 minutes, until smooth.

6 Shape the dough into a ball. Using the floured handle of a wooden spoon, make a hole in the centre, and enlarge.

7 Put the dough ring onto a greased baking sheet and cover with oiled clear film (plastic wrap). Leave in a warm place for about 2 hours or until doubled in bulk.

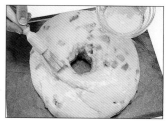

8 Preheat the oven to 180°C/350°F/ Gas 4. Brush the dough with the melted butter and bake for about 30 minutes or until it has risen well and is cooked through and springy.

9 Mix the icing sugar and cream in a bowl. Drizzle the mixture over the bread when it is cool and decorate it with the crystallized fruit and glacé cherries. Dust with icing sugar.

Energy 468kcal/1978kJ; Protein 9.5g; Carbohydrate 84g, of which sugars 48.3g; Fat 12.9g, of which saturates 6.3g; Cholesterol 163mg; Calcium 141mg; Fibre 2.7g; Sodium 180mg

PAN DULCE

THESE "SWEET BREADS" OF VARIOUS SHAPES ARE MADE THROUGHOUT MEXICO, AND ARE EATEN AS A SNACK OR WITH JAM OR MARMALADE FOR BREAKFAST.

MAKES TWELVE

INGREDIENTS
120ml/4fl oz/½ cup lukewarm milk
10ml/2 tsp active dried yeast
450g/1lb/4 cups strong bread flour
75g/3oz/6 tbsp caster (superfine) sugar
25g/1oz/2 tbsp butter, softened
4 large eggs, beaten
For the topping
75g/3oz/6 tbsp butter, softened
115g/4oz/½ cup sugar
1 egg yolk
5ml/1 tsp ground cinnamon
115g/4oz/1 cup plain (all-purpose) flour

1 Pour the milk into a small bowl, stir in the dried yeast and leave in a warm place until frothy.

2 Put the flour and sugar in a mixing bowl. Add the yeast mixture, butter and beaten eggs and mix to a sticky dough.

3 Place the dough on a lightly floured surface and dredge it with more flour. Using floured hands, turn the dough over and over until it is completely covered in a light coating of flour. Cover it with lightly oiled clear film (plastic wrap) and leave to rest for 20 minutes.

4 Meanwhile, make the topping. Cream the butter and sugar in a bowl, then mix in the egg yolk, cinnamon and flour. The mixture should have a slightly crumbly texture.

5 Divide the dough into 12 equal pieces and shape each of them into a round. Space well apart on greased baking sheets. Sprinkle the topping over the breads, dividing it more or less equally among them, then press it lightly into the surface.

6 Leave the rolls in a warm place to stand for about 30 minutes until they are about one and a half times their previous size. Preheat the oven to 200°C/400°F/Gas 6 and bake the breads for about 15 minutes. Allow to cool slightly before serving.

Energy 358kcal/1510kJ; Protein 6.5g; Carbohydrate 65.2g, of which sugars 17.6g; Fat 9.6g, of which saturates 5.6g; Cholesterol 39mg; Calcium 110mg; Fibre 1.9g; Sodium 68mg

ALMOND BISCUITS

ICING SUGAR AND BUTTER COMBINE TO GIVE THESE BISCUITS A LIGHT, DELICATE TEXTURE. THEY CAN BE MADE DAYS AHEAD, AND ARE DELICIOUS WITH DESSERTS OR COFFEE.

2 Put the softened butter in the centre of the flour mixture and use a knife or your fingertips to draw the dry ingredients into the butter until a dough is formed. Shape the dough into a ball.

3 Place the dough on a lightly floured surface and roll it out to a thickness of about 3mm/⅛in. Using a 7.5cm/3in cookie cutter, cut out about 24 rounds, re-rolling the dough as necessary. Place the rounds on baking sheets, leaving a little space between them. Bake for 25–30 minutes until pale golden.

4 Leave for 10 minutes, then transfer to wire racks to cool. Dust thickly with icing sugar before serving, decorated with halved almonds.

MAKES ABOUT TWENTY-FOUR

INGREDIENTS
    115g/4oz/1 cup plain (all-purpose) flour
    175g/6oz/1½ cups icing (confectioners') sugar, plus extra for dusting
    pinch of salt
    50g/2oz/½ cup chopped almonds
    2.5ml/½ tsp almond extract
    115g/4oz/½ cup butter, softened
    halved almonds, to decorate

COOK'S TIPS
Use cookie cutters if you wish. Hearts and crescents are two shapes you might like to try.

1 Preheat the oven to 180°C/350°F/ Gas 4. Combine the flour, icing sugar, salt and chopped almonds in a bowl. Add the almond extract.

Energy 115kcal/481kJ; Protein 1.5g; Carbohydrate 15g, of which sugars 10.1g; Fat 5.8g, of which saturates 2.4g; Cholesterol 9mg; Calcium 24mg; Fibre 0.5g; Sodium 27mg

MEXICAN WEDDING COOKIES

ALMOST HIDDEN BENEATH THEIR VEIL OF ICING SUGAR, THESE LITTLE SHORTBREAD COOKIES ARE TRADITIONALLY SERVED AT WEDDINGS, AND ARE ABSOLUTELY DELICIOUS. SERVE THEM AFTER DINNER WITH COFFEE AND PERHAPS A GLASS OF THE MEXICAN COFFEE LIQUEUR — KAHLÚA.

MAKES THIRTY

INGREDIENTS
225g/8oz/1 cup butter, softened
175g/6oz/1½ cups icing
   (confectioners') sugar
5ml/1 tsp natural vanilla extract
300g/11oz/2¾ cups plain
   (all-purpose) flour
pinch of salt
150g/5oz/1¼ cups pecan nuts, chopped

1 Preheat the oven to 190°C/375°F/ Gas 5. Beat the butter in a bowl until light and fluffy, then beat in 115g 4oz/ 1 cup icing sugar and vanilla extract.

2 Gradually add the flour and salt to the creamed mixture until it starts to form a dough. Add the finely chopped pecans with the remaining flour. Knead the dough lightly.

3 Divide the dough into 30 equal pieces and roll them into balls. Space about 5mm/¼in apart on baking sheets. Press each ball lightly with your thumb, to flatten it slightly.

4 Bake the cookies for 10–15 minutes until they are starting to brown. Cool on the baking sheets for 10 minutes, then transfer to wire racks to cool completely.

5 Put the remaining icing sugar in a bowl. Add a few cookies at a time, shaking them in the icing sugar until they are heavily coated. Serve straight-away or store in an airtight tin.

ALMOND ORANGE BISCUITS

THE COMBINATION OF LARD AND ALMONDS GIVES THESE BISCUITS A LOVELY SHORT TEXTURE, SO THAT THEY MELT IN THE MOUTH. THEY ARE PERFECT WITH COFFEE OR HOT CHOCOLATE.

MAKES THIRTY-SIX

INGREDIENTS
250g/9oz/generous 1 cup lard
125g/4½oz/generous ½ cup
   caster (superfine) sugar
2 eggs, beaten
grated rind and juice of
   1 small orange
300g/11oz/1¾ cups plain
   (all-purpose) flour, sifted with
   5ml/1 tsp baking powder
200g/7oz/1¾ cups ground almonds
For dusting
50g/2oz/½ cup icing (confectioners')
   sugar
5ml/1 tsp ground cinnamon

COOK'S TIP
If you can't be bothered to roll out the dough, just divide it into 36 pieces and roll each one into a ball. Place these on baking sheets and flatten each one into a biscuit (cookie) shape with a fork.

1 Preheat the oven to 200°C/400°F/ Gas 6. Place the lard in a large bowl and beat with an electric whisk until light and aerated. Gradually beat in the caster sugar.

2 Continue to whisk the mixture while you add the eggs, orange rind and juice. Whisk for 3–4 minutes more, then stir in the flour mixture and ground almonds to form a dough.

3 Roll out the dough on a lightly floured surface until it is about 1cm/½in thick. Using cookie cutters, cut out 36 rounds, re-rolling the dough if necessary. Gently lift the rounds on to baking sheets.

4 Bake for about 10 minutes, or until the biscuits are golden. Leave to stand on the baking sheets for 10 minutes to cool and firm slightly.

5 Mix together the icing sugar and cinnamon. Put the mixture in a small sieve or strainer and dust the biscuits well. Leave to cool completely.

Energy 117kcal/490kJ; Protein 1.5g; Carbohydrate 16.9g, of which sugars 7.3g; Fat 5.2g, of which saturates 2g; Cholesterol 7mg; Calcium 24mg; Fibre 0.5g; Sodium 21mg
Energy 131kcal/546kJ; Protein 2.3g; Carbohydrate 9.5g, of which sugars 3.5g; Fat 9.6g, of which saturates 2.9g; Cholesterol 16mg; Calcium 28mg; Fibre 0.7g; Sodium 5mg

FRUIT-FILLED EMPANADAS

IMAGINE BITING THROUGH CRISP BUTTERY PASTRY TO DISCOVER A RICH FRUITY FILLING FLAVOURED WITH ORANGES AND CINNAMON. THESE ARE THE STUFF THAT DREAMS ARE MADE OF.

MAKES TWELVE

INGREDIENTS
  275g/10oz/2½ cups plain (all-
    purpose) flour
  25g/1oz/2 tbsp caster (superfine)
    sugar, plust extra for sprinkling
  90g/3½oz/scant ½ cup chilled
    butter, cubed
  1 egg yolk
  milk, to glaze
  whole almonds and orange wedges,
    to serve
For the filling
  25g/1oz/2 tbsp butter
  3 ripe plantains, peeled and mashed
  2.5ml/½ tsp ground cloves
  5ml/1 tsp ground cinnamon
  225g/8oz/1⅓ cups raisins
  grated rind and juice of 2 oranges

1 Combine the flour and sugar in a mixing bowl. Rub in the chilled cubes of butter until the mixture resembles fine breadcrumbs.

2 Beat the egg yolk and add to the flour mixture. Add iced water to make a smooth dough. Shape it into a ball.

3 Melt the butter for the filling in a pan. Add the plantains, cloves and cinnamon and cook over a moderate heat for 2–3 minutes. Stir in the raisins, with the orange rind and juice. Lower the heat so that the mixture barely simmers. Cook for about 15 minutes, until the raisins are plump and the juice has evaporated. Set the mixture aside to cool.

4 Preheat the oven to 200°C/400°F/ Gas 6. Roll out the pastry on a lightly floured surface. Cut it into 10cm/4in rounds. Place the rounds on a baking sheet and spoon on a little of the filling. Dampen the rim of the pastry rounds with water, fold the pastry over the filling and crimp the edges to seal.

5 Brush the empanadas with milk. Bake them, in batches if necessary, for about 15 minutes or until they are golden. Allow to cool a little, sprinkle with caster sugar and serve warm, with whole almonds and orange wedges.

COOK'S TIP
Use a little of the leftover egg white instead of milk for glazing, if you like.

Energy 276kcal/1161kJ; Protein 4g; Carbohydrate 45.4g, of which sugars 15.7g; Fat 9.9g, of which saturates 5.9g; Cholesterol 40mg; Calcium 59mg; Fibre 1.7g; Sodium 80mg

CHRISTMAS COOKIES WITH WALNUTS

AT CHRISTMAS TIME, THESE ARE INDIVIDUALLY WRAPPED IN SMALL SQUARES OF BRIGHTLY COLOURED TISSUE PAPER AND ARRANGED IN LARGE BOWLS. FOLLOW THE MEXICANS' LEAD, AND TRANSFORM THEM INTO GIFTS BY WRAPPING FIVE OR SIX AT A TIME IN CELLOPHANE AND TYING THE PACKAGES WITH COLOURED RIBBONS.

MAKES TWENTY-FOUR

INGREDIENTS
115g/4oz/½ cup lard, softened and diced
75g/3oz/¾ cup icing (confectioners') sugar
5ml/1 tsp vanilla extract
150g/5oz/1¼ cups unbleached plain (all-purpose) flour
75g/3oz/¾ cup walnuts, chopped
50g/2oz/½ cup icing sugar
10ml/2 tsp ground cinnamon

COOK'S TIP
Polvo means "dust", and these cookies should be crumbly and light to eat. Pecan nuts can be used instead of the walnuts, if you like.

1 Preheat the oven to 190°C/375°F/ Gas 5. Place the lard in a large bowl and beat with an electric whisk until light and aerated.

2 Gradually beat in 25g/1oz/¼ cup of the icing sugar, then add the vanilla extract and beat well.

3 Add the flour by hand, working it gently into the mixture. Do not be tempted to use a spoon or the mixture will be too sticky. Add the walnuts and mix carefully.

4 Divide the dough evenly into 24 small pieces, roll each to a ball, and space well apart on baking sheets. Bake for 10–15 minutes, until golden, switching the baking sheets around halfway through, to ensure even baking. Cool the cookies on wire racks.

5 Put the remaining icing sugar in a bowl and stir in the cinnamon. Add a few cookies at a time, shaking them in the icing sugar until they are heavily coated. Shake off the excess sugar. Serve wrapped in coloured paper.

Energy 141kcal/591kJ; Protein 1.7g; Carbohydrate 15.4g, of which sugars 9g; Fat 8.5g, of which saturates 2g; Cholesterol 4mg; Calcium 22mg; Fibre 0.5g; Sodium 1mg.

DRINKS

Mexicans have some marvellous means of slaking thirst, from refreshing fruit
drinks to rich, satisfying hot chocolate. The traditional drink – pulque – which is
made from the pressed juice of the century plant, is very much an acquired
taste, but tequila has become popular the world over, either enjoyed neat,
in the traditional way, or as the basis for some wonderful cocktails,
such as margaritas and bloody Marias.

Fruity agua frescas, sold from stalls by street traders throughout
Mexico, are the perfect antidote to hot weather. Like licuados and
preparados, they are simple and quick to prepare and make a welcome
change from the ultra-sweet fizzy drinks that are so popular in
Europe. A jug (pitcher) of Lime Agua Fresca is the
perfect way to welcome guests on a warm summer's evening.

Mexican chocolate typically contains almonds and
cinnamon, two ingredients that are widely used in Mexican
cooking, and the milky hot chocolate drinks are absolutely
delicious. Corn-based drinks and coffee laced with cinnamon
are enjoyed with meals or served as substitutes for snacks.

Rompope, the thick, creamy Mexican eggnog, tastes much more
innocent than it should, and provides a wonderful way to unwind at the
end of a stressful day.

TEQUILA

THERE ARE SEVERAL DIFFERENT TYPES OF TEQUILA, MEXICO'S NATIONAL SPIRIT. EACH TYPE OF TEQUILA IS AVAILABLE IN SEVERAL DIFFERENT BRANDS, EACH WITH A DISTINCTIVE FLAVOUR INFLUENCED BY THE SOIL TYPE, SUGAR CONTENT OF THE AGAVE PLANTS, CLIMATE, COOKING AND FERMENTING PROCESS.

There are many different ways of serving tequila. Perhaps the best known of these is the slammer, when shots of chilled tequila are drunk with salt and lime. *Joven* (young) or *reposada* (rested) tequila is often served at room temperature in small shot glasses called *caballitos*, and sipped slowly so that all the flavours can be savoured. *Anejo* (aged) tequila should be served in a small balloon glass (a large glass would allow too much of the aroma to escape). It can be diluted with a little water, but ice should not be added.

TEQUILA SLAMMERS
Mexicans have long enjoyed the taste of lime and salt with their food and drink. Beer is also taken with lime and salt.

INGREDIENTS
  chilled tequila
  salt
  wedges of lime

HOW TO SERVE TEQUILA
Pour a shot glass of tequila. Lick the space between the thumb and the index finger on your left hand, then sprinkle this area with salt. Taking care not to spill the salt, hold a lime wedge in the same hand. Pick up the shot glass in your right hand. Lick the salt, down the tequila in one, suck the lime, then slam down your empty glass. Some drinkers manage salt, lime and tequila in the same hand, but this takes practice.

Energy 111kcal/460kJ; Protein 0g; Carbohydrate 0g, of which sugars 0g; Fat 0g, of which saturates 0g; Cholesterol 0mg; Calcium 0mg; Fibre 0g; Sodium 0mg

TEQUILA SUNRISE

THIS DRINK TAKES ITS NAME FROM THE WAY THE GRENADINE — A BRIGHT RED CORDIAL MADE FROM POMEGRANATE JUICE — FIRST SINKS IN THE GLASS OF ORANGE JUICE AND THEN RISES TO THE SURFACE.

SERVES ONE

INGREDIENTS

25ml/1½ tbsp golden tequila
60ml/4 tbsp freshly squeezed
  orange juice
juice of 1 lime
5ml/1 tsp grenadine

VARIATION

To make a Pink Cadillac, use Grand Marnier instead of orange juice.

1 Half fill a cocktail glass with crushed ice. Pour in the tequila, then the orange and lime juices, which should be freshly squeezed. Don't be tempted to use concentrated orange juice from a carton or bottled lime juice, or the flavour of the finished drink will be spoiled.

2 Quickly add the grenadine, pouring it down the back of a teaspoon held in the glass so that it sinks to the bottom of the drink. Serve immediately.

Energy 88kcal/369kJ; Protein 0.3g; Carbohydrate 6.5g, of which sugars 6.5g; Fat 0.1g, of which saturates 0g; Cholesterol 0mg; Calcium 6mg; Fibre 0.1g; Sodium 6mg

PINEAPPLE TEQUILA

FLAVOURS SUCH AS ALMONDS OR QUINCE HAVE BEEN ADDED TO BLANCO OR REPOSADA TEQUILA FOR SOME TIME. MANY BARS HAVE DEVELOPED UNIQUE FLAVOURS BY COMBINING INGREDIENTS SUCH AS CHILLIES WITH BLANCO TEQUILA AND LEAVING THEM FOR A PERIOD OF TIME. THE METHOD BELOW WILL MAKE A SMOOTH FRUITY DRINK.

<u>SERVES SIX</u>

INGREDIENTS
  1 large pineapple
  50g/2oz soft dark brown sugar
  1 litre blanco tequila
  1 vanilla pod (bean)

1 Rinse a large (about 2 litre/3½ pint) wide-necked bottle or demijohn and sterilize by placing it in an oven and then turning on the oven and setting it at 110°C/225°F/Gas ¼. After 20 minutes remove the bottle from the oven with oven gloves and allow to cool.

2 Cut the top off the pineapple and then cut away the skin, being careful to get rid of all the scales. Cut in half, remove the hard centre core and discard it. Chop the rest of the pineapple into chunks, ensuring they are small enough to fit in the bottle neck.

3 When the bottle is completely cold, put the pineapple into the bottle. Mix the sugar and tequila together in a jug (pitcher) until the sugar dissolves and then pour into the bottle. Split the vanilla pod and add it to the rest of the ingredients.

4 Gently agitate the bottle a few times each day to stir the contents. Allow the tequila to stand for at least 1 week before drinking. When all the tequila has been drunk the pineapple can be used in desserts such as ice cream or warmed with butter and cinnamon and served with cream.

VARIATION
If you like, add a piece of fresh pineapple and some ice to each glass before serving.

Energy 406kcal/1686kJ; Protein 0.1g; Carbohydrate 9.6g, of which sugars 9.6g; Fat 0g, of which saturates 0g; Cholesterol 0mg; Calcium 5mg; Fibre 0g; Sodium 1mg

MARGARITA

THE MOST RENOWNED TEQUILA COCKTAIL, THIS CAN BE SERVED OVER ICE CUBES OR "FROZEN" —
MIXED WITH CRUSHED ICE IN A COCKTAIL SHAKER TO CREATE A LIQUID SORBET EFFECT,
THEN POURED INTO THE GLASS.

SERVES ONE

INGREDIENTS
   45ml/3 tbsp tequila
   25ml/1½ tbsp triple sec
   25ml/1½ tbsp freshly squeezed
      lime juice
   crushed ice or ice cubes
   lime wedge and salt, for
      frosting glass

COOK'S TIP
White tequila is the traditional spirit to
use, but today many people prefer to
make margaritas with reposada tequila,
which gives a more rounded flavour.

1 Frost a cocktail glass by rubbing the
outer rim with the wedge of lime. Dip
the glass in a saucer of salt so that it is
evenly coated. It is important that there
is no salt inside the glass, so take care
that lime juice is only applied to the
outer rim.

2 Combine the tequila, triple sec and
lime juice in a cocktail shaker, add
crushed ice, if using, and shake to mix.
Carefully pour into the frosted glasses.
If crushed ice is not used, place ice
cubes in the glass and then pour the
mixture over.

Energy 160kcal/668kJ; Protein 0.1g; Carbohydrate 7.7g, of which sugars 7.7g; Fat 0g, of which saturates 0g; Cholesterol 0mg; Calcium 3mg; Fibre 0g; Sodium 3mg

MANGO AND PEACH MARGARITA

ADDING PURÉED FRUIT TO THE CLASSIC TEQUILA MIXTURE ALTERS THE CONSISTENCY AND MAKES FOR A GLORIOUS DRINK WHICH RESEMBLES A MILKSHAKE BUT PACKS CONSIDERABLY MORE PUNCH.

SERVES FOUR

INGREDIENTS
   2 mangoes, peeled and sliced
   3 peaches, peeled and sliced
   120ml/4fl oz/½ cup tequila
   60ml/4 tbsp triple sec
   60ml/4 tbsp freshly squeezed
      lime juice
   10 ice cubes, crushed, if necessary
      (see Cook's Tip)
   mango slices, skin on, to decorate

COOK'S TIP
Check that your processor or blender can be used for crushing ice. If you are not sure, break ice cubes into smaller pieces by putting them in a strong plastic bag and pounding them with a meat mallet.

1 Place the mango and peach slices in a food processor or blender. Process or blend until all the fruit is finely chopped, scrape down the sides of the goblet, then blend again until the purée is perfectly smooth.

2 Add the tequila, triple sec and lime juice, process or blend for a few seconds, then add the ice. Process or blend again until the drink has the consistency of a milkshake.

3 Pour into cocktail glasses, decorate with the mango slices and serve.

Margarita Energy 179kcal/754kJ; Protein 1.1g; Carbohydrate 19.1g, of which sugars 18.9g; Fat 0.2g, of which saturates 0.1g; Cholesterol 0mg; Calcium 13mg; Fibre 2.7g; Sodium 4mg

LICUADO DE MELON

AMONG THE MOST REFRESHING DRINKS MEXICANS MAKE ARE FRUIT EXTRACTS MIXED WITH HONEY AND CHILLED WATER.

SERVES FOUR

INGREDIENTS
1 watermelon
1 litre/1¾ pints/4 cups chilled water
juice of 2 limes
honey (see method)
ice cubes, to serve

1 Cut the watermelon flesh into chunks, cutting away the skin and discarding the shiny black seeds.

2 Place the chunks in a large bowl, pour over the chilled water and leave to stand for 10 minutes.

3 Tip the mixture into a large sieve (strainer) set over a bowl. Using a wooden spoon, press gently on the fruit to extract all the liquid.

4 Stir in the lime juice and sweeten to taste with honey.

5 Pour into a jug (pitcher), add ice cubes and stir. Serve in tumblers.

Energy 35kcal/155kJ; Protein 2g; Carbohydrate 7.5g, of which sugars 7.5g; Fat 0g, of which saturates 0g; Cholesterol 0mg; Calcium 25mg; Fibre 1.5g; Sodium 575mg.

SANGRITA

Sipping sangrita and tequila alternately is a taste sensation not to be missed, the warm flavours of the first balancing the harshness of the second. The drinks are often served with Antojitos (nibbles) as an appetizer.

SERVES EIGHT

INGREDIENTS
450g/1lb ripe tomatoes
1 small onion, finely chopped
2 small fresh green fresno chillies, seeded and chopped
120ml/4fl oz/½ cup juice from freshly squeezed oranges
juice of 3 limes
2.5ml/½ tsp caster (superfine) sugar
pinch of salt
1 small shot glass of golden or aged tequila per person

1 Cut a cross in the base of each tomato. Place the tomatoes in a heatproof bowl and pour over boiling water to cover. Leave for 3 minutes.

2 Lift the tomatoes out on a slotted spoon and plunge them into a second bowl of cold water. The skins will have begun to peel back from the crosses. Remove the skins, then cut the tomatoes in half and scoop out the seeds with a teaspoon.

3 Chop the tomato flesh and put in a food processor. Add the onion, chillies, orange juice, lime juice, sugar and salt.

4 Process until all the mixture is very smooth, then pour into a jug (pitcher) and chill for at least 1 hour before serving. Offer each drinker a separate shot glass of tequila as well. The drinks are sipped alternately.

COOK'S TIP
This drink can be made with a 400g/14oz can of chopped tomatoes and tastes almost as good as when made with fresh tomatoes.

SANGRIA

Testament to the Spanish influence on Mexican cooking, this popular thirst-quencher is often served in large jugs (pitchers), with ice and citrus fruit slices floating on top.

SERVES SIX

INGREDIENTS
750ml/1¼ pints/3 cups light red wine
juice of 2 limes
120ml/4fl oz/½ cup freshly squeezed orange juice
120ml/4fl oz/½ cup brandy
50g/2oz/¼ cup caster (superfine) sugar
1 lime, sliced, to decorate
ice, to serve

VARIATION
In some parts of Mexico a less potent version of sangria is served. Fill tall glasses with ice, fill two-thirds full with fresh lime juice diluted with water. Top up with red wine and sweeten to taste.

1 Combine the wine, lime juice, orange juice and brandy in a large jug (pitcher).

COOK'S TIP
To make a convenient sugar syrup for sweetening drinks, heat 50g/2oz/¼ cup granulated sugar in 50ml/2fl oz/¼ cup water. Boil for 3 minutes, chill and store in a tightly sealed jar.

2 Stir in the sugar until it has dissolved completely.

3 Serve in tall glasses with ice. Decorate each glass with a slice of lime.

Energy 72kcal/302kJ; Protein 0.5g; Carbohydrate 3.6g, of which sugars 3.4g; Fat 0.2g, of which saturates 0.1g; Cholesterol 0mg; Calcium 7mg; Fibre 0.6g; Sodium 6mg
Energy 144kcal/602kJ; Protein 0.2g; Carbohydrate 10.4g, of which sugars 10.4g; Fat 0g, of which saturates 0g; Cholesterol 0mg; Calcium 13mg; Fibre 0g; Sodium 9mg

CITRUS AGUA FRESCA

THESE REFRESHING FRUIT JUICES ARE SOLD FROM STREET STALLS IN TOWNS ALL OVER MEXICO. THE VARIETIES OF FRUIT USED CHANGE WITH THE SEASONS.

SERVES FOUR

INGREDIENTS
  12 limes
  3 oranges
  2 grapefruit
  600ml/1 pint/2½ cups water
  75g/3oz/6 tbsp caster (superfine)
  sugar
  fruit wedges and ice cubes, to serve

1 Squeeze the juice from the limes, oranges and grapefruit. Some fruit pulp may collect along with the juice. This should also be used, once any seeds have been discarded. Pour the mixture into a large jug (pitcher).

2 Add the water and sugar and stir until all the sugar has dissolved.

3 Chill for at least 1 hour before serving with ice and fruit wedges. The drink will keep for up to 1 week in a covered container in the refrigerator.

VARIATION
Use pink or ruby red grapefruit instead of white for a slightly sweeter drink with a deeper colour.

Energy 119kcal/506kJ; Protein 0.5g; Carbohydrate 31g, of which sugars 31g; Fat 0.1g, of which saturates 0g; Cholesterol 0mg; Calcium 23mg; Fibre 0g; Sodium 9mg

TAMARIND AGUA FRESCA

TAMARIND, SOMETIMES REFERRED TO AS THE INDIAN DATE, IS NATIVE TO ASIA AND NORTH AFRICA. SEEDS CAME TO MEXICO VIA INDIA. IT IS USED MEDICINALLY AND AS AN ANTISEPTIC. THE FRUIT HAS A SWEET-SOUR TASTE AND MAKES A DRINK SIMILAR TO LEMONADE.

SERVES FOUR

INGREDIENTS

1 litre/1¾ pints/4 cups water
225g/8oz tamarind pods
30ml/2 tbsp caster (superfine) sugar
ice cubes, to serve

COOK'S TIP
Jars of tamarind pulp or paste are sold at Indian food shops and Oriental stores. The dried pulp is also sold in solid blocks. All these products need soaking and straining, but you will be spared the time-consuming task of peeling the pods.

1 Pour the water into a pan and heat until warm. Remove from the heat and pour into a bowl. Peel the tamarind pods and add the pulp to the warm water. Soak for at least 4 hours.

2 Place a sieve (strainer) over a clean bowl. Pour the tamarind pulp and water into the sieve, then press the pulp through the sieve with the back of a wooden spoon, leaving the black seeds behind. Discard the seeds.

3 Add the sugar to the tamarind mixture and stir well until dissolved. Pour into a jug (pitcher) and chill thoroughly before serving in tumblers filled with ice.

Energy 61kcal/259kJ; Protein 0.4g; Carbohydrate 15.7g, of which sugars 15.7g; Fat 0g, of which saturates 0g; Cholesterol 0mg; Calcium 10mg; Fibre 0.5g; Sodium 2mg

PINEAPPLE AND LIME AGUA FRESCA

THE VIVID COLOURS OF THIS FRESH FRUIT DRINK GIVE SOME INDICATION OF ITS WONDERFUL
FLAVOUR. IT MAKES A DELICIOUS MIDDAY REFRESHER OR PICK-ME-UP AT THE END OF A HARD DAY.

SERVES FOUR

INGREDIENTS
  2 pineapples
  juice of 2 limes
  475ml/16fl oz/2 cups still
    mineral water
  50g/2oz/¼ cup caster (superfine)
    sugar
  ice cubes, to serve

COOK'S TIP
When peeling a pineapple cut off the top
and bottom and remove the skin with a
spiral action, cutting deeply enough to
remove most of the "eyes". Any
remaining "eyes" can be cut out using
a small knife.

1 Peel the pineapples and chop the
flesh, removing the core and "eyes".
You should have about 450g/1lb flesh.
Put this in a food processor or blender
and add the lime juice and half the
mineral water. Purée to a smooth pulp.
Stop the machine and scrape the
mixture from the side of the goblet
once or twice during processing.

2 Place a sieve (strainer) over a large
bowl. Tip the pineapple pulp into the
sieve and press it through with a
wooden spoon. Pour the sieved mixture
into a large jug (pitcher), cover and chill
in the refrigerator for about 1 hour.

3 Stir in the remaining mineral water
and sugar to taste. Serve with ice.

Energy 125kcal/537kJ; Protein 0.5g; Carbohydrate 32.7g, of which sugars 32.7g; Fat 0.1g, of which saturates 0g; Cholesterol 0mg; Calcium 20mg; Fibre 0g; Sodium 11mg

LIME AGUA FRESCA

THIS IS THE LIME VERSION OF REAL ENGLISH LEMONADE. TRADITIONALLY, LIME PEEL WOULD HAVE BEEN GROUND IN A MOLCAJETE TO EXTRACT THE OIL. MEXICAN LIMES — LIMONES — ARE HARDER AND MORE TART THAN THE SMOOTH-SKINNED VARIETIES MOST OFTEN SOLD IN WESTERN SUPERMARKETS.

SERVES TWO

INGREDIENTS
    600ml/1 pint/2½ cups water
    30ml/2 tbsp caster (superfine) sugar
    4 limes
    ice cubes, to serve

1 Pour the water into a large jug (pitcher), add the sugar and stir until all the sugar has dissolved. Chill for at least 1 hour.

2 Using a zester or grater, remove the rind from the limes, taking care to take only the coloured zest, not the pith. Squeeze the juice from the limes and add this to the chilled sugar water, with the lime rind. Stir well and chill again until required. Serve with ice in tall glasses, decorated with lime slices.

COOK'S TIP
To extract the maximum amount of juice from the limes, roll firmly between your palms for a few moments, or pierce with a skewer, put in a bowl, and microwave on maximum power for 10–15 seconds before juicing. This works with all citrus fruits.

Energy 62kcal/263kJ; Protein 0.2g; Carbohydrate 16.2g, of which sugars 16.2g; Fat 0g, of which saturates 0g; Cholesterol 0mg; Calcium 10mg; Fibre 0g; Sodium 1mg

STRAWBERRY <u>AND</u> BANANA PREPARADO

SIMILAR TO A SMOOTHIE, THIS IS A THICK, CREAMY FRUIT DRINK. LEAVE OUT THE ALCOHOL IF YOU PREFER.

SERVES FOUR

INGREDIENTS
   200g/7oz/2 cups strawberries, plus
     extra, to decorate
   2 bananas
   115g/4oz block of creamed coconut
   120ml/4fl oz/½ cup water
   175ml/6fl oz/¾ cup white rum
   60ml/4 tbsp grenadine
   10 ice cubes

1 Hull the strawberries and chop them in halves or quarters if they are large fruits. Peel the bananas and chop them into rough chunks.

2 Put the fruit in a food processor or blender, crumble in the coconut and add the water. Process until smooth, scraping down the sides of the goblet as necessary.

3 Add the rum, grenadine, and ice cubes, crushing the ice first unless you have a heavy-duty processor. Blend until smooth and thick. Serve at once, decorated with the extra strawberries.

Energy 211kcal/883kJ; Protein 1.5g; Carbohydrate 23.2g, of which sugars 22g; Fat 0.4g, of which saturates 0.1g; Cholesterol 0mg; Calcium 28mg; Fibre 1.7g; Sodium 41mg

BLOODY MARIA

A NATURAL PROGRESSION FROM SANGRITA, THIS SIMPLE COCKTAIL CONSISTS OF TEQUILA AND TOMATO JUICE MIXED TOGETHER AND SERVED IN THE SAME GLASS.

SERVES TWO

INGREDIENTS

250ml/8fl oz/1 cup tomato
  juice, chilled
5ml/1 tsp Worcestershire sauce
60ml/4 tbsp tequila
few drops of Tabasco sauce
juice of ½ lemon
pinch of celery salt
salt and ground black pepper
ice cubes and 2 celery sticks, cut
  into batons, to serve

1 Pour the chilled tomato juice into a large jug (pticher) and stir in the tequila. Add the Worcestershire sauce and stir the mixture well.

2 Add a few drops of Tabasco sauce and the lemon juice. Taste and season with celery salt, salt and pepper. Serve over ice cubes, with celery batons.

Energy 82kcal/345kJ; Protein 0.9g; Carbohydrate 3.4g, of which sugars 3.4g; Fat 0g, of which saturates 0g; Cholesterol 0mg; Calcium 15mg; Fibre 0.6g; Sodium 260mg

CAFE CON LECHE

MANY MEXICANS START THE DAY WITH THIS SPICED MILKY COFFEE, AND THOSE WHO HAVE ENJOYED A HEARTY MIDDAY MEAL WILL OFTEN OPT FOR A CUP OF IT WITH A PASTRY AS THE AFTERNOON MERIENDA.

SERVES FOUR

INGREDIENTS
50g/2oz/⅔ cup ground coffee
475ml/16fl oz/2 cups boiling water
475ml/16fl oz/2 cups whole milk
4 cinnamon sticks, each about
    10cm/4in long
sugar, to taste

1 Put the ground coffee in a cafetière (press pot) or jug (pitcher), pour on the boiling water and leave for a few minutes until the coffee grounds settle at the bottom.

2 Push down the plunger of the cafetière or strain the jug of coffee to separate the liquid from the grounds. Pour the strained coffee into a clean jug.

3 Pour the milk into a heavy-based pan, add the cinnamon sticks and bring to the boil, stirring occasionally.

4 Using a slotted spoon, lift out the cinnamon sticks and use a smaller spoon to press down on them to release any liquid they have absorbed. Set the cinnamon sticks aside for serving.

5 Add the coffee to the hot milk, then pour into cups. Add a cinnamon stick to each cup. Drinkers should add sugar to taste as required.

HORCHATA

THIS DELICIOUS, AROMATIC RICE DRINK TASTES WONDERFULLY CREAMY, YET DOES NOT CONTAIN A DROP OF MILK. MEXICANS SWEAR BY IT AS A MEANS OF SETTLING STOMACH UPSETS OR CURING HANGOVERS, AND IT IS OFTEN SERVED AT BREAKFAST.

SERVES FOUR

INGREDIENTS
450g/1lb/2¼ cups long grain rice
750ml/1¼ pints/3 cups water
150g/5oz/1¼ cups blanched
    whole almonds
10ml/2 tsp ground cinnamon
finely grated rind of 1 lime, plus
    strips of rind, to decorate
50g/2oz/¼ cup sugar
ice cubes, to serve

1 Tip the rice into a sieve (strainer) and rinse thoroughly under cold running water. Drain, tip into a large bowl and pour over the water. Cover and soak for at least 2 hours, preferably overnight.

2 Drain the rice, reserving 600ml/1 pint/ 2½ cups of the soaking liquid. Spoon the rice into a food processor or blender and grind as finely as possible.

3 Add the almonds to the processor or blender and continue to grind in the same way until finely ground.

4 Add the cinnamon, grated lime rind and sugar to the ground rice and ground almonds. Add the reserved soaking water from the rice and mix until all the sugar has dissolved.

5 Serve in tall glasses with ice cubes. Decorate with strips of lime rind.

Energy 47kcal/198kJ; Protein 3.5g; Carbohydrate 4.8g, of which sugars 4.7g; Fat 1.7g, of which saturates 1.1g; Cholesterol 6mg; Calcium 121mg; Fibre 0g; Sodium 43mg
Energy 707kcal/2955kJ; Protein 16.3g; Carbohydrate 112g, of which sugars 21.2g; Fat 21.5g, of which saturates 1.7g; Cholesterol 0mg; Calcium 121mg; Fibre 2.8g; Sodium 7mg

CAFE DE OLLA

THIS IS ONE OF THE MOST POPULAR DRINKS IN MEXICO. THE NAME MEANS "OUT OF THE POT", WHICH REFERS TO THE CONTAINER IN WHICH THE COFFEE IS MADE. TRADITIONALLY, THE SWEETENER IS PILONCILLO, THE LOCAL UNREFINED BROWN SUGAR, BUT ANY SOFT DARK BROWN SUGAR CAN BE USED. THIS COFFEE IS ALWAYS DRUNK BLACK.

SERVES FOUR

INGREDIENTS
1 litre/1¾ pints/4 cups water
115g/4oz/½ cup *piloncillo* or soft
 dark brown sugar
4 cinnamon sticks, each about
 15cm/6in long
50g/2oz/⅔ cup freshly ground coffee,
 from dark-roast coffee beans

1 Place the water, sugar and cinnamon sticks in a pan. Heat gently, stirring occasionally to make sure that the sugar dissolves, then bring to the boil. Boil rapidly for about 20 minutes until the syrup has reduced by a quarter.

2 Add the ground coffee to the syrup and stir well, then bring the liquid back to the boil. Remove from the heat, cover the pan and leave to stand for around 5 minutes.

3 Strain the coffee through a fine sieve (strainer), pour into cups and serve immediately.

COOK'S TIP
If you do not have a fine sieve (strainer), improvise with a regular sieve lined with coffee filter paper. For a special occasion serve the coffee with chocolate-dipped cinnamon sticks which can be used to stir with.

ATOLE

THIS DRINK, WHICH IS MADE FROM WHITE CORN MASA, IS TRADITIONALLY FLAVOURED WITH PILONCILLO (MEXICAN UNREFINED BROWN SUGAR) AND GROUND CINNAMON. IT HAS THE CONSISTENCY OF A THICK MILKSHAKE. FRESH FRUIT PURÉES ARE OFTEN ADDED BEFORE SERVING AND SOME RECIPES INTRODUCE GROUND ALMONDS OR MILK.

SERVES SIX

INGREDIENTS
200g/7oz/1¾ cups white *masa harina*
1.2 litres/2 pints/5 cups water
1 vanilla pod (bean)
50g/2oz/¼ cup *piloncillo* or soft dark
 brown sugar
2.5ml/½ tsp ground cinnamon
115g/4oz/1 cup fresh strawberries,
 chopped pineapple or orange
 segments (optional)

3 If adding the fruit, purée it in a food processor or blender until smooth, then press the purée through a sieve (strainer).

1 Put the *masa harina* in a heavy-based pan and gradually beat in the water to make a smooth paste.

2 Place the pan over a moderate heat add the vanilla pod and bring the mixture to the boil, stirring constantly until it thickens. Beat in the sugar and ground cinnamon and continue to beat until the sugar has dissolved. Remove from the heat.

4 Stir the purée into the corn mixture and return to the heat until warmed through. Remove the vanilla pod. Serve.

Energy 99kcal/422kJ; Protein 0.2g; Carbohydrate 26.2g, of which sugars 26.1g; Fat 0g, of which saturates 0g; Cholesterol 0mg; Calcium 14mg; Fibre 0g; Sodium 2mg
Energy 250kcal/1050kJ; Protein 4.8g; Carbohydrate 54g, of which sugars 17.4g; Fat 1.7g, of which saturates 0g; Cholesterol 0mg; Calcium 10mg; Fibre 1.1g; Sodium 1mg

AFTER-DINNER COFFEE

A SUPERB END TO A MEAL. KAHLÚA, THE MEXICAN COFFEE LIQUEUR USED IN THIS DRINK, IS ALSO DELICIOUS SERVED IN A LIQUEUR GLASS AND TOPPED WITH A THIN LAYER OF CREAM.

1 Put the ground coffee in a heatproof jug (pitcher) or cafetière (press pot), pour on the boiling water and leave until the coffee grounds settle at the bottom.

2 Strain the jug of coffee through a sieve (strainer) or push down the plunger in the lid of the cafetière to separate the liquid from the grounds. Pour the strained coffee into a clean heatproof jug.

3 Add the tequila, Kahlúa and vanilla extract to the coffee and stir well to mix. Add the sugar and continue to stir until it has dissolved completely.

4 Pour the mixture into small coffee cups, liqueur coffee glasses or tall glasses that will withstand the heat of the coffee.

SERVES FOUR

INGREDIENTS
  50g/2oz/⅓ cup strong ground coffee
  475ml/16fl oz/2 cups boiling water
  120ml/4fl oz/½ cup tequila
  120ml/4fl oz/½ cup Kahlúa liqueur
  5ml/1 tsp natural vanilla extract
  25g/1oz/2 tbsp soft dark brown sugar
  150ml/¼ pint/⅔ cup double cream

VARIATIONS
If you prefer you can use Tia Maria instead of Kahlúa, or even a chocolate liqueur if you wish.

5 Hold a teaspoon just above the surface of one of the coffees. Pour the double (heavy) cream very slowly down the back of the spoon so that it forms a pool on top of the coffee. Repeat with the remaining coffees. Serve at once.

Energy 511kcal/2116kJ; Protein 1g; Carbohydrate 19g, of which sugars 19g; Fat 36.5g, of which saturates 19.5g; Cholesterol 80mg; Calcium 40mg; Fibre 0g; Sodium 43mg

ROMPOPE

LEGEND HAS IT THAT THIS RICH EGGNOG WAS FIRST MADE IN THE KITCHENS OF A CONVENT IN PUEBLA. SOME VERSIONS ARE THICKENED WITH GROUND ALMONDS OR SERVED WITH FRESH SOFT FRUITS SUCH AS RASPBERRIES. IT IS TRADITIONAL TO SEAL BOTTLES OF ROMPOPE *WITH ROLLED CORN HUSKS OR CORN COBS WHICH HAVE BEEN STRIPPED OF THEIR CORN.*

MAKES 1.5 LITRES/2½ PINTS/6¼ CUPS

INGREDIENTS
   1 litre/1¾ pints/4 cups milk
   350g/12oz/1½ cups sugar
   2.5ml/½ tsp bicarbonate of soda
   1 cinnamon stick, about 15cm/6in
   12 large egg yolks
   300ml/½ pint/1¼ cups dark rum

4 Return the mixture to a clean pan, place over a low heat and cook until the mixture thickens and the back of the spoon is visible when a finger is drawn along it.

5 Stir in the rum, pour into sterilized bottles and seal tightly with stoppers or clear film (plastic wrap). Chill until required. Serve *rompope* very cold. It will keep for up to 1 week in the refrigerator.

1 Pour the milk into a pan and stir in the sugar and bicarbonate of soda (baking soda). Add the cinnamon stick. Place the pan over a moderate heat and bring the mixture to the boil, stirring constantly. Immediately pour the mixture into a bowl and cool to room temperature. Remove the cinnamon stick, squeezing it gently to release any liquid.

2 Put the egg yolks in a heatproof bowl over a pan of simmering water and whisk until the mixture is very thick and pale.

3 Add the whisked yolks to the milk mixture a little at a time, beating after each addition.

Energy 397kcal/1666kJ; Protein 10.5g; Carbohydrate 38.5g, of which sugars 38.5g; Fat 13.3g, of which saturates 4.6g; Cholesterol 411mg; Calcium 223mg; Fibre 0g; Sodium 77mg

CHAMPURRADA

THIS POPULAR VERSION OF ATOLE IS MADE WITH MEXICAN CHOCOLATE. A SPECIAL WOODEN WHISK
CALLED A MOLINOLLO IS TRADITIONALLY USED WHEN MAKING THIS FROTHY DRINK.

SERVES SIX

INGREDIENTS
115g/4oz Mexican chocolate, about
2 discs
1.2 litres/2 pints/5 cups water or
milk, or a mixture
200g/7oz white *masa harina*
30ml/2 tbsp soft dark brown sugar

1 Put the chocolate in a mortar and
grind with a pestle until it becomes a
fine powder. Alternatively, grind the
chocolate in a food processor.

3 Place the pan over a moderate heat
and bring the mixture to the boil,
stirring all the time until the frothy
drink thickens.

COOK'S TIP
If you can't locate Mexican chocolate,
improvise by mixing 115g/4oz dark bitter
chocolate (minimum 70 per cent cocoa
solids) with 25g/1oz/¼ cup ground
almonds, 50g/2oz/¼ cup caster
(superfine) sugar and 10ml/2 tsp ground
cinnamon in a food processor. Process
until a fine powder is obtained.

2 Put the liquid in a heavy-based pan
and gradually stir in all the *masa harina*
until a smooth paste is formed. Use a
traditional wooden *molinollo*, if you have
one, or a wire whisk for a frothier drink.

4 Stir in the ground chocolate, then add
the sugar. Serve immediately.

MEXICAN HOT CHOCOLATE

MEXICAN CHOCOLATE IS FLAVOURED WITH ALMONDS, CINNAMON AND VANILLA, AND IS SWEETENED
WITH SUGAR. ALL THE INGREDIENTS ARE CRUSHED TOGETHER IN A SPECIAL MORTAR, AND HEATED
OVER COALS. THE POWDERED MIXTURE IS THEN SHAPED INTO DISCS. MAKING THE CHOCOLATE IS
QUITE A FIDDLY BUSINESS, BUT FORTUNATELY THE DISCS CAN BE BOUGHT IN SPECIALIST STORES.

SERVES FOUR

INGREDIENTS
1 litre/1¾ pints/4 cups milk
50–115g/2–4oz Mexican chocolate
(1–2 discs)
1 vanilla pod (bean)

1 Pour the milk into a pan and add
the chocolate. Precisely how much to
use will depend on personal taste. Start
with one disc and use more next time
if necessary.

3 Heat the chocolate milk gently,
stirring until all the chocolate has
dissolved, then whisking with a wire
whisk or a *molinollo* until the mixture
boils. Remove the vanilla pod and
divide the drink among four mugs or
heatproof glasses. Serve at once.

VARIATION
If you prefer, you can use dark bitter
chocolate instead of Mexican chocolate.
You will need slightly less, as the flavour
will be more intense.

2 Split the vanilla pod lengthways using
a sharp knife, and add it to the milk.

Energy 250kcal/1048kJ; Protein 6g; Carbohydrate 41.6g, of which sugars 18.8g; Fat 6.8g, of which saturates 3.5g; Cholesterol 5mg; Calcium 89mg; Fibre 1.1g; Sodium 30mg
Energy 220kcal/924kJ; Protein 8.1g; Carbohydrate 25.3g, of which sugars 25.1g; Fat 10.4g, of which saturates 6.4g; Cholesterol 13mg; Calcium 248mg; Fibre 0.6g; Sodium 88mg

INDEX

achiote, 58
adobo seasoning, 89
after-dinner coffee, 250
albondigas, 145
alcoholic drinks, 60–63
allspice, 58
almonds, 33
  almond biscuits, 225
  almond orange biscuits,
    226–7
  almond pudding with
    custard, 211
  prawns with almond
    sauce, 166–7
almuerzo, 14
America, Mexican food in, 18
ancho chillies, 48
  see also chillies
asadero, 12, 56
atole, 248–9
avocados, 40–41
  avocado soup, 99
  guacamole, 41, 71

baked salmon with a guava
  sauce, 160–61
Bajio, 12
banana: strawberry and banana
  preparado, 244
banana leaves, 44
barbecuing: chargrilled swordfish
  with chilli and lime sauce,
  164–5
  corn with cream, 192
bass see sea bass
beans: 11, 15, 30–31
  black bean salsa, 72
  chicken and tomato
    chimichangas, 126
  eggs motulenos, 114–5
  frijoles charros, 11, 195
  frijoles de olla, 14, 193, 194
  pinto bean salsa, 73
  refried beans, 194
beef: albondigas, 145
  beef enchiladas with red
    sauce, 147
  machaca, 55
  sopes with picadillo, 107
  stuffed butterfly of beef with
    cheese and chilli and
    sauce, 148–9
  tacos with shredded beef,
    146
  taquitos with beef, 103
beer, 60
biscuits: almond biscuits, 225
  almond orange biscuits,
    226–7
  Christmas cookies with
    walnuts, 229
  Mexican wedding cookies,
    226–7
black bean salsa, 72
bloody Maria, 245
bread: king's day bread, 222–3

  pan dulce, 224
broad beans: green lima beans
  in a sauce, 184–5
buñuelos, 214–5
burritos, 11, 28
  burritos with chicken and
    rice, 124–5
  red snapper burritos, 158
  see also tortillas

cactus pear see nopales salsa;
  pork in green sauce
  with cactus
caesar salad, 203
cafe con leche, 246–7
cafe de olla, 248–9
cakes: garbanzo cake, 220
  king's day bread, 222–3
  pecan cake, 221
capirotada, 216–7
caramel custard, 208–9
carne seca, 11, 54
carnitas, 12, 138–9
carnival, 16
cascabel chillies, 48
  see also chillies
cauliflower, red, 183
cebollas en escabeche, 86
Central Mexico, 12–13
ceviche, 11, 13, 15, 153
chalupas, 28
champurrada, 252–3
chargrilled swordfish with chilli
  and lime sauce, 164–5
chayotes, 15, 53
  chayote salad, 202
  chayote salsa, 84
  chayotes with corn and
    chillies, 198
  see also squash
cheese, 11, 56–7
  chicken flautas, 110–11
  chillies in cheese sauce,
    112–3
  quesadillas, 108
  stuffed butterfly of beef with
    cheese and chilli sauce,
    148–9
chick peas: garbanzo cake, 220
chicken: and tomato
  chimichangas, 126
  burritos with chicken and

  rice, 124–5
  chicken fajitas, 128–9
  chicken flautas, 110–11
  chicken with chipotle
    sauce, 130–31
  drunken chicken, 127
  panuchos, 106
  Tlalpeño-style soup, 94–95
chilaquiles, 140
chiles con queso, 11
chiles en nogada, 12–13
chilled coconut soup, 98
chillies, 12, 46–49
  adobo seasoning, 89
  beef enchiladas with red
    sauce, 147
  black bean salsa, 72
  chayotes with corn and
    chillies, 198
  chicken with chipotle sauce,
    130–31
  chilli strips with lime, 87
  chillies in cheese sauce,
    57, 112–3
  chillies rellenos, 100–101
  chipotle sauce, 74–5
  classic tomato salsa, 68–9
  courgette with cheese and
    green chillies, 186
  fried potatoes, 190–91
  green lima beans in a sauce,
    184–5
  guacamole, 71
  guajillo chilli sauce, 74–5
  habañero salsa, 88
  jicama, chilli and lime salad,
    201
  lamb stew with chilli sauce,
    144
  mushrooms with chipotle
    chillies, 178–9
  pinto bean salsa, 73
  potatoes with chorizo and
    green chillies, 182
  red salsa, 90–91
  stuffed butterfly of beef
    with cheese and chilli
    sauce, 148–9
  stuffed chillies in a walnut
    sauce, 180–81
  tortas, 102
  Veracruz-style red snapper,
    157
chimichangas, 28
chipotle chillies, 48–9
  chipotle sauce, 74–5
  see also chillies
chocolate, 32
  champurrada, 252–3
  ice cream with Mexican
    chocolate, 218–9
  Mexican hot chocolate, 252–3
choko see chayotes
chorizo, 54
  eggs with chorizo, 112–3
  potatoes with chorizo and

  green chillies, 182
  tortilla pie with chorizo, 140
Christmas, 16, 17
  Christmas cookies with
    walnuts, 229
christophene see chayotes
churros, 14, 206–7
cilantro see coriander
cinco de mayo, 16
cinnamon, 58
citrus agua fresca, 240
classic tomato salsa, 68–9
cloves, 58
coconut, 11, 39
  coconut custard, 213
  coconut soup, chilled, 98
  fruit platter, 218–9
cod: fisherman's stew, 174–5
  see also salt cod
coffee: after-dinner coffee, 250
  cafe con leche, 246–7
  cafe de olla, 248–9
comal, 20
comida, 14–15
cookies see biscuits
coriander, 58–9
corn, 24–29, 50
  chayotes with corn and
    chillies, 198
  corn soup, 94–5
  corn tortillas, 26
  corn with cream, 192
courgette: courgette torte, 187
  courgette with cheese and
    green chillies, 186
crab with green rice, 170
cumin seeds, 59
custards: almond pudding with
    custard, 211
  caramel custard, 208–9
  coconut custard, 213

day of the dead, 17
desayuno, 14
desserts and sweetmeats,
  205–29
día de candelaria, 17
día de los santos reyes, 16
drinks, 231–253
drunken chicken, 127
drunken plantain, 216–7

Easter, 16

eggs: almond pudding with
custard, 211
caramel custard, 208–9
eggs motulenos, 114–5
eggs rancheros, 14, 116–7
eggs with chorizo, 112–3
rompope, 251
empanadas: empanadas with
ropas viejas, 104–5
fruit-filled empanadas, 228
enchiladas, 15, 28
beef enchiladas with red
sauce, 147
enchiladas with pork and
green sauce, 134
epazote, 13, 59
equipment, 20–21
escabeche, 152

Europe, Mexican food in, 18–19

fajitas, 28
chicken fajitas, 128–9
feasts and festivals, 16–17
festivals and feasts, 16–17
fish and seafood, 11, 12, 13, 15,
151–175
fisherman's stew, 174–5
flan see caramel custard
flautas, 28
fresno chillies, 47
see also chillies
fried plantain, 190–91
fried potatoes, 190–91
fried sole with lime, 160–61
frijoles, 15
frijoles borrachos, 11
frijoles charros, 11, 195
frijoles de olla, 14, 193, 194
see also beans
fruit-filled empanadas, 228
fruit platter, 218–9
fruit vegetables, 40–53
see also fruits; vegetables
fruits, 34–39
see also fruit vegetables

garbanzo cake, 220
garlic: frijoles de olla, 193, 194

prawns in garlic butter, 168
scallops with garlic and
coriander, 171
granadillas, 35
green beans, 50
green beans with eggs, 184–5
green lima beans in a sauce,
184–5
green rice, 196–7
green tomatillo sauce, 70
see also enchiladas with pork
and green sauce; pork in
green sauce with cactus
guacamole, 41, 71
guajillo chillies, 49
guajillo chilli sauce, 74–5
see also chillies
guavas, 35
baked salmon with a guava
sauce, 160–61
guayabas see guavas

habañero chillies, 13, 49
habañero salsa, 88
see also chillies
herbs, seasonings and spices,
58–59
history of cooking in Mexico, 8–9
hochata, 246–7
huevos rancheros, 14, 116–7

ice cream with Mexican
chocolate, 218–9
Independence Day, 17
ingredients, 23–63

jalapeño chillies, 46
see also chillies
jicama, 12, 15, 51
fruit platter, 218–9
jicama, chilli and lime
salad, 201
jicama salsa, 78

kahlúa, 61
king's day bread, 16, 222–3

lamb stew with chilli sauce, 144
lemons, 34
licuado de melon, 237
lima beans: green lima beans in
a sauce, 184–5
limes, 34
citrus agua fresca, 240
lime agua fresca, 243
pineapple and lime agua
fresca, 242
los días de los muertes, 17

machaca, 54–5
mangoes, 36
fruit platter, 218–9
mango and peach
margarita, 236
mango salsa, 82–3
margarita: 235

mango and peach
margarita, 236
masa/masa harina, 13, 25, 26
meal patterns, 14–15
meat, preserved, 54–5
meat dishes, 123–150
see also beef; chicken;
lamb; pork
melon: chayote salsa, 84
fruit platter, 218–9
merienda, 14
mescal, 61–2
metate, 20
Mexican chocolate, 32
Mexican hot chocolate, 252–3
Mexican rice, 109
Mexican-style green peas, 178–9
Mexican sugar, 33
Mexican wedding cookies,
17, 226–7
minguichi, 57
molcajete and tejolote, 21
mole poblano, 13, 17
molettes, 114–5
molinollo, 21
Monterey Jack, 57
mozzarella, 56
mushrooms with chipotle
chillies, 178–9
mussels: fisherman's stew,
174–5

Navidad, 17
nopales, 12, 45
nopales salsa, 80–81
see also nopalitos; prickly
pears
nopalitos: nopalitos salad, 200
pork in green sauce with
cactus, 135
see also nopales; prickly
pears
nuts and seeds, 33

ollas, 21
onion relish, 86
oranges, 34
almond orange biscuits,
226–7
citrus agua fresca, 240
fruit-filled empanadas, 228
oregano, 59

pan dulce, 14, 224
panuchos, 106
papayas, 39
fruit platter, 218–9
pasada chillies, 49
see also chillies
pasilla chillies, 49
see also chillies
peaches: mango and peach
margarita, 236
peas: Mexican-style green peas,
178–9
pecan cake, 221

pepitas, 118–9
peppers see sweet peppers
pescado y legumbres, 15
picadillo, sopes with 107
piloncillo, 15, 20, 33
piñas, 61–2
pineapples, 36–37
fruit platter, 218–9
pineapple and lime agua
fresca, 242
pineapple tequila, 234
pink cadillac, 233
pinto bean salsa, 73
plantains, 44
drunken plantain, 216–7
fried plantain, 190–91
fruit-filled empanadas, 228
spiced plantain chips 120
platillo fuerte, 15
poblano chillies, 46–7
see also chillies
pomegranates, 39
popcorn with lime and chilli, 121
pork, 12
albondigas, 145
carnitas, 138–9
chorizo, 54
eggs with chorizo, 112–3
empanadas with ropas viejas,
104–5
enchiladas with pork and
green sauce, 134
pork in green sauce with
cactus, 135
stuffed loin of pork, 136–7
tamales filled with spiced
pork, 142–3
tortilla pie with chorizo, 140
tostadas with shredded pork
and spices, 141
postre, 15
potatoes: fried potatoes, 190–91
potato cakes, 189
potatoes with chorizo and
green chillies, 182
prawns: ceviche, 153
fisherman's stew, 174–5
prawn salad, 169
prawns in garlic butter, 168
prawns with almond sauce,
166–7
prickly pears, 38
see also nopales salsa; pork

in green sauce with cactus
Pueblo fish bake, 172–3
pulque, 12, 61
pumpkin: pepitas, 118–9
    pumpkin in brown sugar, 212
    pumpkin seed sauce, 85
    pumpkin with spices, 188
    see also squash

quesadillas, 15, 28, 108
queso anejo, 57
queso chihuahua, 57
queso de oaxaca, 57
queso fresco, 56

rainbow trout: Pueblo fish bake,
    172–3
recados, 13
red cauliflower, 183
red rub, 90–91
red salsa, 90–91
red snapper: Veracruz-style red
    snapper, 157
    red snapper burritos, 158
    red snapper with coriander
        and almonds, 156
refried beans, 194
regional cooking, 10–13
restaurants, Mexican food in, 19
rice, 14–15, 31
    burritos with chicken and
        rice, 124–125
    crab with green rice, 170
    green rice, 196–7
    hochata, 246–7
    Mexican rice, 109
    rice pudding, 210
    yellow rice, 196–7
roasted tomato and coriander
    salsa, 82–3
roasted tomato salsa, 76–7
rompope, 251
rub, red, 90–91
rum: drunken plantain, 216–7

salads: caesar
    chayote, 202
    nopalitos, 200
    prawn, 169
    spinach, 199
salmon: baked salmon with a
    guava sauce, 160–61
    salmon with tequila cream
        sauce, 162

salsas, 67–92
salt cod, 54–5
    salt cod for Christmas Eve,
        154–5
    see also cod
sangria, 238–9
sangrita, 238–9
sapodillas, 39
sapote, 39
sauces see salsas
scallops: ceviche, 153
    fisherman's stew, 174–5
    scallops with garlic and
        coriander, 171
sea bass with orange chilli
    salsa, 159
seafood and fish, 11, 12, 13,
    15, 151–75
seasonings, spices and herbs,
    58–9
seeds and nuts, 33
semana santa, 16
serrano chillies, 46
    see also chillies
shark: Yucatan-style shark
    steak, 163
snacks and soups, 14, 15,
    92–122
sole, fried with lime, 160–61
sopaipillas, 206–7
sopes with picadillo, 107
soups and snacks, 14, 15,
    92–122
spiced plantain chips, 120
spices, seasonings and herbs,
    58–9
spinach salad, 199
squash, 52–3
    see also chayote; pumpkin
squid: ceviche, 153
steak see beef
strawberry and banana
    preparado, 244
string beans see green beans
    with eggs
stuffed butterfly of beef with
    cheese and chilli sauce,
    148–9
stuffed chillies, 100–101
stuffed chillies in a walnut
    sauce, 180–81
stuffed loin of pork, 136–7
sweet peppers, 44–45
    guajillo chilli sauce, 74
sweet potatoes, 51
    sweet potato salsa, 79
sweetcorn see corn
sweetmeats and desserts,
    205–29
swordfish: chargrilled swordfish
    with chilli and lime sauce,
    164–5
    swordfish tacos, 164–5

tacos, 28, 29
    tacos with shredded beef,

146
tamales, 12, 15, 17, 24
    tamales filled with spiced
        pork, 142–3
tamarind, 59
    tamarind agua fresca, 241
taquitos with beef, 103
tejolote and molcajete, 21
tequila, 11, 62–3, 232
    after-dinner coffee, 250
    bloody Maria, 245
    drunken chicken, 127
    mango and peach
        margarita, 236
    margarita, 235
    pineapple tequila, 234
    pink cadillac, 233
    salmon with tequila cream
        sauce, 162
    sangrita, 238–9
    tequila slammers, 232
    tequila sunrise, 233
Tex-Mex food, 18–19
tiger prawns see prawns
Tlalpeño-style soup, 14, 94–5
tomate verde see tomatillos
tomatillos, 42–43
    crab with green rice, 170
    enchiladas with pork and
        green sauce, 134
    green tomatillo sauce 70
    pork in green sauce with
        cactus, 135
    salsa cruda de tomatillo, 43
tomatoes, 11, 42
    bloody Maria, 245
    chipotle sauce, 74–5
    classic tomato salsa, 68–9
    guajillo chilli sauce, 74–5
    pumpkin seed sauce, 85
    quick fresh tomato salsa, 42
    red salsa, 90–91
    roasted tomato and coriander
        salsa, 82–3
    roasted tomato salsa, 76–7
    sangrita, 238
tortas, 102
tortilla equipment: comal, 20
    tortilla press, 20
    tortilla warmer, 21
tortillas, 14, 18–19
    burritos with chicken and
        rice, 124–5
    chicken and tomato
        chimichangas, 126
    chicken fajitas, 128–9
    chicken flautas, 110–11
    corn tortillas, 26
    eggs motulenos, 114–5
    eggs rancheros, 116–7
    empanadas with ropas viejas,
        104–5
    enchiladas with pork and
        green sauce, 134
    flour tortillas, 27
    folding and cooking, 28

panuchos, 106

quesadillas, 108
ready-made tortillas, 29
red snapper burritos, 158
sopes with picadillo, 107
swordfish tacos, 164–5
tacos with shredded beef,
    146
taquitos with beef, 103
tortilla chips, 118–9
tortilla pie with chorizo, 140
tortilla soup, 96–7
tostadas with shredded pork
    and spices, 141
tostadas, 28
    tosadas with shredded pork
        and spices, 141
totopos, 28, 118
trout see rainbow trout
turkey mole, 132–3
    see also moles

USA, Mexican food in, 18

vanilla, 59
    vanilla sugar, 59
vegetable pear see chayote salsa
vegetables, 50–53, 177–203
    see also fruit vegetables

walnuts: Christmas cookies with
    walnuts, 229
watermelon: fruit platter, 218–9
    licuado de melon, 237
    see also melon
weddings, 17
wine, 60–61

yam bean see jicama
yellow rice, 196–7
Yucatan-style shark steak, 163